DEBATING
THE 1960s

Debating Twentieth-Century America
Series Editor: James T. Patterson, Brown University

DEBATING
THE 1960s
LIBERAL, CONSERVATIVE, AND RADICAL PERSPECTIVES

MICHAEL W. FLAMM
and
DAVID STEIGERWALD

ROWMAN & LITTLEFIELD PUBLISHERS, INC.
Lanham • Boulder • New York • Toronto • Plymouth, UK

Permission to reprint the material in the Documents sections is gratefully acknowledged.

ROWMAN & LITTLEFIELD PUBLISHERS, INC.

Published in the United States of America
by Rowman & Littlefield Publishers, Inc.
A wholly owned subsidiary of The Rowman & Littlefield Publishing Group, Inc.
4501 Forbes Boulevard, Suite 200, Lanham, Maryland 20706
www.rowmanlittlefield.com

Estover Road, Plymouth PL6 7PY, United Kingdom

Copyright © 2008 by Rowman & Littlefield Publishers, Inc.

British Library Cataloguing in Publication Information Available

Library of Congress Cataloging-in-Publication Data
Flamm, Michael W., 1964-
    Debating the 1960s : liberal, conservative, and radical perspectives / Michael W. Flamm and David Steigerwald.
        p. cm. — (Debating twentieth-century America)
    Includes bibliographical references and index.
    ISBN-13: 978-0-7425-2212-1 (cloth : alk. paper)
    ISBN-10: 0-7425-2212-1 (cloth : alk. paper)
    ISBN-13: 978-0-7425-2213-8 (pbk. : alk. paper)
    ISBN-10: 0-7425-2213-X (pbk. : alk. paper)
    1. United States—History—1961–1969—Sources. 2. United States—Politics and government—1961–1963—Sources. 3. United States—Politics and government—1963–1969—Sources. 4. Right and left (Political science)—History—20th century—Sources. I. Steigerwald, David. II. Title.
    E841.F53 2008
    973.923—dc22

                                                                2007011070

Printed in the United States of America

♾ ™The paper used in this publication meets the minimum requirements of American National Standard for Information Sciences—Permanence of Paper for Printed Library Materials, ANSI/NISO Z39.48-1992.

CONTENTS

INTRODUCTION

The turbulent period that has gone down in history as "The Sixties" began on a note of liberal optimism, with John F. Kennedy calling Americans to put aside the narrow, self-satisfied quest for material goods and commit their energies instead to the national well-being. "Ask not what your country can do for you," he famously counseled, "ask what you can do for your country." As it happened, millions of Americans did just that, and the ensuing period witnessed an extraordinary outpouring of public activism. Yet that activism hardly resulted in the kind of orderly public-spiritedness that Kennedy had in mind. Instead by 1968, raw political conflict had so badly ruptured public life that otherwise sensible people were genuinely convinced that America was descending into fascism, or anarchy, or race war, depending on their position on the political spectrum. The period that began with liberal optimism ended with Richard Nixon in the White House, having manipulated public fears that America had gone berserk. A period that began with a wave of buoyant liberalism—seen in the Democratic Party's dominance of national politics through mid-decade, in the surge of liberal legislation that permanently altered American society, and in the widespread support for racial justice and other liberal causes—ended in the emergence of contemporary conservatism. What seemed at the time like a new stage in the history of modern liberalism turned out to be the last stage of that history.

This trajectory from liberal optimism to the rise of contemporary conservatism has become the prevailing interpretation of the period among historians of the Sixties. Historians have generally agreed that the period witnessed the collapse of modern liberalism. From that foundation, scholarship on the period has filled out the wider parameters of public life, and the result is something like a three-paneled mosaic. Instead of a narrative of liberalism against conservatism, current scholarship generally has created a picture of a nation with an official liberalism at its center and a left and right that defined themselves largely by their mutual contempt for that center;

1

within each of these broad sensibilities, furthermore, were divisions, factions, and keen disagreements. Thus the general picture of this intriguing moment in American history places liberalism in the dominant center. The New Left, composed of the student rebellion, the antiwar movement, and the schismatic eruption of black nationalism, feminism, gay rights, and the counterculture, posed assorted radical challenges to the center. Meanwhile, what looked at the time like a quixotic movement among intellectual snobs such as William F. Buckley and the odd-ball presidential run of Barry Goldwater in 1964 we now recognize as the origins of the contemporary conservatism that has dominated in America from Ronald Reagan in 1980 to George W. Bush.

We have crafted the two essays here in an effort to describe this three-way confrontation of liberalism, the New Left, and the modern conservative movement. Our hope is to convey the breadth of political conflict, while providing a general outline of the debates between liberals, radicals, and conservatives over four crucial issues of the day: the civil rights movement, the Great Society program of reform, the Vietnam War, and American mores and values.

THE LIBERAL-RADICAL DEBATES
OF THE 1960s

David Steigerwald

LIBERALISM, THE LEFT, AND THE
"NEW MOOD" OF AMERICAN LIFE

Surveying the terrain of American public life at the opening of the 1960s, Arthur M. Schlesinger, Jr., Harvard historian, charter member of the earnestly liberal Americans for Democratic Action, and influential liberal guru, detected a "new mood" filtering into the nation's consciousness. The 1950s, he wrote, had been a period of "passivity and acquiescence" during which Americans "have been largely absorbed in themselves—in their own careers, their own lives, their own interests." This self-involvement, Schlesinger thought, was not from avarice but was instead the natural response of a people who had been asked to disregard their personal lives for a series of great and strenuous national undertakings. "During the '30's, '40's and into the '50's the American people went through the worst depression of their history, the worst war of their history, the worst cold war of their history, the most frustrating limited war of their history," Schlesinger noted. "During these decades, two aggressive Presidents kept demanding from us a lively interest in public policy. . . . But no nation can live in tension indefinitely. By the early '50's, the American people had had it. . . . We wanted a vacation from public responsibilities." And Dwight D. Eisenhower, the military hero turned aging politician whose second presidential term was then drawing to a close, was the "perfect man" for them. "Where his predecessors had roused the people, he soothed them; where they had defined issues sharply, he blurred them over; where they had called for effort and action, he counseled patience and hoped things would work themselves out." Eisenhower's gift was that he made "politics boring at a time when the people wanted any excuse to forget public affairs."

This retreat from great public activity was not unusual in American life, Schlesinger suggested. Indeed, American history might be well understood as a cyclical turn of activism and passivity, a cycle that he thought was a constant turning of liberalism and conservatism, "positive" government and "negative" government. Under normal circumstances, a historian might be blasé about this state of affairs. But, the Harvard scholar insisted, in the midst of "the grim and unending contest with communism," which "was the central international fact of the decade," American lethargy was downright dangerous: "The Communists took no time out to flop in the hammock. We did, and we have paid a cruel price for it."

As the Sixties opened, Schlesinger detected a whiff of dissatisfaction with Eisenhower's America and speculated that "new forces, new energies, new values are straining for expression and for release." This rising sense was scattered, to be sure, but could be seen "in freshening attitudes in politics; in a new acerbity in criticism; in stirrings, often tinged with desperation, among the youth; in a spreading contempt everywhere for reigning clichés." Schlesinger hoped that these new energies would burst forward in a great effort to improve the quality of American life and thus allow an ever-sharper contrast between American democracy and Soviet communism. In contrast to the 1930s, when the Great Depression gave rise to most of the ideas that liberals of Schlesinger's generation embraced, "the '60's will confront an economy of abundance." While "there still are pools of poverty which have to be mopped up, . . . the central problem will be increasingly that of fighting for individual dignity, identity, and fulfillment in an affluent mass society." Liberals after the 1930s fought for the economic security of the average American. But in the affluent society, "the new issues will be rather those of education, health, equal opportunity, community planning. . . . A guiding aim, I believe, will be the insistence that every American boy and girl have access to the career proportionate to his or her talents and characters, regardless of birth, fortune, creed, or color."

Schlesinger's brief essay was remarkably prescient. Indeed, a new mood was afoot. As he predicted, the new mood would erupt into a wave of public activism, much of which was aimed at just the sort of goals he described. He was also prophetic in warning that "the '60's will probably be spirited, articulate, inventive, incoherent, turbulent, with energy shooting off wildly in all directions." What that meant for Schlesinger personally turned out to be unbearably painful. Two close associates and admired friends, John and Robert Kennedy, were assassinated. The war in Vietnam, which Schlesinger himself concluded was unwise, tore the nation apart. A civil rights cause that Schlesinger believed was the logical next step in expanding American justice grew into a mass movement that veered toward radicalism and pulled many liberals along with it, while it also engendered a conservative reaction. Perhaps most directly to the point, the new mood gave rise to a form of politics, principally among young Americans, that Schlesinger found absurd, irrational, and potentially totalitarian.[1]

What went wrong?

It has to be said at the outset that the "lull" in American life that Schlesinger described as part of the conservative turn of the 1950s had put liberals to sleep too. Having been in control of national government through the Roosevelt years and into the early Cold War, liberals had settled into a period of consolidating the legislative and political gains that they had made in the twenty years after 1932. Adlai Stevenson, the Democratic Party's leader through the 1950s, spoke of "the strange alchemy of time" that "converted the Democrats into the truly conservative party of this country—the party dedicated to conserving all that is best, and building solidly and safely on these foundations."[2]

Those foundations of what I will call establishment liberalism had been laid during Franklin Roosevelt's New Deal. The building blocks included programs such as Social Security that aimed at alleviating the worst forms of distress in a wide portion of the population. It is important to understand that the liberal state was never genuinely a welfare state. The New Deal aimed at providing secondary insurance against disaster, rather than guaranteeing against poverty. The fundamental principle behind the New Deal was that the federal government became an active participant in shaping the capitalist economy. The real legacy of the New Deal was that it gave birth to what historian Alan Brinkley has dubbed a "compensatory" state, which used the federal government's powers to tax and spend to "redress weaknesses and imbalances in the private economy without directly confronting the internal workings of capitalism. Such a state," Brinkley concludes, "could manage the economy without managing the institutions of the economy."[3] To establishment liberals, the economy was not to be controlled; it was to be regulated and influenced through enlightened management.

Having abandoned any interest in either attacking corporations through antitrust law or in extensive national planning, the establishment Sixties liberals did not see themselves as antibusiness. American business leaders, however, remained wary of liberals' penchant for federal spending and regulation and had a pronounced tendency to support Republicans.

Democratic Party leaders had to work hard against the antiliberal biases among business leaders. When he entered office at the outset of the Sixties, for example, John F. Kennedy found himself in a tussle with American steel manufacturers who were determined to raise prices, even though the new president had pressured steel workers to keep wage demands down. Kennedy eventually prevailed, then tried to soothe strained relations with business by calling for a program of tax reductions and reform. The experience moved

Kennedy to call for a truce between his administration and corporate America. In a June 1962 commencement address at Yale, the president complained that the relationship between business and government had become "clogged by illusion and platitude and fails to reflect the true realities of contemporary American society." After running off a list of economic myths about federal spending and fiscal irresponsibility, Kennedy invoked the liberal conception of equilibrium: "It is true—and of high importance—that the prosperity of this country depends on the assurance that all major elements within it will live up to their responsibilities. If business were to neglect its obligations to the public, if labor were blind to all public responsibility, above all, if government were to abandon its obvious—and statutory—duty of watchful concern for our economical health," then the process of smooth growth would collapse. In what historian Allen Matusow describes as the very "premise of postwar American liberalism," Kennedy concluded: "What is at stake in our economic decisions today is not some grand warfare of rival ideologies which will sweep the country with passion, but the practical management of a modern economy."[4]

The moderation of liberalism was not just a function of politicians making the normal compromises of democratic governance. As Schlesinger noted in his "New Mood" essay, the socioeconomic terrain had changed dramatically since the 1930s. During the Depression, widespread economic distress created grass-roots support for Roosevelt's New Deal programs. By contrast, the prosperity of postwar America encouraged a "dominant tone . . . of satisfaction" among workaday people, as Richard Hofstadter, another liberal historian turned social and political critic, observed. "A large part of the New Deal public, the jobless, distracted and bewildered men of 1933, have in the course of the years . . . become home-owners, suburbanites and solid citizens."[5]

This satisfied sensibility was most vividly seen in the condition of organized labor. During the 1930s, American labor fought pitched battles against company goons and local police for the right to organize. The 1935 National Labor Relations Act, which protected the right to organize, began the process of institutionalizing labor in the process of economic management. By the early 1950s, the intense class conflict of the Depression had given way to a steady, if not amicable, pattern of negotiations between labor and capital that ran according to generally accepted rules. Establishment liberals such as Harvard economist John Kenneth Galbraith argued that this arrangement allowed labor unions to shed the radicalism of the past and accept a role as a regular counterbalance against corporate power. In exchange for this institutionalization, the unions avoided radicalism, booted communists out of their ranks, and supported American foreign policy.

The payoff was clear. Wages and benefits grew dramatically after World War II; real wages for factory hands were 65 percent higher in real terms in the 1950s than they had been in the 1920s. Union membership ballooned to its highest point in 1955 when roughly a third of the nonagricultural American labor force was unionized. Certainly unions had their enemies among business leaders and conservative Republicans, but this opposition further cemented organized labor's relationship to the Democratic Party. Sixty-four percent of union workers voted for Kennedy in 1960; four years later, 86 percent voted for his successor, Lyndon Johnson. Labor leaders prided themselves on their ability to corral voters and regularly took responsibility for keeping the House of Representatives in Democratic hands from 1954 through the entire 1960s, and the Senate Democratic from 1956 onward as well. That pride was well-founded: through the Sixties and beyond, union households remained among the most reliable Democratic voters.

If the United States had achieved a prosperous domestic equilibrium and reached, as many observers at the time believed, a general consensus among governing and institutional elites about the ground rules for managing prosperity, the international situation was far different. There, the Soviet Union posed a fundamental threat. The Roosevelt administration had led the United States out of its Depression Era isolationism and through a successful war against Nazi fascism. The postwar confrontation with the Soviet Union convinced Roosevelt's successors in the Truman administration to expand American military commitments and put in place a global strategy that ensured a constant American presence throughout the world. By the late 1940s, Truman officials put in place the policy of Containment and, with it, American diplomatic and military alliances around the periphery of the Soviet Union; Containment pledged the United States to check communist aggression wherever it erupted. While conservatives accused liberals of being "soft" on communism, the truth is that establishment liberals such as Arthur Schlesinger believed that defeating the communists was without doubt the most urgent cause of the 1950s.

Thus when Democrats regained the White House in 1961, staking out an aggressive Cold War posture was uppermost in John F. Kennedy's mind. His famous inaugural address was almost entirely focused on the international scene. "Let every nation know," he declared, "whether it wishes us well or ill, that we shall pay any price, bear any burden, meet any hardship, support any friend, oppose any foe, in order to assure the survival and the success of liberty." Curiously, the press coverage of the speech hailed it as a farsighted attempt to break through the stalemate of U.S.-Soviet relations and noted that Soviet Premier Nikita Khrushchev and the new Cuban leader, Fidel Castro, both welcomed the new tone they heard. It is true that Kennedy called for a new "quest for peace, before the dark powers of destruction unleashed by science engulf all humanity in planned or accidental self-destruction." But his overtures were qualified: "Civility is not a sign of weakness, and sincerity is always subject to proof. Let us never negotiate out of fear. But let us never fear to negotiate." Even his most optimistic visions were laced with militaristic language, as when he hoped that "a beachhead of cooperation may push back the jungle of suspicion."

With its moderate model of political economy and its steadfast commitment to the Cold War, establishment liberalism was a philosophy forged through the bitter experiences of Depression, World War, and Cold War. In a sense, it was a triumph of practical experience over theory and naïve idealism and a hard-won adjustment to the sobering realities of the mid-twentieth century—to the limitations of even the best intentioned reformers; and to the frightening lengths to which men and nations would go to exert power over others. Once Kennedy moved into the White House, establishment liberals, heeding Schlesinger's prediction of a new mood among the public, were poised to make another long run at legislative accomplishment, the management of prosperity, and victory in the Cold War.

To say, however, that Sixties liberalism was a pragmatic adjustment to the realities of midcentury is not to say that liberals were well prepared for the realities that soon confronted them. Because their experience had revolved around class conflict at home and great-power conflict abroad, liberals of Schlesinger's generation were not ready for the two explosive forces that developed after 1960. First, they did not instinctively understand how profoundly a movement for genuine racial justice would reshape America. They were in no position, therefore, to anticipate either the revolutionary nature of the black liberation struggle or the lengths to which defenders of white supremacy were prepared to go to maintain the system of legal segregation and racial oppression. Second, their devotion to global anticommunism boxed them into a disastrous foreign-policy corner—almost literally in a tiny corner of the world in Southeast Asia. The Vietnam War was a serious foreign policy blunder. More important, it opened up fissures in the public arena that tore the nation apart. In the end, therefore, the center of American political life—the liberal center—could not hold.

In detecting the new mood in American life, Arthur Schlesinger counted several indications of changing sensibilities that were fundamental to the quickened activism of the Sixties. He noted that the disenchantment among "youth" seemed to grow from a yearning for "a renewal of conviction" as an alternative to the chase after mere "material comforts." In a single observation, Schlesinger caught both the youthful makeup of the emerging activism and the young generation's unique relationship to the affluent society.

As a straightforward sociological fact, the new activism was bound to be youthful. Probably the most important sociological development of the period was the baby boom, that demographic oddity in which, roughly from the mid-1940s to the early 1960s, American couples produced a historic bumper crop of children, seventy-five million in all. In violation of the rules of demographic history, they did so at a time of increasing material affluence; and they managed to do so with only a modest increase in the size of the average family. This equation was possible because, on returning from war to a consistently improving economic situation, young Americans married younger and in greater numbers than at any time in the twentieth century.

The consequences of the baby boom for the 1960s are hard to exaggerate. As the baby boom children grew in numbers and matured, they exerted a gravitational pull on American society. Marketers from Hollywood to toy manufacturers to recording companies began to craft products and advertisements for the "youth market." American mass culture flattered young people in their generational self-consciousness. Whatever else they shared with their parents, according to Todd Gitlin, affluence created a "divide of experience which could never be erased." Gitlin, one of the small handful of students who launched the New Left political movement in the early Sixties, thought that this cultural condition bred an incongruous mixture of conformist messages and self-aware satire that mocked the American cornucopia. "America was mass-producing images of white youth on the move yet with nowhere to go," he remembered. In *Mad* magazine and James Dean movies, Gitlin found the pose of alienated anticonformity, which seemed a sensible reply to the consumer rat race. Though also products of the mass-consumption society, these voices of uneasiness amidst prosperity "pried open cultural territory which became available for radical transmutation. . . . In a world that adult ideologies had defined as black and white . . . they did help establish the possibility of gray."[6]

The unique historical place of the baby boomers boiled down to this: They were children of the most affluent society on earth and were therefore the first generation to discover that television and teen music and suburban homes did not impart meaning to life. They were the first generation to have to conduct an experiment with living in a society that emphasized consumption instead of work, leisure over labor. No wonder that many among them broke out into a search for a "radical transmutation" of society.

While the radical activism of the Sixties is usually associated with white college students, the first major outbreak of protest by baby boomers came in February 1960, when four freshmen African-American students at North Carolina Agricultural and Technical College decided, more or less on their own, to stage a sit-in demonstration against the segregated lunch counters in the downtown Greensboro Woolworth's store. Within days, more than a hundred other protesters joined them. Meanwhile, through spring 1960, the sit-in movement spread west to Nashville and down the eastern seaboard.

Something new, clearly, was in the works. There had been sit-ins before, but few had generated even newspaper stories, much less region-wide imitations. Timing was everything; the Greensboro Four had caught the new mood, primarily among other college-aged African-Americans. The heightened expectations that greeted their generation made them ripe for political activism. Not only had they witnessed the improving economic conditions of the country, but they were the generation that was supposed to benefit first from the Supreme Court's 1954 ruling in *Brown v. Board of Education*, which destroyed the constitutional underpinnings of segregation. In spite of *Brown*, they had attended segregated high schools and found themselves attending segregated colleges. The white South had thumbed its collective nose at the Supreme Court and was getting away with it, partly because many older civil rights leaders and establishment liberals remained confident that, eventually, the law would bring change. With the older generation either resisting racial justice or sitting on their hands, members of this particular generation decided that it was their duty to confront the system of segregation.

Perhaps there is no better example of this generation's position than that of John Lewis. Born and raised on a remote family farm in Pike County, Alabama, Lewis parlayed a youthful piety into a college education at Fisk University in Nashville, something that his parents could never have dreamed of. In Nashville, this deeply provincial young man—a rube, really—became familiar not only with the big city but the world as a whole. He had become an admirer of Martin Luther King, Jr., after the Montgomery Bus Boycott of 1955, and when he had the chance to involve himself in the Nashville sit-in movement, he grabbed it. Within a year he had made himself one of the core activists in the student wing of the civil rights movement. In his memoirs, he remembers how the gap between what his generation had been promised and the endless talk about how segregation would "eventually" fall created "a sense of urgency and awareness spreading among my classmates and friends, and, indeed, among black students throughout the city. There was a growing feeling that this movement for civil rights needed—no, *demanded*—our involvement."[7]

Lewis and his peers moved to sustain the momentum of the sit-ins by organizing the Student Non-Violent Coordinating Committee (SNCC) in April 1960. While they accepted the tutelage of older activists including King himself, SNCC became the main organizational vehicle through which this small handful of students—a mere 150 at the first meeting in Raleigh, North Carolina—changed American society. From the outset, SNCC approached its cause in ways that reflected a zealous, youthful idealism. A serious religious intensity fired their enthusiasm, steeled their commitment to action, and led them to create a unique group. With some important exceptions, SNCC members were born and bred southerners with no political experience. That lack of experience meant a fresh approach to protest. SNCC adopted a loose, informal organizational structure that relied on collective decision-making and discouraged individual leadership. Yet group decisions were not binding on anyone; a member's commitment to any given action depended ultimately on individual conscience. The group's motto caught this open-ended quality: "Do what the spirit say do, go where the spirit say go." They were contemptuous of institutionalized politics, which they believed was full of compromise and hypocrisy.

SNCC had only a few guiding principles. Initially, they were committed to the principle of nonviolent protest; at the same time, they were determined to use that method to confront segregation directly and immediately. This combination of religious conviction, generational urgency, and willingness to confront authority made SNCC a radical group in the purest sense of that term. They were unaffiliated with any party or ideology and free of obligations to any form of institutionalized power; all of the standard means of controlling a group were therefore filtered away. Even Martin Luther King found it difficult to influence the students once the momentum of protest began to unroll.

The young people of SNCC were unencumbered by organizational attachments or ideological predispositions, but their generational counterparts among white college students could not say the same thing. The students who convened what became known as the New Left were, like it or not, connected to the old radical politics of the past. By and large, the earliest pioneers of radicalism among young whites were "red-diaper babies," young people whose parents had been active in left-wing politics during the Great Depression. The baby boomers took from their parents an interest in political activism and a certain degree of comfort with nonconformity. Many of the red-diaper babies were from the East Coast; many, like Todd Gitlin, were Jewish and had grown up in an environment of intellectual and political sophistication. There were important exceptions to this type, particularly Tom Hayden, who was raised in a middle-class Catholic family outside Detroit.

Being a "new" left required that the baby boom radicals escape from the Cold War orthodoxies of both liberals and communists. They looked for alternatives to their parents' Marxism. One course of inspiration came from an independent radicalism of French existentialist philosophers Jean Paul Sarte and Albert Camus. The existentialists emphasized the absurdity and meaningless of modern life and thereby appealed to the disenchanted children of affluence. From Camus, the aspiring young radicals took the lesson that individual action in defiance of the order of things would make life worth living. This conviction became extremely important to the New Left. In the short term, it imparted a sense of urgency to young people who already enjoyed the blessings of abundance; in the long term, it meant that political action was an end in itself, rather than a means to an end.

A second, more important source of independent thought was C. Wright Mills, a sociologist at Columbia University who established a reputation during the 1950s as a fiercely independent critic of the status quo. It hardly hurt that Mills, the motorcycle-riding renegade sociologist who carried Texas panache into the stuffy Ivy League, was the New Left's godfather in style as well as in ideas. According to Tom Hayden, the New Left leader who wrote his master's thesis on Mills, the sociologist combined "the rebel life-style of [the actor] James Dean and the moral passion of Albert Camus, with the comprehensive portrayal of the American condition we were all looking for."[8] In a series of powerful books published during the 1950s, Mills demonstrated his independence from both the staid world of academia and conventional political categories. He made his name by denouncing the technocratic elites who dominated contemporary capitalism, detailed the bleak world of the new white-collar worker, and denounced the Cold War as an insane race to the death. Mills had also become a vocal critic of the "Old Left," the generation of radicals who had embraced the textbook version of Marxism and followed the official Communist Party line. More than anything else, however, he insisted to the end of his brief life—he died suddenly in March 1962—that affluent America made genuine democracy impossible because its large-scale bureaucracies destroyed the sort of face-to-face relationships that alone could provide people with practical control of their everyday lives.

It was Mills, in fact, who convened the American New Left rather by invitation in an autumn 1960 essay, "Letter to the New Left," where he urged radical youth to be unabashedly utopian and idealistic. The old politics of left and right were simply exhausted, he wrote. The left-right divide between communism and capitalism had become the dogma of the Cold War. In this stale confrontation, the real victor was an official version of liberalism that excused its own emptiness by merely dismissing all ideological competitors. Cold War liberalism, Mills snapped, was not a political philosophy but merely "liberal rhetoric," an "approved style" that often appeared "simply as snobbish assumptions" about the world. It was hard to see what radical traditions were left for young people to draw from. The "old left" was obsolete, particularly in what Mills famously derided as the "labour metaphysic," the idea that radicalism had to come from the working class. In an era when the trade unions were incorporated into the system, Mills insisted that radical energy had to come from another source. It was clear to him who would lead a New Left: "Who is it that is getting disgusted with what Marx called 'all the old crap'? Who is it that is thinking and acting in radical ways? . . . It is the young intelligentsia." Sounding much the same note as Arthur Schlesinger, Mills proclaimed that "the Age of Complacency is ending. We are beginning to move again."[9]

By singling out the "young intelligentsia" as the potential agents of a new radicalism, Mills was extending advice to that handful of college students who had launched scattered efforts at campus organizing. At Harvard, the University of Michigan, and the University of California at Berkeley, left-wing students had begun to rally fellow dissenters around a variety of issues—the nuclear arms race, the fraternity system on their campuses, and once the sit-in movement began, racial injustice. But Mills was also trying to locate the potential base of a broad social movement, one that would serve the same purpose for the New Left that the working class served for the Old Left under the sway of conventional Marxism—that is, as the social sector out of which the forces for radical change would emerge. Mills was correctly diagnosing the important social changes brought about by the simultaneous growth of the corporate economy and the baby boom. Because corporations needed a workforce of college graduates, the numbers of college students would grow quickly. Enrollments had increased steadily during the 1950s and by 1961, more than 3 million students were enrolled in American colleges and universities; by 1969, that number reached 7.75 million. As Todd Gitlin has argued, the scientific-bureaucratic character of the American economy, coupled with the baby boom, guaranteed an explosion in university enrollments. It was an indication of the nation's affluence, he suggested, that "by 1960 the United States was the first society in the history of the world with more college students than farmers."[10]

For the New Left's theorists, this connection between the nature of contemporary capitalism and the university was fundamentally important. Just as the working class was essential to the era of industrial capitalism, the New Left figured that college graduates would become necessary to the affluent society and therefore had leverage to wield. Just as conventional Marxist theory had assumed that workers would become radicalized because of the brutal treatment they received at the hands of industrialists, so New Left thinkers expected that college students and graduates would resent living in a bureaucratized economic system that stifled their individual creativity and bound them to the production of the Cold War military machine. The system did not produce miserable poverty, as the older system had done; it produced individual alienation within a dangerously militarized state. The cause of the New Left, as Tom Hayden wrote in a mix of Mills and Camus, "was to prevent the coming of the cheerful robot by transforming these drifting individuals into self-aware citizens, the amorphous mass into an educated public."[11]

At the time Mills called for a New Left, the pioneers of the student movement had been searching for a suitable organization to which to attach themselves. They agreed to collaborate with a venerable old left-wing student organization, the Student League for Industrial Democracy, which traced its origins back to the World War I era. Principally funded by the United Auto

Workers, the organization was renamed Students for a Democratic Society (SDS) in 1959 and drew into it many of the fledging student groups from around the country. Between early 1960 and June 1962, when a mere one hundred or so students met at an AFL-CIO camp at Port Huron, Michigan, to establish the direction and strategy for SDS, the two specific causes that galvanized a new radical activism emerged: President Kennedy quickly proved that he intended to fight the Cold War aggressively; and SNCC had reignited far-reaching civil rights protests in the South. The new mood was picking up. Some of the students had participated in civil rights demonstrations in the South; some had begun protests against the rigid rules at their respective campuses; and still others had joined in protests against the arms race. All these issues were on their mind when they gathered at Port Huron, where they produced nothing less than a manifesto for their generation.

The famous Port Huron Statement, among the most extraordinary political manifestos in American history, was largely the work of Tom Hayden, who had been editor of the student paper at the University of Michigan and an outspoken activist. Hayden's genius was to capture the mood not just of his activist colleagues, not even just of his fellow college students across the nation; he caught the mood of an age. The opening sentence of the Port Huron Statement summed up the essence of the young radicals: "We are people of this generation, bred in at least modest comfort, housed now in universities, looking uncomfortably to the world we inherit." In a single statement, Hayden indicated the New Left's specific generational sensibility; conceded that he and his peers had enjoyed the material benefits of the affluent society; expressed the sense of alienation that they believed was the product of that society; and referred to their status as students. They were not oppressed. They were "uncomfortable." Repudiating the dogmas of everyone before them—the communists, the liberals, and certainly business-minded conservatives—Hayden and his colleagues called for a revolution in heart and mind to unleash the "unrealized potential for self-cultivation, self-direction, self-understanding, and creativity." They insisted that a society that gave rise to such self-realization would not be a world of competitive individualism. Rather, it would recognize the modern reality of human interdependence and move from the appreciation that self-realization, in the proper sense, must inherently foster "human brotherhood . . . as a condition of future survival and as the most appropriate form of social relations." At a time when the survival of humanity was held hostage to a balance of terror built on the rickety frame of American and Soviet nuclear arsenals, the radical students believed that sweeping social and political changes were the only solutions to their discomfort.

As a manifesto for a "new left," the Port Huron statement aimed at America's liberal establishment. Liberals, the students claimed, liked to take credit for the improvements for African-Americans. Yet as of 1962 most "improvements" had come because of the general prosperity of the nation, and to say that the Kennedy administration had done more for civil rights than the Eisenhower administration was to compare "whispers to silence when positively stentorian tones are demanded." Liberal Democrats were hopelessly compromised, moreover, by their habit of placating the segregationists in their party. Liberals were also the architects of the Cold War, which had turned America into a "Warfare State," instead of a welfare state. Indeed, the problems of education and urban poverty were largely ignored because national priorities focused on shoveling money to arms makers. Committed to the Cold War, liberals only gave lip service to necessary social reforms. Hypocrisy, when all was said and done, was liberalism's most prominent characteristic.

The New Left's alternative to the affluent society was a world where "participatory democracy" flourished. They wanted to "replace power rooted in possession, privilege, or circumstance by power and uniqueness rooted in love, reflectiveness, reason, and creativity." Participatory democracy would create a society in which individuals shared directly in all those decisions that affected their lives and in which they did so in common with one another. Connected to one another and empowered to control their own lives, people would lift the modern curse of alienation, which the depersonalized, bureaucratized world of the liberal establishment had imposed.

As SDS saw the situation, none of the established liberal systems were working toward such a decent world. The economy was on "remote control" and working to benefit huge corporations, rather than for human beings. The political system paired two parties that were more in collusion than competition, with very little substantive difference between them. American government was nothing more than "organized political stalemate" that protected the status quo. Far from the "democratic model of which its glorifiers speak," the party system "frustrates democracy by confusing the individual citizen, paralyzing policy discussion, and consolidating the irresponsible power of military and business interests." And there were no corrective ingredients in the system any longer. Borrowing from Mills, the students insisted that the last best hope of the old left, the trade union, that "historic institutional representative of the exploited," had become enfeebled. If unions remained "the most 'liberal' mainstream institution," still "its liberalism represents vestigial commitments, self-interestedness, unradicalism. . . . Labor has succumbed to institutionalization, its social idealism waning under the tendencies of bureaucracy, materialism, [and] business ethics."

Who would emerge to bring this change about? Drawing directly from Mills, they answered plainly, university students. Because the university was so central to the bureaucratic, scientific character of the affluent society, it contained a paradox. On the one hand, the universities produced the knowledge and the engineers that ran the warfare state; on the other hand, the university's indispensability made it a choke point where "new levers of change" could exert pressure. The universities were therefore ideally suited to act as the breeding grounds of a radical vanguard. They were the only true homes of pure knowledge in America. And they contained the "younger people who matured in the post-war world" and who were the natural constituents of a new left. While it would still be necessary to reach outside the university and link up with progressive unions, peace activists, and the civil rights movement, the Port Huron students announced themselves "committed to stimulating this kind of social movement, this kind of vision and program in campus and community across the country."

This was the New Left as the Sixties dawned.

CIVIL RIGHTS FROM THE LEFT

Sixties liberalism is inextricably connected to the civil rights movement. On the surface, it is only sensible that the two should be so linked. The movement did much to shape the presidencies of John F. Kennedy and Lyndon Baines Johnson. And it was during these two administrations that the hallmark civil rights victories, especially the 1964 Civil Rights Act and the 1965 Voting Rights Act, were realized.

It was, after all, John F. Kennedy who threw the crucial weight of the federal government behind the movement to dismantle racial segregation. His Justice Department, headed by his brother Robert Kennedy, mediated between civil rights activists and state and local authorities in the South. At times that mediation required rare courage from federal officials, not just political courage either, but personal physical courage. One thinks of John Seigenthaler, the Justice Department lawyer beaten into a coma in the parking lot of the Montgomery, Alabama, bus station while trying to rescue Freedom Riders from a snarling white mob. Or of John Doar, who put himself between black protestors and riot police during Medgar Evers's funeral in 1963. Kennedy himself made the decisive departure away from federal indifference to racial repression in June 1963. In the aftermath of the brutal treatment of protestors in Birmingham and Alabama Governor George Wallace's defiance of federal court demands that the University of Alabama admit black students, Kennedy delivered an unambiguous declaration of support for the movement. Declaring to a national television and radio audience that "we are confronted primarily with a moral issue . . . as old as the scriptures and . . . as clear as the American Constitution," the president made it clear that he intended to ask Congress for new civil rights legislation that, in effect, would prohibit racial segregation in public places once and for all. Kennedy evoked the golden rule to put the matter plainly: "The heart of the question is whether all Americans are to be afforded equal rights and equal opportunities, whether we are going to treat our fellow Americans as we want to be treated." (See document 2.) Kennedy was assassinated before this new legislation was passed, but Lyndon Johnson continued the effort. No matter what else is said about liberal waffling and compromises in the arena of civil rights, Lyndon Johnson's decision to impose the Voting Rights Act and its accompanying enforcement measures on the South was one of the foremost acts of political courage in American history. A Southerner himself, he knew full well that the act would sever white southerners from the Democratic Party and imperil the party's long-standing electoral majority.

Yet the relationship between civil rights and liberalism is not so natural as this impression suggests, nor were Kennedy or Johnson heroes. If anything, given the singular importance of the black liberation struggle to the history of America in the Sixties, it is startling how slow liberals were to engage fully the civil rights issue. To be sure, a wide spectrum of convictions existed among liberals on civil rights; the further left someone was, the more likely he or she was to support racial equality. The progressive wing of the party won an important victory at the 1948 convention when it managed to interject into the platform relatively frank language in opposition to all racial discrimination; in response, Southern segregationists bolted to Strom Thurmond's third-party candidacy as the States' Rights Party nominee. Yet the divisions of 1948 put a pall over the issue. Perhaps bowing to the age of acquiescence, the Democrats spent the 1950s mending their regional divisions. Adlai Stevenson was the favored candidate of liberal idealists in 1952 and 1956, but he was decidedly conservative on racial issues.

It can be argued in defense of liberals that as late as 1960 the civil rights movement had not yet pressed itself on the conscience of the nation. Of course there had been important outbreaks of protest—among them, the successful African-American protests against Montgomery, Alabama's segregated bus system in 1955. Across the breadth of white America, however, such events registered little. Kennedy said nothing about racial justice in his inaugural address, even though the speech was crafted around a demand for universal freedom. An even more telling anecdote concerns Kennedy's jockeying for the African-American vote during the 1960 campaign. Frustrated with his inability to secure the support of any recognized black spokesmen, Kennedy paid a visit in May to singer Harry Belafonte, an important supporter of black causes. When Belafonte urged Kennedy to seek support from Martin Luther King, Jr., the candidate replied: "Why do you see him as so important? . . .What can he do?"[12] To Kennedy the Harvard-bred sophisticate, Martin Luther King, Jr., was at most a regional figure, a southern preacher who had once made the news by leading a successful bus boycott down in Alabama. To Kennedy the Boston-Irish politician, King was a leader of a people who could not vote and who therefore could not "do" anything for a candidate in a tight race.

Many liberals assumed that the Supreme Court's decision in *Brown v. Board of Education (of Topeka)* in 1954, which ruled the "separate-but-equal" doctrine unconstitutional, should have been enough to initiate the dismantling of formal Jim Crow. Writing a few years before *Brown*, for example, Arthur Schlesinger insisted that "law is an essential part of the enterprise of education which alone can end prejudice." Because it was "foolish to think that we can transform folkways and eradicate bigotry overnight,"[13] Schlesinger and his colleagues did not support a grass-roots social movement for civil rights. There was a double meaning buried here. On the one hand, the expectation was that American institutions were functioning properly and, under the control of political elites, were moving toward the orderly establishment of racial justice; it also implied, however, that a grass-roots movement to push that justice along more urgently was beyond the bounds of legitimate politics. It should be said as well that this liberal perspective was not confined to Kennedy insiders. Indeed a large wing of African-American leaders who were associated with civil rights shared this view. Stalwart figures such as Roy Wilkins, head of the National Association for the Advancement of Colored People (NAACP) after 1955, and Thurgood Marshall, one of the lead attorneys in the *Brown* case and eventually the first African-American Supreme Court Justice, were similarly distrustful of the social movement that erupted in force beginning in 1960.

It was this embedded cautiousness that the young activists of SNCC intended to challenge and that Martin Luther King, Jr., sought to coax liberals away from. Both the students and King understood that in the equation of power in America, they needed the help of the federal government. SNCC hoped they could shame establishment liberals into supporting them; King struggled to persuade. Either way, civil rights activists maneuvered Kennedy into gradual support. They did so through an elaborate game of pressure and counterpressure that began in earnest when SNCC, in conjunction with an older organization, the Congress for Racial Equality (CORE), launched the so-called Freedom Rides in May 1961.

For two years, between the Freedom Rides and spring 1963, when southern resistance had become so utterly unacceptable that Kennedy cast off political considerations, the president tiptoed carefully around the use of federal power on behalf of civil rights. Though sympathetic to the protestors—he admired their courage, if nothing else—he knew that imposing federal authority would create immediate resentment among Southerners; federal intervention might obscure the basic justice of the issue and provoke howls of Southern indignation against "outside agitators." Ultimately, any federal action on behalf of civil rights activists, Kennedy assumed, could be counterproductive. During those early years, whenever activists clashed with Southern authorities, Kennedy worked behind the scenes to cover over the fundamental conflict. During some of the movement's most dramatic moments, the Freedom Rides and the efforts to desegregate the Universities of Mississippi and Alabama, the administration strained to persuade the states' governors to use their own police forces to ensure public order and the safety of the activists. The governors, plying their own political interests, insisted that if the activists were to have protection it would have to come from federal officials.

Yet in at least three high-profile instances, it was Kennedy's caution that proved counterproductive. The Freedom Riders who battled their way through Alabama in spring 1961 were viciously attacked at the Montgomery bus depot after the state's governor reneged on a deal to protect them. In fall 1962, Mississippi Governor Ross Barnett played up his opposition to the integration of Ole Miss after federal courts ordered that one African-American man, James Meredith, be registered. But Barnett cut a deal with the administration behind the scenes to have Meredith registered. With no leader willing to quell segregationist opposition, mob violence erupted that left two people shot to death. In 1963, when young activists undertook a voter-registration drive in Mississippi that Kennedy's Justice Department had encouraged, they were subjected to constant police harassment, arrest, and beatings. Kennedy's attempts at moderation obviously failed to prevent violence. It also helped stoke the increasing radicalism of both black and white civil rights activists, who derided the administration's habit of subordinating the greatest moral issue of the day to petty political calculations.

By June 1963, Kennedy had taken his limit. Martin Luther King's Birmingham protests had produced mass arrests and provoked local authorities to attack protestors with police dogs and high-powered fire hoses. When a repeat of the Battle of Ole Miss threatened in Alabama, Kennedy, finally, threw his weight to civil rights. But it was not only the justice of the cause that moved him. As president, he was constitutionally bound to uphold the supremacy of the federal government. He believed, moreover, that the media coverage of the protests embarrassed the United States in world opinion and undermined the ideological campaign of the Cold War. It was difficult to criticize the Soviet Union for its political repression or make appeals to anticolonial movements on the basis of American ideals when the media was carrying pictures of Southern whites pummeling black protestors. As he explained in his June 1963 address, "we preach freedom around the world, and we mean it. . . . [B]ut are we to say to the world . . . that we have no second-class citizens except Negroes; that we have no class or caste system, no ghettoes, no master race except with respect to Negroes?"

And what of Martin Luther King? Where did he fall on the spectrum of Sixties politics? If having a "moderate" temperament made one a liberal, then King was a liberal. If seeking inclusion for his constituents into the mainstream of American life meant that King was a liberal, then so he was. He was a public figure who insisted on nonviolence, often invoked the U.S. Constitution, and lauded American democracy as a political ideal. King's great rhetorical strength was his insistence on the universality of his cause. He almost never spoke of the civil rights movement as a movement just for African-Americans but, rather, as a movement that helped America realize her finest ideals for everyone. As a realist, he knew he had to work closely with the institutional civil rights leaders such as the NAACP's Roy Wilkins, as well as conventional politicians in the liberal wing of the Democratic Party. The movement's ultimate dependence on federal support entailed the risks of forced compromises, hollow victories, and bitter disappointment. For someone who never ran for an office, King developed extraordinary political skills; he carefully calibrated his approach to both presidents with their political limitations in mind. Perhaps, then, King was a stalwart liberal.

Yet in more important ways, he was not. Every move he made, every slight equivocation or bend in tactics in deference to the immediate political situation was intended to further the movement's ends—and such compromises were remarkably few, considering that King had no army behind him, no power of the state, or any of the other mechanics of power. If the term "revolutionary" means anything substantive, it surely applies to those who seek to transform the world they live in fundamentally. By this definition, Martin Luther King, Jr., was a revolutionary. If succeeding in transforming one's world is the mark of the successful radical, then King was among the most important radicals in American history and on par with Ho Chi Minh and Fidel Castro as the most influential radical of his generation. The great difference between King and these contemporaries was that he led a revolution that was remarkably nonviolent. True, people lost their lives in civil rights activism, probably more than the forty names memorialized on Maya Lin's civil rights monument in Birmingham. But compare that to the three million who died in Vietnam, and King's accomplishment looks very impressive.

Even if we judge King by the strained measures of the period, he looks more radical than most of the noisy youngsters who ridiculed his nonviolence and his moderation. His strategy of nonviolent protest was never intended to be cautious or even moderate; on the contrary, it was designed to provoke direct confrontation with authorities and to incite violence from segregationists. Though it was rooted in religious conviction, the strategy also took into account the concrete realities of power. Blacks were a minority in the South as a whole, and the other side had all the advantages of power—more law, more government, more guns. Nonviolent confrontation was not just the most Christian approach to social change; under the circumstances it was the only effective approach.

Certainly there were flaws and shortcomings in King's tactics. Nonviolent protest created expensive and time-consuming legal hassles. It required extraordinary collective self-discipline. It was hard to ask whole communities of people to sacrifice day-to-day life over weeks and months. And because the tactics relied on community protest, they were largely localized, and what was achieved in Montgomery, therefore, had little to do with what was gained or lost in Memphis.

These realities made the SNCC activists ambivalent about King. They admired him enormously but could not understand why he spent more time fund-raising than protesting; indeed they couldn't help but notice that King himself rarely joined in protest actions. At the very least, he seemed to need a nudge.

By choice and by conviction, SNCC believed that protest had to be relentless. Thus they plunged into a five-year hell that began with the Freedom Rides and ended with the battle of Lowndes County and the Selma march for voting rights in 1965. During the Freedom Rides, SNCC activists endured a Klan firebombing, the frightful beatings in Birmingham and Montgomery, and eventual arrest and imprisonment in Mississippi's infamous Parchman Prison, where they were again physically abused. During the voting-registration drives that Bob Moses began in 1961, activists often roamed through very isolated areas to make contact with the most impoverished African-Americans, the tenant farmers and small-property holders who had always been denied the right to vote. Because the activists worked either alone or in groups of two or three, the Justice Department could not provide protection, and the media lacked the temperament to cover an effort that could not provide regular drama. Under these circumstances, the activists were badly vulnerable. During 1963, nearly all of the voter-registration workers spent some time in Mississippi jails. The charismatic Moses, a 26-year-old New Yorker who had been drawn South by the sit-ins, survived at least one assassination attempt, and the state's NAACP director, Medgar Evers, was murdered in his own driveway. Still, 1964 was worse, in spite of the influx of seven hundred white volunteers, a handful of FBI agents, and national media. Segregationists responded to the Freedom Summer campaign, Moses's bold attempt to expand the registration drives to all of Mississippi, with over one thousand arrests, at least eighty beatings, and eight people badly wounded or killed. Perhaps the most notorious civil rights era murders took place very early in the campaign when a Klan group that included police officers from the small town of Philadelphia executed volunteers James Chaney, Andrew Goodman, and Michael Schwerner. It was almost an understatement for SNCC's James Forman to write of those years in Mississippi "that we lived and worked on the fine line between life and death in the back roads of the South."[14]

The cumulative effects of this ongoing violence carried the young activists from a fellowship of idealists dedicated to King's Christian nonviolence to radical black nationalism. This transformation began through the Freedom Rides, which imparted a sturdy self-confidence, if not self-righteousness, in the young activists. After their release from Parchman Prison, they became intolerant of equivocation and impatient with any caution. They had lost faith in the legal approach of the national NAACP and grew deeply cynical about federal help, even when they sought it out. Except for the most dedicated King devotees, such as John Lewis, SNCC members even became critical of the wider movement's most esteemed leader. They refused to appreciate the delicate politics that King had to play with Kennedy and Johnson. Having dedicated themselves to confrontational activism of the most intense sort, they could not see why the movement needed other kinds of activity. When movement elders pointed out that King was far more valuable out of jail than in, the young activists scoffed. As their impatience with King grew, so did their criticism, which became cutting and personal. They began to mock him as a celebrity who sought the limelight. They noted that when King did spend time in jail, as he did during the Albany, Georgia, campaign of 1962, he wore silk pajamas, as though he was of the movement's aristocracy. SNCC members began to speak about King's "Christ-complex" and refer to him sarcastically as "De Lawd."

The mounting tension between King's wing of the movement and SNCC expressed itself most crucially on the issue of nonviolence. King clung to the strategy of nonviolence as an inalterable principle, as did some of his protégés, such as John Lewis. But through the voter-registration drives, many other SNCC members began to abandon it, some in favor of what they called "armed self-defense," others in favor of full-scale guerrilla warfare. No one showed that effect more clearly than James Forman, who as a Chicago native in his thirties during the early 1960s was not typical of SNCC members but who was among the organization's founders. Older and more worldly than most of his counterparts, Forman was never enthralled with King. He was willing to accept nonviolence as a reasonable tactic, but, as he put it, "I did not believe in nonviolence as a way of life."[15] As SNCC executive secretary, he oversaw the Mississippi Freedom Summer campaign to recruit white college students to help with the registration drives. In order to protect volunteers in Mississippi, he briefly considered allowing guns at local offices but, along with Bob Moses, decided it would be an invitation to police raids if word got out about weapons caches. The violence of Freedom Summer, however, pushed him to think not just in terms of armed self-defense but of revolution, violent if necessary.

An understandable bitterness, if not cynicism, enveloped many of the original SNCC members. After years of living under extreme pressure, they developed burnout. John Lewis never flagged in his devotion to King's vision.

But it is a measure of how radicalized SNCC was growing that the speech he proposed to deliver as the group's representative at the renowned August 1963 March on Washington was so radical that Bayard Rustin, the march organizer, had to plead with him to temper it, lest it offend moderate allies. Indeed the Catholic archbishop of Washington threatened to remove himself from the program if Lewis promised to "march through the South, through the heart of Dixie, the way Sherman did" and "burn Jim Crow to the ground." Lewis agreed to alter this passage, but the speech was nonetheless a pointed critique of moderate liberalism and institutional gridlock. "The party of Kennedy is also the party of [Mississippi senator James] Eastland," he declared, referring to the Democrats. But the Republican Party, which contained both the liberal Jacob Javits and the Arizona senator Barry Goldwater, who had already taken a states' rights stance, was no better. "Where is the political party that would make it unnecessary to march on Washington?" Lewis asked.[16] Two years later, when Lewis lobbied his colleagues to stick to the original vision of an integrated, nonviolent organization, he was ousted from the chairmanship in something of a coup.

For many of the activists, the last straw of disillusionment came at the end of Freedom Summer in August 1964. In spite of successfully registering fewer than 10 percent of the seventeen thousand black Mississippians who dared to attempt the feat, the Freedom Summer organizers launched the Mississippi Freedom Democratic Party (MFDP). The idea was that this new, integrated party would challenge the all-white state delegation to the Democratic National Convention of August 1964 on the grounds that the regulars were unrepresentative of Mississippi as a whole. Beyond that, organizers expected that the MFDP would remain as a permanent, independent power base made up of and led by those same downtrodden Mississippians who had risked their lives to register to vote.

At the Democratic convention in Atlantic City, New Jersey, MFDP organizers worked with progressives within the national party, including Joseph Rauh, who as head of Americans for Democratic Action had been trying for years to undermine the segregationist hold in the Democratic Party. Rauh arranged for television coverage of MFDP members' testimony before the Democratic Party credentials committee. One such member was Fannie Lou Hamer, a sharecropper whose family was evicted from their home and who was beaten by police for having tried to register. With the instinctive, roof-raising oratory of someone raised in the rural black church, Hamer raised the fever of the proceedings with soaring testimony. Lyndon Johnson kept an eye on the proceedings from the White House and preempted the television coverage by calling a bogus press conference. When the party offered the MFDP a compromise package of two at-large delegates and a promise to establish a nondiscriminatory selection process for 1968, the activists, their hopes and ideals forged through that brutal summer, erupted in anger and potent disillusionment. Not only had the segregationists won again, as they saw it, but their liberal friends had betrayed them again.

Thus for a brief time, roughly from 1962 through 1964, establishment liberals in the Kennedy and Johnson administrations, moderate civil rights leaders such as Roy Wilkins, the radical nonviolent activists associated with King, and the still more radical SNCC activists, all managed to coordinate their interests for the cause of racial justice. Together they accomplished great things. King had succeeded in pushing Kennedy and then Johnson to ram through the comprehensive Civil Rights Act of 1964 over the strenuous opposition of the southern wing in Congress. Liberals from both parties joined to support the measure. In one dramatic moment, California Senator Claire Engle, who was recovering from brain surgery for cancer, had himself wheeled on to the chamber floor, where, unable to stand or speak, he slowly lifted his hand and pointed to his eye to signal his "aye" vote. The 1964 Civil Rights Act effectively compelled the destruction of legal segregation not only by outlawing discrimination in all public accommodations and employment but by setting up an enforcement mechanism through the Justice Department. It was a sweeping piece of legislation; indeed the prohibition on discrimination in employment included a provision covering gender as well as race, religion, and national origin.

The main weakness in the Civil Rights Act revolved around voting registration. While the act outlawed discrimination in registration, it failed to outlaw the various gimmicks, such as the poll tax and literacy tests, that long had been used to deny blacks (as well as poor whites) the ballot. Moreover, its enforcement mechanisms were weak.

More was needed, and King launched another round of large protests directed at pushing the Johnson administration toward a second piece of legislation. Again King chose a dramatic setting: a fifty-mile march for voting rights from Selma, Alabama, to the state capital, Montgomery, where petitions for justice could be placed before the segregationist champion, Governor George Wallace. When Alabama state troopers attacked King and fellow marchers on Selma's Edmund Pettus Bridge on "Bloody Sunday," March 7, 1965, the violence spurred Johnson much as the Birmingham violence had motivated Kennedy two years before. Perfectly aware that he was writing off the white southern vote, Johnson nonetheless pushed Congress to develop a bill that completed the civil rights revolution in the South. The following week, Johnson spoke before Congress and a national television audience. He reviewed the history of white supremacy and put the civil rights movement dead center at the heart of American ideals. "Their cause must be our cause too," the President said. Then he invoked the movement's most famous slogan: "And we shall overcome!" Southern Congressmen sat benumbed in un-comprehending silence. Martin Luther King, watching the speech with friends in Atlanta, wiped a tear from his cheek as the magnitude of what Johnson had just done settled in on him.

The essential part of the Voting Rights Act of 1965 was the audacious enforcement provisions, which provided for federal supervision of the reg-istration and voting processes in those areas of the country where discrimi-nation had been practiced. This was nothing less than a form of ongoing, long-term federal intervention into those states' rights that segregations held so sacrosanct. The Voting Rights Act was the key to the permanent destruc-tion of white supremacy; in this bill, American liberalism met and made good on the demands of radical activists who understood that black politi-cal power was essential to a successful revolution. Its effects were dramatic and sudden. Whereas roughly a third of Mississippi's eligible blacks were registered to vote in the 1964 presidential election, nearly 60 percent were registered by 1968. Because Mississippi was always the worst case, the swings in other states were not so immense. But across the South, black voting moved to parity with white voting, and "black power" began to make itself felt in local and state politics in ways that have been inalterable.

The Voting Rights Act completed the successful revolution against for-mal white supremacy in the American South. America was permanently transformed. Yet even as it produced this victory, that broad collection of civil rights champions was cracking apart. It had been difficult enough to destroy Jim Crow, but the issues confronting African-Americans after the removal of legal discrimination were more daunting in part because they were more ab-stract and more deeply embedded in the nation's economic system—namely, the problems of urban poverty, unemployment, family disruption, housing, and education. Most of the participants in the movement up to that point recognized that a new stage had been reached. They could not agree, how-ever, on how to take that next step. In fact they stopped walking together.

The breakdown of any consensus was apparent in the year after the Vot-ing Rights Act was signed. Johnson himself recognized the need for new strategies in a commencement address at Howard University in June 1965. There he argued that it was hardly fair to claim that blacks and whites stood on an even playing field just because segregation had been struck down. The "next stage" of the civil rights movement, he insisted, would work toward moving African-Americans to the starting line. But any momentum he had generated toward that end was threatened in August 1965, when the Watts section of Los Angeles erupted in a five-day riot that killed thirty-four people and caused $35 million in property damage. Watts marked the point at which public sympathy for "Negro causes" began to decline. Johnson felt betrayed and worried aloud to his aides that "Negroes will end up pissing in the aisles of the Senate and making fools of themselves, the way . . . they had after the Civil War."[17] Still, Johnson quietly funneled reconstruction money to Los Angeles and began to formulate plans for a broad conference, which would consider how to move to a new stage of the movement under the banner, "To Fulfill These Rights."

In early June 1966, that long-planned White House conference brought some 2,400 delegates representing government officials, corporate leaders, politicos, and activists to Washington. The conference was a near fiasco that illuminated crisscrossing tensions. SNCC refused to participate on the grounds that, as the new chairman Stokely Carmichael explained to reporters, integration was "an insidious subterfuge for white supremacy. . . . Political and economic power is what black people have to have."[18] A group calling itself ACT picketed in front of the conference headquarters and ridiculed King as the "Black Jesus" when he arrived. New York Mayor John Lindsay and Robert F. Kennedy both used the conference as a platform for establishing their progressive *bona fides* by calling for a much more far-reaching agenda than the administration had set down. Inside the conference, progressives tried to tie the prospects for the "next stage" to Vietnam by arguing that the intensifying war was both morally wrong and soaking away money better used for social programs. Determined to prevent any such expression, the administration stacked the conference with moderates. Johnson delivered a brief but enthusiastically received speech, but one that seemed to indicate the limits of his power, if not his patience. Johnson told the delegates that the federal government could help but could not change the conditions of people's lives alone. Thurgood Marshall followed the president with a keynote address that dismissed public protests as irritants, at best. King, meanwhile, ignored and seemingly irrelevant, spent much of the conference in his hotel room.

The conference revealed that the movement was breaking up into at least three directions: the moderate center was trying to hold its institutional power; the radical left was refusing to cooperate at all; and King was seemingly lost.

On the left, the concept of "black power" was emerging among the radicalized remnants of SNCC, who aligned themselves with the ghetto uprisings and the urban spokesman for aggressive black action. This radical shift owed much to Stokely Carmichael, who had risen to prominence in SNCC in 1965 and 1966 during a factional struggle between his black-power contingent and King devotee John Lewis. Of Caribbean origin by way of New York and Howard University, Carmichael's cosmopolitan background encouraged the view that activism in the American South was but a piece of a global struggle against white domination. Flamboyant, brash, unwilling to bite his tongue especially around whites, Carmichael had been with SNCC since the Freedom Rides but had never been a King man.

Carmichael had gained influence among the young activists when he led SNCC's early 1965 efforts in Lowndes County, Alabama, an effort that was supposed to be coordinated with King's Selma-to-Montgomery march. Determined to build local institutions of political power, Carmichael and his colleagues discovered obscure state laws that outlined the proper way to form a new political party. Among its odd stipulations was that the new party had to have a symbol; the locals decided on a black panther, a symbol of sleek, stealthy power. There at the birth of the original Black Panther Party, Carmichael ridiculed those who argued that independent organization undermined the civil rights coalition with the Democrats. "To ask the Negroes to get in the Democratic Party," he remarked when he assumed the SNCC chairmanship, "is like asking Jews to join the Nazi Party."[19] As for King's vision, he declared frankly that "we don't want to integrate." Thus mocking the overarching goal of the mainstream movement, Carmichael proceeded to banish King to obsolescence: "Non-violence is irrelevant. . . . We're building a force to take power. We're not a protest movement."[20] Within a month of taking the helm of SNCC, Carmichael began invoking the slogan "black power" during marches through Mississippi, and he did so in ways and at times that he knew would be interpreted as a rebuke to King.

Carmichael spent a good deal of energy the next few years trying to explain just what black power meant, but while he struggled to give the concept some theoretical weight, it took on a rhetorical might all its own. Black power became both a rallying cry in and a romantic explanation for the urban riots that followed Watts. From 1965 through 1967, almost 150 episodes of urban violence erupted; the worst riot, in Detroit in July 1967, ended in forty-three deaths, over one thousand injuries, and seven thousand arrests. That same year, Huey Newton and Bobby Seale organized the Black Panther Party as a sort of paramilitary group in Oakland that eventually engaged in shoot-outs with local police.

Black power advocates were quick to defend the violence on the grounds that the African-American cause was part of the colonial struggle of people of color against European imperialism. Thus Floyd McKissick, who became head of the traditionally pacifist CORE in 1966, argued that the riots were rebellions of "black people demanding that they no longer be exploited." Though they had fled to the suburbs, according to McKissick, whites kept the ghetto under a state of colonial control. "White landlords, white storekeepers, white corporate managers, and a white, Anglo-Saxon Wall Street, conspire to keep the black man in his place." Not only do they control the ghetto's economic structure, whites also "maintain control of the city agencies and the political scene. They determine what opportunities will be available and what will be reserved for whites only." Against such control, the episodes of urban violence were not riots but "a liberation struggle." Dismissing establishment liberals and conventional civil rights at once, McKissick insisted that "we cannot look elsewhere for help. We cannot lean on the crutch of religion. We cannot depend on phony 'coalitions.' We must work out our own methods."[21]

For his part, Martin Luther King felt pressure from every direction: from the left, from the establishment, from the riots. As his experience at the White House conference suggested, by 1966 he was unsure that he could even remain relevant. In the hopes of reviving nonviolent protest, he decided to redirect his efforts from the South to the northern cities. Just as he chose to attack segregation at its heart by going to Birmingham in 1963, so King decided that his efforts to improve the living conditions of urban blacks would be most dramatic if he could succeed in Chicago. The African-American population there was nearly nine hundred thousand, the bulk of whom had been confined to the south and west sides and the poorest of whom had been exiled into the nation's worst public housing projects. Chicago Mayor Richard Daley was a classic big-city machine politician—Irish, Democrat, and pro-union. As the African-American community grew dramatically from the Great Migration of rural folk, Daley dealt with its problems in the only way he knew how: by relying on black ward bosses whose neighborhood power depended on their loyalty to the city political machine. This traditional form of power sharing was hardly up to the task of addressing the deep problems in Chicago's African-American neighborhoods.

King decided to focus first on the issue of housing. He moved into a westside tenement and began to organize community groups to pressure city hall to enforce zoning and building regulations as well as enforce open-housing laws to open up white neighborhoods to integration. As part of the strategy, King led marches into several neighborhoods notorious for their hostility to blacks. The marches were met by mobs that rained down bricks and rocks on them and were as hostile as anything King and his associates had seen in the South. In fact, King himself was clobbered by a rock during the march into the Gage Park neighborhood. Meanwhile, he took a constant rhetorical pounding from Chicago's black power radicals. At every point, King found himself having to deflect criticism over his negotiations with city hall, while trying to explain to the press that the anger expressed in black power rhetoric was a legitimate response to miserable conditions. When King accepted a very modest agreement with Daley and Chicago area realtors that all of Chicago's neighborhoods would have at least 1 percent African-American population over the next few years, the local radicals denounced it as a sellout and King as useless. When King agreed to suspend a planned march into Cicero, Chicago's most infamously hostile neighborhood, the black-power advocates insisted on going ahead with it. When they did, in early September 1966, they were met by over 3,000 snarling whites and 2,700 national guardsmen who kept the two groups apart.

The Chicago campaign, often neglected in the memories of the civil rights movement, contained some of the most important forces at work in the late Sixties. There was a solid grain of truth in the black-power radicals' claim that King had sold out; the so-called pillow agreement was so soft because King had privately conceded defeat and was looking for a face-saving deal that would allow him to retreat. Their failure demonstrated the limits of King's nonviolent protest: when arrayed against legal segregation supported by the power of Southern law, it was effective; when conducted with the protection and public approval of authorities who were only partially willing to meet his demands, King found it impossible to muster the moral outrage necessary to success. Chicago exposed the limits of liberalism as well, because it nationalized the race issue. The nation's dirty little secret—that antiblack racism existed everywhere—was now laid bare.

Chicago led King to reevaluate his fundamental purpose. He was sincere in his tempered view of black power, which he regarded as the predictable result of deep frustration. He thought the idea of independent black political clout was fine, but he insisted that other ethnic and racial groups had gained their clout by appealing to general American ideals, not to race-specific demands. Because black power was built on the delusion that an independent black political movement could win power, it was ultimately counterproductive in his view. Its countenance of violence was bound to fracture the liberal-left coalition that King had created. So when the black-power left increased its notoriety—in Oakland, California, the Black Panther Party emerged as the end point of armed, racially conscious politics; elsewhere, black-power advocates demanded control of territories for a "black homeland" in America—King responded by directing his organization toward a class-based, rather than race-based, movement.

King's 1967 decision to develop his Poor People's Campaign, designed to bring the problems of poverty, joblessness, and marginalization all into a singular protest movement, was as much a product of despair as hope. In the spring of that year, he had taken an unequivocal stand against the Vietnam War, and in doing so, he incurred the White House's wrath, as well as the heated criticism of moderate civil rights leaders. He had broken with the liberal middle. Years of FBI harassment and persistent death threats had made him fatalistic. A prolonged period of little sleep and irregular diet had taken a physical as well as a mental toll. His sermons became darker, more pessimistic, and increasingly reflective of the Christian conviction in humanity's inherent depravity. Yet it speaks to the potency of that other Christian conviction in King, the one which never relinquishes hope, that he believed that he could cut through the thicket that had grown up around him by leading an interracial movement of America's poor. This was the cause he committed himself to at the end of his life; the one he was engaged in when he defended wage demands of Memphis sanitation workers; and the one he was pursuing in April 1968 when an assassin's bullet found him.

LIBERAL REFORM AND THE NEW LEFT

The trajectory of liberal reform in the Sixties paralleled the civil rights movement in a few important ways. Just as they shared with civil rights activists the general conviction that racial justice was a necessary cause, so establishment liberals shared with the young activists of the New Left the belief that the conditions of life could be improved for many of the nation's people. As an ideological matter, liberals and young radicals largely saw eye to eye on the need for social reform, at least during the first half of the decade. Indeed it was one point on which a handful of operatives in the Kennedy and Johnson administrations were far to the left of their presidential bosses. As with civil rights, the liberal reforms that burst out of Lyndon Johnson's domestic Great Society programs and his War on Poverty beginning in 1964 achieved lasting and important benefits—not least Medicaid and Medicare, the closest Americans have managed to come to universal health care. Yet as with civil rights, Johnson's reforms, paradoxically, had adverse political consequences. The most politically volatile programs in the War on Poverty raised expectations that could not practically be met, and the apparent failure ensured condemnation from the left; the right, meanwhile, effectively and persistently claimed that liberals were simply throwing money at problems that undeserving people had created for themselves. As with civil rights, establishment liberals got very little credit at the time for their achievements.

There was, however, at least one crucial difference between social reform and civil rights. Whereas the civil rights movement was a grass-roots effort to correct a glaring injustice, the liberal reforms of the Sixties were top-down efforts. Undertaken at a time when the conditions of life for Americans were generally good, the reforms of the period were not responses to the clamoring of large sections of the population for solutions to urgent needs.

Indeed, why the Sixties became a period of extensive social reform is not self-evident. The Sixties was not a time of economic distress. Throughout the decade, for example, unemployment, the most politically volatile economic problem, was relatively low. True, Kennedy entered office during a recession and inherited a rate that hovered beneath 7 percent; after 1961, the unemployment rate declined until it bottomed out beneath 4 percent in the latter half of the decade. Overall wages were healthy and continued the long-term increases that had begun after World War II.

Curiously, establishment liberals saw this prosperity as a reason to enact, rather than avoid, reform. As we have seen, they believed that the American economy was fundamentally sound. Poverty remained, but as influential thinkers such as John Kenneth Galbraith argued, "it can no longer be presented as a universal or massive affliction. It is more nearly an afterthought."[22] As establishment liberals saw it, poverty survived in one of two forms: as a result of individual dislocation; or as "pockets" limited to a specific geographic area. There were always individuals who needed extra help to secure a foothold. Meanwhile and more important, there were regions of the country where affluence had never quite reached, such as the rural south and southwest, and others where industrial changes had generated regional depressions, such as in the Pennsylvania coal regions. Inner cities, deluged by the flood of black and white migrants from rural areas and unable to provide adequate employment, housing, or education were especially hard hit. Another stream of thought, which collected around urban sociology, suggested that poverty in these two forms could be alleviated, if not virtually eliminated, if those specific areas and marginalized individuals were targeted with programs that helped pull them into the mainstream. Put together, prosperity, liberal economic expertise, and innovative social science held out the possibility that poverty might be all but wiped out.

These streams of thought provided both a diagnosis and a treatment, exactly the sort of combination Kennedy was keen for. And he had ideas of his own. He had shown interest in such issues as health care for the poor during his senatorial career, and it is often said as well that he was shocked when he came face-to-face with the deep poverty of Appalachia during the 1960 presidential primary in West Virginia. His sister Eunice helped ensure that the problem of juvenile delinquency, which had become a politically fashionable cause during the late 1950s, got consideration.

Given poverty's supposedly limited breadth, Kennedy's domestic program was piecemeal and modest. On entering office, he proposed health care for the elderly poor; a minimum wage hike that also expanded the types of workers who were covered by the law; an Area Redevelopment Act designed to provide federal money for communities struggling with dying industries or chronic marginalization; an ambitious job training bill designed to encourage updated work skills for both victims of technological displacement and young adults who lacked skills in the first place; and, finally, a juvenile delinquency program that was intended as an experiment in how best to wean ghetto youth from self-destructive behaviors by providing opportunities.

The last three programs essentially constituted the Kennedy administration's attack on that "afterthought" of poverty, and together they yielded results befitting their modest purposes. The Area Redevelopment program ran into political opposition from congressional conservatives and into the economic reality that areas that had lost major industries were not very attractive places for new business investment. The job training program had been born amidst concerns that high-tech, "cybernetic" machinery would displace large groups of manufacturing workers, who would need retraining. But the prosperity of the mid-Sixties delayed large-scale technological displacement until the 1970s, and thus the program, while popular with Congress because it stressed the virtue of work, gradually focused on trainees whose skills were rudimentary and whose prospects were limited to the lowliest jobs.

The juvenile delinquency program, meanwhile, took on a life of its own. When administration officials began to consider a program, they characteristically looked for the "cutting edge" ideas about the problem. The hottest idea, "opportunity theory," came from Columbia University sociologists Lloyd Ohlin and Richard Cloward, whose 1960 book, *Delinquency and Opportunity*, had argued that juvenile crime was a rational response to inner-city conditions. Denied access to the normal rewards of society, ghetto youths were tempted toward whatever paid, including drug dealing and petty crime. Because delinquent behavior was a predictable response to the inner-city environment, it stood to reason that if the environment were changed, the behavior would change too. The key to this change, Ohlin and Cloward argued, was to provide tangible opportunities for ghetto youths. While the theory had its critics, it was alluring to Kennedy officials for several reasons: it explained delinquency in a way that was not moralistic; it suggested a solution; and it could possibly apply as well to the more general problem of urban poverty. Indeed, the more they pondered the issue, the more Kennedy's juvenile delinquency officials thought they were shooting at two birds with one stone. Program head David Hackett explicitly linked delinquency and poverty: "We saw no distinction between the two."[23] Soon enough the theory was seen to pay a third dividend. As the civil rights movement picked up steam in 1962 and 1963, Hackett and his colleagues aimed the juvenile delinquency program primarily at black youth. As Hackett explained to the president in 1963, "most of the programs in action or being developed will affect primarily minority youth—Negroes in almost every city."[24]

These were considerable virtues indeed for a program that was modest in scope but laden with liberal optimism. Within the Kennedy White House, the program had still another important strength: the steady support of the U.S. Attorney General, the president's brother and closest advisor, Robert F. Kennedy. The attorney general took an intense personal interest in the program, in part because he identified with the alienated youth he kept hearing the sociologists theorize about. He appointed Hackett, a trusted boyhood friend, to run it. Together, Kennedy and Hackett brought into the administration of the juvenile program men who were remarkably radical for Washington. Hackett's men hated bureaucracies only slightly less than they despised the bureaucrats who made their comfortable living by ensuring that nothing got done. From early on, they saw themselves at war with the established agencies, especially the Labor Department. Indeed, they gained a reputation as cunning players in the maze of executive branch agencies. "Hackett's guerrillas," as one critic wrote with some admiration, saw themselves as "living off the administrative countryside, invisible to the bureaucratic enemy but known to one another, hitting and running and making off with the riches of the established departments."[25]

These bureaucratic renegades were radical in another way as well. They extended the logic of opportunity theory to the political sphere. If poor people were poor because the system denied them proper opportunities, they reasoned, then at bottom the issue was not the lack of job skills but, rather, the lack of political power to change the system. Just as job training was supposed to empower poor people to pick themselves up, so this decidedly radical notion assumed that if poor people were encouraged to develop political skills, they would grab power and help themselves. This was the genesis of what became known as "community action," and none of Hackett's men were so aggressive in promoting it as the sociologist Richard Boone, whom Robert Kennedy brought from the Ford Foundation. Like his colleagues, Boone was contemptuous of the federal bureaucracies. But he was even more critical of local institutions, from city hall to welfare agencies, that provided services to the poor; these Boone considered simply oppressive, existing for their own purposes, and organized in defense of the status quo.

During John Kennedy's presidency, the administration's caution and the relatively paltry $30 million budget of the fledgling juvenile delinquency program kept these bureaucratic renegades in check. When Lyndon Johnson assumed the presidency, he moved almost immediately to expand domestic programs. Johnson's motives were complex. He was at heart a New Deal liberal and fervently believed that the federal government had a mission, if not a moral obligation, to help those at the bottom of the social ladder. As a politician, Johnson believed that federal money not only helped the poor but could be directed in ways that benefited friends. His was a simple calculus: the more federal programs, the more friends. Another motive grew out of Johnson's peculiar relationship to John F. Kennedy. Johnson was almost Kennedy's opposite—ungainly rather than dashing; a modest Texas background against Kennedy's wealth and breeding—and he was burdened with a sense of inferiority. Coming to the presidency as he did in the midst of national trauma only heightened this sense. Accordingly, Johnson sought to build a legacy of accomplishment greater than Kennedy's. The day after the assassination, Johnson met with Kennedy economic advisor Walter Heller and gave him the green light to expand domestic spending. "I want you to tell your friends—Arthur Schlesinger, Galbraith and other liberals that . . . I'm no budget slasher," Johnson exclaimed. "If you look at my record, you would know that I am a Roosevelt New Dealer. As a matter of fact, to tell the truth, John F. Kennedy was a little too conservative to suit my taste."[26]

Finally, there was the issue of civil rights. Having thrown his power behind the Civil Rights Act and planning to do the same for the 1965 Voting Rights Act, Johnson understood that the Democrats were writing off the white South. It was all the more important, therefore, that African-American and liberal votes be locked up. To do so, Johnson was willing to go beyond what Kennedy had promised in domestic reforms aimed at African-Americans.

Johnson threw himself into his Great Society reform program. In short order, he rammed through Medicaid/Medicare, which provided health care to the poor and elderly; the Elementary and Secondary Education Act, which vastly increased the federal funds available to public school districts; the Appalachian Redevelopment Act, designed to encourage economic development and job growth in that poor region; and the National Housing Act, intended to make home ownership possible for low-income Americans. Under the Great Society, the federal government established the National Endowment for the Humanities. Johnson established a new cabinet department, Housing and Urban Development, dedicated to a panorama of social programs and led by the first African-American cabinet head, Richard Weaver. It was a breathtaking legislative run, and it contained, as the *Chicago Tribune* sarcastically remarked at the time Johnson proposed it, "everything for everybody."[27]

While the grab-bag quality of the Great Society invited such criticism, the fact is that because Johnson threw so much at so many entrenched interests, these programs became his legacy. They worked, at least in the sense that many of them have survived.

The same cannot be said for the administration's second line of reform, the War on Poverty. The keystone of the War on Poverty, announced with great fanfare in Johnson's maiden address to Congress in January 1964, became the 1964 Economic Opportunity Act (EOA). The act created the Office of Economic Opportunity (OEO), which was given oversight of an array of programs more or less intended to address urban poverty, including the Job Corps job training program, the VISTA program (a domestic version of the Peace Corps), and all the various programs lumped under the Community Action Program. To ensure that the act had a link to Kennedy, Johnson chose Sargent Shriver, the Kennedys' brother-in-law and an heir to the Chicago Merchandise Mart fortune, to administer the agency. Because it was a new bureaucracy dedicated to the administration of the War on Poverty, OEO was in effect an end run around the existing agencies, and its independence supposedly ensured that the programs would be simpler to oversee and effectively delivered in the spirit of uplifting the poor.

In formally proposing the act in March 1964, Johnson emphasized that the programs would provide "opportunity" to those in need. The act "will give almost half a million young Americans the opportunity to develop skills, continue education, and find useful work." It would give "dedicated Americans the opportunity to enlist as volunteers in the war against poverty." It was intended to give the nation itself "the opportunity for a concerted attack on poverty." (See document 3.) The EOA also proposed to "give every American community the opportunity to develop a comprehensive plan to fight its own poverty."

But here was the fingerprint of Hackett's guerrillas. Though Johnson himself was deeply suspicious of the abstract theorizing of the academics and even more suspicious of anything associated with Robert Kennedy, he grudgingly agreed to permit Richard Boone to fasten a mandate to the act that insisted that local programs had to be developed with the "maximum feasible participation" of the poor themselves. Boone thought that such participation would empower the poor to stand up to those institutions that presumably kept them in abject dependence. By placing this command in the legislation itself, the radicals expected to funnel money directly to agencies organized by or for residents of poor neighborhoods, thereby skirting all the existing local bureaucracies. No one stated the case for community action better than Robert Kennedy himself as he testified on behalf of the bill: "The institutions which affect the poor . . . are huge, complex structures. . . . They plan programs for the poor, not with them." Sounding every bit the existential radical, Kennedy explained that "part of the sense of helplessness and futility comes from the feeling of powerlessness to affect the operation of these organizations." The purpose of the community action component was nothing less than to "change these organizations by building into the program real representation for the poor."[28]

Community action had the effect Boone and Kennedy had hoped, and it turned out to be a political disaster. In order to get federal money from OEO, city governments had to include representatives of the poor, but it was never clear just how much "representation" was the "maximum feasible," who could claim to "represent" the poor, or how much control over a given pot of money "representation" guaranteed. While some grants went directly to independent citizens' groups, others were funneled through city governments. In some of the former cases, independent groups felt empowered to challenge local institutions; in the latter, the local political machines controlled the purse strings and essentially stymied real community representation. It was only with a little exaggeration that Daniel Patrick Moynihan wrote that these incompatible forces caused "all hell to break out all over the place."[29] In Chicago, OEO funds made their way to a criminal street gang that set up a Head Start program. In Syracuse, the program paid for the organization of a tenants' union in public housing projects that made the city's mayor livid. In Harlem, it funded a black nationalist theater group under the radical poet Le Roi Jones. In San Francisco, black-power advocates tried to use OEO money to fund an independent political party. Within a year, Johnson was receiving heated protests from some of his most loyal big-city friends, including Chicago's Richard Daley, who with Los Angeles Mayor Sam Yorty led the National Conference of Mayors to denounce community action for stoking class struggle. In the off-year congressional elections of that year, the Democrats lost forty-seven House seats, many in the South, but the party took a beating in state elections across the Midwest, which the White House interpreted as a rebuke to the War on Poverty. A politician above all else, Johnson was quickly losing whatever taste for radical grass-roots politics he had.

For a brief time in 1965, community action gave Lyndon Johnson's reforms an undeniably radical bent. For that brief time, establishment liberals and the activists of the New Left seemed to be allies, not enemies. This was not too surprising, since on the issue of social reform, the New Left distinguished itself from liberals only by matters of degree, not kind. In the Port Huron Statement's conclusion, for example, the pioneers of Students for a Democratic Society called for an ambitious housing act, universal health care, more generous Social Security payments for the poor, and a raised minimum wage. They applauded the Area Redevelopment Act. They were not that far from the establishment on these issues. As it turned out, the New Left shared something else with the official portion of the War on Poverty: a fairly brief and incomplete commitment to the practice of community organization.

Even though the Port Huron Statement said relatively little about social reform, the cause became increasingly important to SDS in 1962. They had dabbled in the civil rights struggle, either in sympathy protests in the North or some by going south. But civil rights was not their cause. Looking for a parallel issue, SDS radicals began to look to the inner cities of the North as the terrain of struggle. As urban Northerners, they believed that that cities were at least familiar territory, though few had any experience living or working in poor neighborhoods.

In 1963, SDS used a grant from the United Auto Workers to launch the Economic Research and Action Project (ERAP). SDS intended to use ERAP, the group's first effort at radical activism, to gain organizing experience and, hopefully, secure some concrete improvements for the urban poor. They took their method directly from SNCC. The group envisioned more or less independent efforts taken up in different cities—essentially wherever an SDS chapter or a group of activists chose—that would develop out of local conditions. There were to be no SDS "leaders"; the organizers were to make all decisions through discussion, debate, and democratic consensus. The local people were to be encouraged to take up their own causes and learn the science of self-empowerment. Todd Gitlin and Nancy Hollander, who participated in the group's Chicago effort, maintained that "by winning some victories, the organizers could show that 'a whole lot of people is strong', could break the cycle of private hopelessness and plant the seeds for a political movement, for the self-determination of the poor."[30]

The theory behind ERAP, such as it was, came from Port Huron's main author, Tom Hayden. Writing with SDS colleague Carl Wittman, who already had helped organize groups of poor blacks in the declining industrial town of Chester, Pennsylvania, Hayden argued that ERAP projects should seek to generate "an interracial movement of the poor." Hayden and Wittman anticipated that civil rights activism would move north once segregation was destroyed. The problem of black poverty would become the focus of the protest movement, which would pit, the authors feared, poor whites against poor blacks. The "contending forces" of race had created "a crisis and a paralysis among the liberal organizations," they wrote, "and behind it all is the Federal Government encouraging mild concessions and preparing to maintain order." The hope was that seasoned organizers might help bridge the racial chasm, and the surest way to do so, they theorized, was by emphasizing those two things that poor folk had in common: "a widespread feeling of alienation and a discouragement with existing economic policies." Whatever the differences between them and African-Americans, "the 50 million or more 'non-Negroes' who now are in a state of poverty or economic insecurity" might still be organized in an interracial movement. (See document 4.)

On the strength of such thinking, SDS established "action" projects in thirteen cities, the most important of which were in Chicago, Newark, Cleveland, and Boston. Each project was to tailor the organizing effort around whatever local needs and issues seemed keenest among their prospective constituents. The initial idea was that the organizers would live in the neighborhoods they hoped to organize and study the problems that might be used to bring people together. The young radicals learned a few lessons very quickly. In contrast to the theory behind ERAP, theoretical notions of poverty did not particularly move the poor; they rarely thought of themselves as "alienated." Instead, poor people had very specific, local grievances. They did not hate capitalism, but they despised their landlords, who charged high rents for apartments in ill-repair. The poor were not opposed to the "Establishment," but they feared and loathed the local police who both harassed and failed to protect them. ERAP activists came to see these concrete, everyday concerns as the organizational focus for local movements. Where theory failed, practicality might succeed. A punning play on project acronyms caught this shift in strategy: the Chicago project, which began on the original notion of organizing around unemployment, was known as JOIN, for Jobs or Income

Now!; the Cleveland project, which aimed at neighborhood problems, was dubbed GROIN, for Garbage or Income Now!

Even with this practical approach, the young radicals confronted the daunting tasks of organizing their communities. Their neighbors were instinctively suspicious of them, among other reasons because ERAP's communal houses generated gossip about communism, group sex, and drug use. America's poor might have been organized to battle for economic improvement but as a lot were culturally conservative and disapproved of the students' living arrangements. That conservatism also showed itself in ethnic and racial insularity. When they chose neighborhoods, project organizers looked for "poor" areas; once in the neighborhoods, they found that a good deal of self-segregation by race, ethnicity, and background created a divisive heterogeneity. As Hayden and Wittman feared, the civil rights movement strained those divisions in a twofold way. As African-American political organization intensified through 1964, various white groups, such as the Appalachians, grew jealous of blacks' new-found clout. They fell back on an age-old racism and yet wanted to imitate black political methods. ERAP activists must have anticipated some of this hostility, but they never expected to discover that their neighborhoods were not really "communities" in any meaningful sense. Many residents came and went. Generally, the residents lacked a stake in the neighborhoods and tended to adopt a strategy of keeping their heads down, minding their own business, and just getting by. These were not people who made good material for a political movement.

Through the ERAP experience, however, one group in particular did emerge as likely material, and they were the exception that proved the new rules: single mothers, often on welfare. Women activists found it possible to build relationships with white and black mothers in ways that eluded the men in the projects. The welfare system was also an apt example of an unresponsive bureaucracy that wielded power over voiceless constituents. As it existed then, welfare case officers had significant power over those on their case rolls and were often accused of using it capriciously to regulate the private lives of their welfare cases. Recipients were not permitted to have men living in the home, even if the man was the father of their children. Caseworkers could launch what one recipient who became involved in the Chicago movement called a "midnight raid" whenever they pleased. "If a woman's by herself and ain't got her husband with her," declared one woman who became involved with ERAP, "they never leave you alone and act like it's a sin or something."[31] Activists accused caseworkers of intentionally obscuring welfare regulations to prevent recipients from complaining about abuse or exercising their own management of available resources. ERAP's women found an innate feminism alive among welfare mothers, who proved eager to accept the activists' help in dealing with caseworkers and mastering the regulations in order to understand their rights. The hassles with the system were a source of very immediate trouble for many women, and they were easily motivated to organize. Mothers on welfare had to stay put in order to receive regular benefits. And just as New Left theory held that politicizing the poor could also express the subjective needs of the activists themselves, so the successful contacts with welfare mothers reinforced an intensifying feminism among New Left women.

The end result was that with the radicals' help, welfare mothers organized their own national body, the National Welfare Rights Organization, which mounted widely noted protests beginning in 1966 and continuing into the next decade. For their own part, New Left women moved closer to the radical feminism that was brewing in other parts of "the movement."

This singular success notwithstanding, ERAP projects began to fold up by 1966, though some dedicated activists remained far longer than most. The war and the burgeoning antiwar movement drew the energies of many away from the projects; those few who tried to have a foot both in the inner cities and the peace movement were irresistibly drawn toward the latter as the war went on. Some SDS leaders, most notably Paul Potter, insisted that ERAP was not really in keeping with the spirit of the New Left. It was another effort to participate in someone else's cause, rather than attending to their own need of authentic public activism. Worse, the theory behind "The Interracial Movement of the Poor," Potter insisted, smacked too much of the Old Left's "labor metaphysic." They had made the mistake of concentrating on the economic injustices of capitalism, he wrote rather scornfully, and found themselves "with a slightly different portion of the same well-chewed piece of gristle so many American radicals had gnawed and choked on before."[32]

Though the peripatetic Tom Hayden was unable to devote much attention to the Newark project, he had a different view of ERAP than Potter. In his view ERAP's failure reflected the hypocrisy of liberal reforms, which were never meant in good faith to help the poor. Instead, the Great Society was only intended to smooth over the worst injustices of capitalism in order to save the system from itself. When Hayden surveyed the Newark project in 1965, he found it bogged down in the hypocrisy of an antipoverty program designed, he said, to ensure "the dominance of established interests, especially those with the Democratic Party machine and middle-class reform groups"—the dominance of liberals, in other words. For the city's poor, Hayden claimed, "the President's programs would be another cruel joke were [they] not so irrelevant to their lives."[33]

Fellow New Left theorists argued that the War on Poverty reflected a distinct and identifiably new sort of establishment thinking that they began calling "corporate liberalism." By gathering together a liberal consensus in favor of reform, Richard Flacks wrote in 1966, Lyndon Johnson created a facade for "the preservation of a corporation economy." The president sought "to harness an extensive social welfare system to a centrally coordinated but privately controlled economy." It was bad enough that reforms were aimed at "the *co-optation* of dissent," but the programs also allowed corporate interests to gorge themselves at the public trough. "As long as corporate interests dominate" liberal government, Flacks insisted, "as long as power is badly skewed, every public venture becomes a subsidy for special interests, every regulatory agency becomes a lobby for the industry it regulates, every social reform is twisted and diluted to avoid jeopardizing private greeds."[34] If this were true, then the deck was stacked against the poor even within community action programs.

Because the New Left believed that liberal compromises corrupted even the reform programs, then the poor had no other recourse than outright rebellion. Following the lead of the black-power radicals, New Left theorists insisted that the urban riots were akin to anticolonial rebellions. Hayden even argued that the Newark riot, the largest of 1967 aside from Detroit, fulfilled the New Left's dreams of existential action. It generated community involvement in a way that none of the federal reforms ever could, he claimed. Violence might have been unfortunate, but the riot was a legitimate form of participatory democracy among people whose lives were otherwise lived under the boot of public authorities. New Left writer Andrew Kopkind insisted that the riots were in fact "rebellions [with] an authenticity beyond chaotic mob action." As he saw it, the riots "mocked the materialism of the suburbs and the legal violence committed in the name of the government." They were "scenes in a vast, spontaneous morality play, staged by guerrilla actors in the only real theater," and those actors were on their way to becoming a new cadre of black leadership, "half guerrilla, half ward heeler."[35]

It is worth noting that this kind of inflammatory thinking emerged among radicals after SDS had folded up ERAP and left the arena of community organizing. It was a cheap sort of radicalism, therefore, that Kopkind was peddling. It was far easier to imagine that the riots were a self-organized form of revolutionary politics than commit to the long and invariably frustrating process of grass-roots organization. As such, Kopkind and Flacks both revealed the New Left's mounting tendency to denounce everything associated with the liberal center. That tendency, however, was less a result of the left's disappointment with the Great Society. Rather, it was an indication of how the deepening crisis of the Vietnam War was radicalizing the ways in which the New Left understood all of American life.

THE NEW LEFT AND THE LIBERAL WAR IN VIETNAM

For all the differences that emerged between the New Left and establishment liberals over race and poverty, these two wings of American public life probably would have maintained a civil, working relationship had it not been for the Vietnam War. Vietnam blew everything apart.

From its inception, the New Left seized on liberal Cold War policy as both the most important and most emblematic distortion in American life. The establishment's preoccupation with communism lay beneath a policy of nuclear deterrence that contemplated, as a matter of publicly stated planning, a nuclear exchange with the Soviet Union in which an estimated 130 million Americans would die. This, the policymakers announced, would be a victory, since some Americans would survive, while the Soviet Union would be totally destroyed. Could there be a better example, SDS asked, of the insanity of a society that had put its fate in the hands of a militarized government? In order to wage the Cold War, meanwhile, the United States was forced to spend money that might otherwise be used for social programs at home and alleviating poverty abroad. As the young radicals at Port Huron put it, the United States had developed not into a welfare state but a "Warfare State," which mobilized the bulk of the nation's technological genius and economic resources in the competition with the Soviets. Most of the nation's institutions were bound up in the warfare state, and this was particularly true of the universities, many of which were engaged in various sorts of Pentagon research and development. The mass media toed the line too by loyally repeating official pronouncements; the media merely "mimics conventional Cold War policy," declared the Port Huron Statement. But what was most disturbing to the young radicals—and most revealing about the state of American society—was that the vast majority of Americans accepted the Cold War as the normal state of affairs. Because all the decisions about foreign policy were "more and more the property of the military and industrial arms race machine," the average citizen felt powerless to alter even such a suicidal course.

Almost as soon as he entered the presidency, John F. Kennedy delivered proof that his inaugural promise to wage the Cold War aggressively was not mere rhetoric. In his first major foreign policy decision, Kennedy approved a hopelessly flawed invasion of Cuba that the Eisenhower administration had been planning in the vain hopes of toppling the new regime of Fidel Castro. The infamous Bay of Pigs invasion of April 1961 deeply embarrassed the new president, not, however, because he was worried about its legality. Kennedy was upset that the plan's failure made him look like an amateur, and he carried an almost obsessive resentment against Castro thereafter. Indeed, the administration conducted an ongoing program of CIA assassination attempts against Castro.

In setting American policy so directly against Castro's revolution, Kennedy helped solidify what had been then only a loose coalition of radicals into an increasingly vocal opposition to U.S. Cold War policy in general. There had been, as historian Van Gosse has observed, a fair amount of sympathy for Castro's 1959 revolution in the United States, at a time when Castro had shown neither an ideological inclination toward the Soviet Union nor the authoritarianism that eventually came to characterize his regime. Kennedy's overt hostility to Cuba garnered support in the general public but quickly and deeply disillusioned those on the left. Staughton Lynd, a young Yale professor who became a fixture in the movement against the Vietnam War, recalled at the end of the 1960s that his own consciousness was piqued in 1956 when Martin Luther King, Jr., led the Montgomery Bus Boycott and Fidel Castro launched his armed challenge to the dictatorship of Fulgencio Batista in Cuba. Sympathy for the Cuban revolution was strong among older left-wingers, particularly those with independent streaks such as C. Wright Mills and the irascible journalist I. F. Stone. Mills's indictment of American policy, *The Causes of World War III* (1958), had already become required reading among the young radicals when, in 1960, he published *Listen, Yankee*, a strident defense of the Cuban revolution's legitimacy. Assuming the voice of a Cuban revolutionary, Mills assured American readers that they need not fear that Cuba would become a Soviet satellite: "We haven't done all this fighting to get out from under one tyranny just to stick our necks into some other yoke," his Cuban protagonist maintained.[36] Similarly, Stone insisted that the revolutionary spirit appearing throughout Latin America was independent from the Cold War. "We see Castro as a pawn in our global struggle with the U.S.S.R.," Stone wrote several months before the Bay of Pigs. "The Latin American masses see him as their first honest champion since the Mexican Revolution and a man who dared defy American oil and sugar firms. The Latins couldn't care less about our cold war."[37]

When the Bay of Pigs invasion was launched, the American sympathizers with Cuba were prepared to protest. Though he already had concluded that Castro was not interested in democracy, Stone still rebuked Kennedy for engaging in what was plainly old-fashioned Yankee imperialism. Street protests in New York and San Francisco brought out thousands, while smaller rallies were held in Boston, Chicago, Los Angeles, and Washington. Students at many of the nation's elite campuses, already organized in fledgling activist groups that had been inspired by the sit-in movement, were primed to disrupt their placid campuses. Though puny by the standards of the huge protests against the Vietnam War later in the decade, in retrospect the Bay of Pigs protests were important for several reasons. They brought together a diverse group of people and therefore provided the first step toward the broad movement against the Vietnam War. In so doing, the conflict over Cuba was the starting point of a decisive and, as it turned out, irreparable breach between the progressive left and those erstwhile liberals who saw so much promise in John F. Kennedy.

These developments came into play again when, some eighteen months after the Bay of Pigs disaster—an interlude during which the young radicals met at Port Huron and composed their famous manifesto—Cuba returned in dramatic fashion as the focal point of the Cold War. In mid-October 1962, American surveillance planes photographed the construction of what appeared to be Soviet missile silos in Cuba, and thus began the Cuban Missile Crisis that for thirteen days held the world in a state of alarmed suspense. On the evening of October 22, Kennedy explained to a national television audience that he would not permit the Soviets to place missiles on the island and that he would consider an attack from Cuba reason for the United States to launch a full attack on the Soviet Union itself. The administration had considered bombing the missile site or invading Cuba; instead, Kennedy opted for a preventive naval blockade to stop Soviet ships from delivering warheads. For several days, full nuclear war loomed as an almost irresistible reality—indeed, we now know it was even closer than some of the actors in the drama appreciated at the time—only to be turned away in a last-minute, backdoor diplomatic arrangement between the superpowers. To most Americans, it looked as though their young president had stood toe to toe with the blustering Soviet premier, Nikita Khrushchev, and stared him down. Kennedy, meanwhile, regained the confidence he had lost in the Bay of Pigs defeat.

For those on the left, however, the Cuban Missile Crisis bore out almost everything they had come to think about the Cold War. Kennedy had been as belligerent as Khrushchev. He already had proved willing to engage in violence against the Cuban revolution, and it was difficult to believe that his aggressiveness in this case was not connected to his desire to avenge himself against Castro for the Bay of Pigs. For those few who harbored the romantic notion of world revolution, Kennedy's opposition to the apparent solidarity growing between the Soviets and the Cubans smacked of capitalist imperialism. A simpler critique considered it sheer lunacy to destroy the world to make points in international one-upmanship.

The missile crisis stirred to action Americans who were far outside the insular orbit of the scrawny New Left and eventually made possible a broad-based movement against the war in Vietnam. Two groups in particular, Citizens for a Sane Nuclear Policy (SANE) and Women Strike for Peace (WSP), were mostly composed of middle-class professionals of conventionally liberal attitudes. Both had been founded several years before, but the missile crisis brought home to the members of each group the need for intensified activism. The Fellowship of Reconciliation (FOR), meanwhile, a venerable old Christian pacifist group, underwent a revival as the antinuclear movement picked up steam. These were among those varied groups that began to coalesce, fused together by the heat of youthful energy.

Attuned though they were to the Cold War, the New Left radicals did not yet foresee that America's long-running involvement in the civil war in Vietnam was about to explode into a full-scale U.S. military commitment.

True, Kennedy had expanded the American military effort in Southeast Asia, but he showed little taste for full-scale war there. If anything, he was growing increasingly impatient with South Vietnamese dictator Ngo Dinh Diem, whose regime managed to be simultaneously repressive and militarily inept. In late August 1963, a group of South Vietnamese army officers contacted the CIA in Saigon to sound out whether the United States would support a coup against Diem. At first, administration officials gave the generals a green light by indicating U.S. support, but then second thoughts within the Kennedy inner circle generated weeks of debate. Kennedy's men were still arguing over the wisdom of a coup when, on November 1, the generals overthrew the regime, murdering Diem in the process. Three weeks later, Kennedy himself was assassinated in Dallas, Texas.

With very little experience in foreign policy, far more interested in his domestic reform program, Lyndon Johnson stayed the course that Kennedy had set in Vietnam. All of the main players on Kennedy's team stayed in place for Johnson: Robert McNamara as Secretary of Defense; Dean Rusk as Secretary of State; McGeorge Bundy as National Security Advisor. So too did many subordinate yet influential advisors such as Walt Rostow, William Bundy, George Ball, and Maxwell Taylor. Johnson's Texas common sense nagged him like a guilty conscience and constantly warned him not to expand American involvement. But like nearly all American politicians of the 1950s, he embraced Cold War orthodoxies. He believed in the domino theory, which held that if communism was not stopped in Vietnam it would spread to all of Asia and eventually isolate the United States in the world. He thought that withdrawing from Vietnam when things looked bad would only appease the Soviets and make them more likely to increase their aggressiveness. And he assumed that if he failed to stand up to communism, his domestic opponents would destroy his grand dreams for domestic reform. So when Kennedy's men began to urge Johnson to expand American military responsibility in Vietnam, Johnson figured he had no options.

The first decisions to Americanize the war in Vietnam were made in summer 1964. Ongoing political chaos in South Vietnam convinced administration officials that the United States had to assume more military responsibility just to keep what semblance of a government remained in Saigon afloat. They concluded that an air war against North Vietnam would stymie North Vietnamese support for the southern guerrillas and boost the morale of the South Vietnamese government.

But they needed a pretext to begin the bombing campaign. That excuse came in early August when an altercation between North Vietnamese patrol boats and American surveillance vessels off the North Vietnamese coast allowed the administration to accuse the North of an unprovoked attack. Concealing key facts, the president presented a gullible Congress with the Gulf of

Tonkin resolution, which essentially gave him a free hand in Southeast Asia. With virtually unanimous congressional support, Johnson hoped that he could exert enough military pressure against the North Vietnamese that they would withdraw their support of the war in the South and thereby make an even larger American military effort unnecessary. Like so many of the administration's assumptions, this one proved badly misguided, in part because the Vietnamese Communist Party decided to match American escalation in the equally misguided assumption that they would raise the cost of fighting above what Johnson was willing to pay.

After sporadic bombing failed to alter North Vietnamese behavior, Johnson came to the fateful decision, announced in mid-February 1965 after an attack on an American air base at Pleiku, to approve a policy of regular and extensive bombings and to dispatch American ground troops. Even as he upped the military ante, the president attempted to placate his liberal supporters by assuring them that he intended to fight the Communists while keeping the best interests of the Vietnamese people in mind. His "Peace Without Conquest" address at Johns Hopkins University on April 7 mixed Woodrow Wilson with Franklin Delano Roosevelt. Disavowing any hostile intentions toward the Vietnamese, he announced his intention to ask Congress for "a billion dollar American investment" in Southeast Asia. Among other things, the investment would go toward developing the Mekong River delta and providing electric power to the region, much as the American Tennessee Valley Authority did for Appalachia during the 1930s. Marshalling the same rhetoric he used for the Great Society, Johnson promised that this investment would help replace "despair with hope, and terror with progress." (See document 5.)

Up to that point, the voices raised against U.S. policy in Vietnam were few and far between. But with the expansion of American military operations, the young radicals of SDS began to rethink their focus on domestic activism. During a meeting at the end of 1964, at which Stone made a cogent case that Vietnam was fast becoming the main tumor of America's cancerous policies toward the Third World, advocates of a peace march on Washington persuaded just enough SDS colleagues to support the effort. It was neither an easy nor an uncontroversial shift in the group's focus. At the time, few SDS members thought antiwar activity would overshadow their other efforts, and those who did believed that would be unfortunate. None of them foresaw just how important what they were about to undertake would turn out to be.

What eventually became the Easter March on Washington was a watershed moment in the history of the New Left. It was the first protest march that SDS planned, organized, and led. And the manner in which the young radicals did so was both illustrative of the style of activism they intended to deploy and a prelude to many of the problems that the New Left would create for itself.

As SDS leaders began to plan the march, they decided that they would not exclude any groups sympathetic to the antiwar cause, including communist ones. To do so, they argued, would tie them to the obsolete anticommunism of their elders. Yet this decision made the leaders of SANE and FOR deeply uneasy, because they thought that any participation by communist groups would give the administration reason to dismiss the protest out of hand and invite the media to see the march as anti-American, rather than antiwar. Moreover, whereas the students seemed to think that protest was an existentialist act and therefore an end in itself, the older activists believed that the point of protest was to persuade fellow citizens. It was a means to an end. Many members of SANE maintained friendships with congressmen, prominent editors and journalists, and even administration officials, and they believed they could persuade these acquaintances of the folly of U.S. policy in Vietnam.

In April 1965, American military escalation in Vietnam allowed the antiwar coalition to paper over these differences—not the last time Lyndon Johnson's decisions actually helped protests along. As the first of many, the Easter 1965 march was inherently important. It drew far more people—at least twenty thousand—than organizers had hoped. It set the format for most subsequent marches, and it was a format drawn from the large civil rights gatherings. Many luminaries spoke, including I. F. Stone. Bob Moses, the esteemed civil rights activist, compared the killing of Vietnamese to the murders of civil rights workers in the South. Folk singers Judy Collins, Joan Baez, and Phil Ochs sang and marched. But the most important moment came when SDS president Paul Potter delivered the keynote address. Potter and his colleagues had carefully worked over the speech, and their care was borne out in a rambling yet evocative address that updated the ideas of Port Huron and directed them at the war.

Potter began by trying to puncture the basic claim of the administration as to its purpose in Vietnam, to unveil, so to speak, the basic untruth. The administration insisted that it was defending freedom in Vietnam, but the United States had supported an antidemocratic dictator who abused his own people. Comparing the Vietnamese to the people who joined the civil rights movement in Mississippi and Alabama, Potter insisted that the root of the conflict rested in "the demand of ordinary people to have some opportunity to make their own lives, and of their unwillingness . . . to give up the struggle against external domination." Certainly the president could not seriously claim that fighting in Vietnam enhanced freedom at home. Not only was it impossible to see how American freedom improved by putting down the legitimate aspirations of another people a world away, but the war already had "led to even more vigorous governmental efforts to control information, manipulate the press and pressure and persuade the public through distorted and downright dishonest documents." Recalling Port Huron's critique of the

Warfare State, Potter quipped that "the only freedom this war protects is the freedom of the warhawks in the Pentagon and the State Department to experiment with counter-insurgency and guerrilla warfare in Vietnam."

As he rose to his crescendo, Potter combined two claims that symbolized the nature of the New Left: that the bureaucracy was out of control; and that liberals, given their bureaucratic power, were implicated in bureaucratic horrors. The war, Potter maintained, was the product of the "remote-control" society that had created militarized institutions that existed for themselves and had spun out of the control of the very people who were supposed to be in charge of them. Such a society ran on a process of dehumanization, a process that ground down everyone, the Vietnamese, American citizens, even administration officials. After all, Potter insisted in his most piercing comment, the war "depends on the construction of a system of premises and thinking that insulates the President and his advisors thoroughly and completely from the human consequences of the decisions they make. I do not believe," Potter acknowledged, "that the President or Mr. Rusk or Mr. McNamara or even McGeorge Bundy are particularly evil men." But that was just the point: "If asked to throw napalm on the back of a ten-year-old child they would shrink in horror. But their decisions have led to mutilation and death of thousands and thousands of people." The question was, therefore, what sort of society led decent men to such obscene acts. "What kind of system is it that allows good men to make those kinds of decisions?" Rallying his listeners to existential witness, Potter exhorted the crowd to "name that system. We must name it, describe it, analyze it, understand it and change it." (See document 6.)[38]

Potter intentionally never "named the system." At that first stage, SDS leaders did not want to alienate further their elder colleagues. Yet as early as the following November, SANE sponsored another large Washington gathering at which then-SDS president Carl Oglesby promised the crowd that he would name the system. He began where Potter left off by pointing out that the war managers were "fundamentally *liberal* men." "Since it is a very bad war," he argued, "we acquire the habit of thinking that it must be caused by very bad men." But the roster of those who had made American policy in Vietnam was filled with men drawn from "mainstream liberal[ism]. . . . They are not moral monsters. They are all honorable men. They are all liberals." If good men made evil policy, then there had to be something wrong with liberalism, and this was exactly his point. Oglesby admitted that he thought of himself as a liberal, but he had in mind a liberalism that promoted authentic humanism and was dedicated to the promotion of human rights. The liberal war managers, by contrast, were committed to squelching all revolutions as a threat to America's international interests. They could not say as much, because the United States had been born through a violent revolution. So the liberal power elite used anticommunism to "hold together our twin need for richness and righteousness." They could simply denounce the anticolonial revolutions as communist and oppose them on those grounds. "This is the action," Oglesby concluded, not of humanist liberalism but of *"corporate liberalism,"* of liberals who were committed not to "human values" but to the expansion and protection of large corporations.[39]

True to the New Left indictment, this bureaucratic system ground its way into a relentlessly widening war. American troop levels steadily increased. Over 150,000 in 1965, American personnel in Vietnam doubled in numbers in 1966 and hit their peak of 536,000 by 1968. The *Rolling Thunder* bombing campaign eventually included some three million sorties that unleashed nearly eight million tons of bombs, more than had been used in the entire combined history of warfare. Conservative estimates assumed that U.S. bombing caused one thousand civilians casualties a week. While it is true that the United States did not use nuclear weapons or systematically bomb Hanoi, North Vietnam's capital and main population center, the American effort was a "limited war" only in an academic sense. North Vietnam was extensively bombed outside of Hanoi. And though the United States did not deploy its ultimate weapon, it used an extensive arsenal of high-tech weapons, napalm, and chemical weapons such as the defoliant Agent Orange.

As it ramped up the war abroad, the administration intensified its attacks on antiwar activists, just as Paul Potter predicted. The White House approved a series of official moves against dissenters, which included FBI surveillance and infiltration of radical groups and Internal Revenue Service audits of outspoken opponents. The administration was publicly contemptuous of opponents, whom they branded as either communists or ignoramuses or both.

The more the administration hardened, the more even moderate activists began to see wisdom in SDS's positions and the more SDS moved to the left. From 1965 to 1967, the antiwar movement gradually picked up energy, gathered adherents, and widened its activities. As it did so, it gathered a coalition of groups with SDS in the lead into a decentralized web that took the name of the National Mobilization to End the War in Vietnam, or MOBE. Like SDS, MOBE was committed to keeping the antiwar movement in the mold of the civil rights movement. Large-scale protests were essential, but individual acts of witness were just as valuable. People could decide for themselves how to protest, and there should not be any "leaders." Beneath the copious shelter of this broad conception, the movement was content to urge people to "resist" the war directly.

Resistance took many forms, the most important of which emphasized individual action, most often against the draft. The Selective Service required all males to register for the draft at age eighteen, and consequently the draft card was an almost universal possession of American men. To the young existentialists, the draft symbolized how an impersonal government could intrude into the individual's life without his consent; beyond that, of course, it was a constant reminder that if the government called, the young man, by law, had to give up his freedom and pick up a gun.

One means of resisting was to reject the draft card, and this was done both through draft card turn-ins and draft card burnings. Both acts were illegal and brought the direct possibility of imprisonment—indeed Congress passed a stiff bill in 1965 that set a five-year prison term and $10,000 fine for destroying a draft card. Doing so, therefore, amounted to individual rejections of the government's supremacy. It was a highly charged, emotional act that had to be measured against the backdrop of a wide generational crisis in America: men who took these steps typically had fathers, uncles, and brothers who had served in the military, and to reject the draft often was a form of repudiating one's family heritage. While thousands of young men "dodged" the draft, either by dropping out of sight or going into self-exile in Canada or Europe, those few who publicly resisted through draft card destruction challenged the system head on, rather than merely evading it. In the best civil rights tradition, they invited the consequences, whether that meant imprisonment or mob attacks. As simple as it may seem, destroying a draft card was a step not easily taken, which is why draft evasion of various sorts was common but direct resistance was not.

Indeed, resisters, as distinguished from evaders, often were moved more by religious convictions than by political or personal motives. The religious element in the antiwar movement has often been overlooked, as historians, much like many of the media commentators of the 1960s, have focused instead on the political radicalism of the student wing of the movement. More recently, both Doug Rossinow and Michael Foley have shown how religious values inspired activists at the University of Texas and in the Boston resistance movement, respectively. While religious activists steered away from overarching political theories and the divisive schisms of left-wing politics, their sense of moral urgency could lead to actions that can only be described as radical. In November 1965, for example, Norman Morrison, a Quaker pacifist moved by reports he had read of U.S. bombing runs on Vietnamese villages, committed suicide by self-immolation within sight of Secretary of Defense McNamara's Pentagon office window. Seeing themselves as acting in the radical tradition of the city's abolitionists, Boston draft card burners memorialized Morrison when they destroyed their cards. Two of the most notorious opponents of the draft, Daniel and Philip Berrigan, were Catholic priests—at least at the time they started their solitary campaign of breaking into selective service offices and pouring red paint over the files to symbolize the blood being spilled in Vietnam.

After 1965, opposition to Johnson's Vietnam policy grew steadily and emerged from many different sources. The establishment itself produced important critics. The august journalist Walter Lippmann began a regular critique of the war in his columns. Political scientist Hans Morgenthau, the dean of American international relations scholars, insisted that it was the wrong war in the wrong place at the wrong time. Most important, Arkansas Senator J. William Fulbright, chairman of the Senate Foreign Relations Committee and the most influential congressman on foreign affairs, announced his intention to hold extended hearings into administration policies in 1966. The Fulbright hearings, some of which were televised over the next year and a half, maintained a steady venue for Fulbright and other senators increasingly dubious about the war to expose the irrationality of the administration's policy. By doing so, Fulbright did much to legitimize antiwar opinions. Religious and political groups grew more emboldened in holding protests in communities across the country.

SDS benefited from its participation in the movement, even when its leaders remained wary of association with liberals who merely opposed the war and not the entire system. Almost in spite of itself, by 1967 SDS became the antiwar movement's center of gravity. The relentless escalation of the war and the Johnson administration's persistent refusal to acknowledge its critics were clearly the main causes of the movement's growth. As the liberal strands of the movement gravitated to the left, as the movement's success on campus brought as many as one hundred thousand students into SDS, antiwar protests grew larger and more boisterous. Originally conceived on the model of civil rights protests, the early antiwar marches emphasized the importance of orderliness and a certain decorum—participants often wore suits, ties, and dresses. By 1967, however, the sort of public image that came to define "The Sixties" was emerging, as marches became unruly events with participants decked out in jeans, T-shirts, headbands, and other accoutrements of the "counter-culture." One could reasonably look at the famous march of late-October 1967 and think that maybe a revolution was in the offing.

That particular march, which ended with a "siege" of the Pentagon, was the high point in the history of the New Left and the antiwar movement. To cap off Stop the Draft Week in dramatic fashion, MOBE leaders had decided to embrace the tactics of the Berkeley, California, antiwar wing, which had been using running street battles with local police to disrupt the functioning of the Oakland induction center, the largest depot for shipping soldiers out to the Far East. Jerry Rubin, the pioneer in these tactics, fed the increasingly rebellious inclinations of SDS leaders by insisting that his approach to confrontation was based on active resistance to the system and that using them in a prominent national march in Washington would sow such confusion that the whole system would begin to unravel. Rubin's intention was audacious: create havoc around the Pentagon and take the movement to the very citadel of the Warfare State.

The Pentagon March was a celebration of color and boisterousness, a sort of participatory democracy in action. Even the standard parts of the protests, the usual rounds of speeches by the usual big names, had a combustible feel to them. The protests began with William Slone Coffin, Jr., and his colleagues defying arrest with their draft card turn-in. The writer Paul Goodman, speaking to businessmen at a State Department function, denounced his audience as the main agents of worldwide menace; former SNCC president John Lewis stopped his speech for a moment of silence in remembrance of Che Guevara. Little of the well-organized choreography of most marches took hold. To the delight of many, the event seemed utterly without any leaders. An estimated one hundred thousand protesters milled about, listening to a speech here, teasing Capitol police there. Once a long debate about which route to take to the Pentagon was resolved, perhaps as many as fifty thousand made their way toward the place that the authorities had prepared for them. There, entirely in keeping with "the tactics of resistance," marchers did whatever happened to move them. Some tried to storm the building—a couple dozen actually got inside, where they were beaten and arrested. Another group, including novelist Norman Mailer, breached a fence below the Secretary of Defense's office window and were promptly (and courteously, much to Mailer's chagrin) arrested. Most of the others remained in the large parking lot, where they spent hours heckling soldiers who were sent in to act as crowd control. The interplay between the crowd and the troops became part of Sixties mythology when marchers planted daisies in gun barrels and invited the soldiers to come join them. As night fell and the organization of the march completely disintegrated, federal marshals serving alongside the troops began to pick off marchers and subject them to ferocious beatings before heaving them into police vans; they were particularly severe with young women in the hopes that male marchers would try to intervene and provide an excuse for their own vicious beatings. By the time the protest wound to its chaotic finish, 683 had been arrested, and the Pentagon siege became instant lore.

To the typical American looking at these goings-on, the antiwar movement probably came off as a bunch of lunatics, with their pot smoking, their efforts to "levitate" the Pentagon with Buddhist chants, and their kamikaze missions against the building. President Johnson shared that sentiment. But Johnson thought enough about the protests to rig a CIA report that linked march organizers to Vietnamese Communist officials, which he revealed to a handful of selected congressmen.

To the radicalized wing of the antiwar movement, however, the siege was everything they had hoped for. Sidney Peck, the main organizer, thought that the event proved that a mass movement against the war was evolving. The pacifist journal *Liberation* glowingly reported on the march. In the longest essay, George Dennison argued that the march was a thorough success, whether or not it actually influenced policy. To Dennison, the purpose of the protests was action itself, because action induced psychic liberation from social constraints. "The troops in front of us represented great force," Dennison claimed. "But it was obvious that they were quite without power, for their force can only destroy. Power, however, was brimming in the faces and shining in the actions of those around me."[40]

This logic allowed the radicals to declare victory according to their own standards of judgment, and thereafter the tactics aimed at boisterous disruption became the rule in antiwar protests. Within weeks, in fact, New York activists, with SDS members front and center, launched similar street battles with city police aimed at disrupting an appearance of Secretary of State Dean Rusk and sticking it to what one participant described as those "liberal fascists."

The year 1968, that most tumultuous year of a tumultuous decade, began with a large-scale Communist offensive in Vietnam, the TET Offensive of late January. TET was an audacious Communist effort at fomenting complete disorder in the urban areas of South Vietnam through coordinated attacks in thirty-six provincial capitals and five major cities. In the South Vietnamese capital of Saigon, the guerrillas seized the main radio station, and a handful even forced their way into the American embassy. In the old imperial city of Hue, North Vietnamese troops slaughtered several thousand South Vietnamese officials and family members. In spite of its boldness, the offensive was quickly put down everywhere but in Hue, which U.S. Marines took back after six weeks of intense urban combat. The final tally left the Communists badly bloodied—five thousand killed and more than thirty thousand wounded or captured, as against five hundred deaths among the combined U.S.-South Vietnamese forces. In addition, the guerrilla infrastructure inside of South Vietnam had been exposed and largely destroyed.

Though TET was a military failure for the Communists, the whole operation belied the Johnson administration's constant promises that the war was well in hand and the end was in sight. Inside the administration, the long-standing consensus on Vietnam began to crack. Indeed, the war's architects, Secretary of Defense McNamara and National Security Advisor McGeorge Bundy, left office. The antiwar forces in the Democratic Party, organized in a subterranean movement to "dump Johnson," threw its weight behind Minnesota Senator Eugene McCarthy, who decided to challenge the president on an antiwar platform. After McCarthy nearly beat Johnson in the March 1968 New Hampshire primary, Robert Kennedy, himself a recent convert to the antiwar cause, also entered the race for the Democratic presidential nomination. Johnson bent under the cumulative pressures of politics and war and made the surprising announcement at the end of March that he would not seek reelection.

From there, a cascade of grave events unrolled. Martin Luther King, Jr., was assassinated in Memphis on April 4. A spasm of rioting wracked dozens of cities, including Washington. Within the month, student protestors shut down Columbia University. Robert Kennedy was murdered in June while on the campaign trail in California. Dramatic events elsewhere mirrored those in the United States: a democracy movement in Czechoslovakia was brutally suppressed by the Soviets; in France, a nationwide strike that brought together the French New Left with the trade unions nearly brought down the government of Charles De Gaulle; students took over Tokyo University; and later in the year, the Mexican government murdered hundreds of democracy activists protesting one-party rule in that country.

In the United States, the Democratic Party embodied this chaos, which carried into the 1968 presidential convention in Chicago. All of the forces of the antiwar movement, from the MOBE to the cultural rebels behind Jerry Rubin and his sidekick Abbie Hoffman to the mainstream McCarthy Democrats, came together as the party fought a war within. The FBI predicted widespread disruptions, in part because they took on faith Hoffman's prediction that one hundred thousand of his followers would show. Inside the convention, Eugene McCarthy lacked sufficient support to challenge Johnson's handpicked successor, Vice President Hubert Humphrey, so he settled for a platform fight over an antiwar plank. The fight over the plank degenerated into expletive-laced harangues.

While nowhere near one hundred thousand hippies came to town, there remained many angry opponents of the status quo who responded to the defeat of the McCarthy movement and Humphrey's nomination with a massive march on Michigan Avenue. With some coming in from the north, some from the south, some from across the street, the protestors began to merge in the bottleneck in front of the Hilton Hotel. In the tight quarters around the Hilton, the Chicago police, already warmed up in earlier confrontations, unleashed wave attacks. With nightsticks flailing, they lunged into the crowd, grabbing whoever came closest to hand, pulling hair, choking throats, picking people up by their clothes, and chucking them into waiting paddy wagons. As people tried to squeeze up against the hotel facade in hopes of avoiding the melee, a large window cracked, and a stream of humanity flowed through it into the hotel's Haymarket Lounge, ironically named for the famous bombing at an anarchists' rally during the late nineteenth century. The police followed; not only did they continue to beat those inside the bar, they chased people to the upper floors, where the McCarthy campaign was set up. (See document 7.)

As has often been noted, opinion polls taken after the convention showed that most Americans supported the actions of the Chicago police. When Richard Nixon won the 1968 election, it appeared to some radicals that the country was turning decidedly to the right. While a new conservatism certainly was congealing at the time, it is important to remember that Nixon campaigned as a moderate and had promised to find a way to end the war in Vietnam. What in the long term was an important moment in the development of contemporary conservatism was, at the time, an indication that the antiwar movement had achieved some important goals. The movement always had been a diverse one, and after 1968 the moderate elements within it began to reassert control. Meanwhile, public opinion, that elusive creature, turned against the war after TET, and thereafter, antiwar attitudes became the norm, rather than the exception. Opposition to the war had become respectable—hence Nixon's campaign promise.

Ironically, once opposition to the war became something of a mainstream stance, the New Left splintered. It was as though opposition to the war, and to the "corporate liberalism" they had discovered behind Vietnam, provided much of whatever coherence the New Left managed to acquire. True, some of the largest antiwar marches came after 1968, and the events at Kent State and Jackson State universities, in which students were killed during spring 1970 protests, testified to the ongoing crisis in America. But as the Republican Richard Nixon took office, his policies of Vietnamization reduced the numbers of American troops in Vietnam and thus the number of casualties. Nixon managed to bleed away, so to speak, one of the main causes of public anxiety with the war and thereby isolate the New Left.

To some extent as well, New Left activists were suffering from a burnout by 1968 not unlike that which appeared among SNCC leaders. Port Huron veterans Mickey and Richard Flacks and Todd Gitlin looked to settle into routine, if not necessarily apolitical, academic lives. Tom Hayden remained ever the activist, but his participation in the October 1969 "Days of Rage" was simply strange. Hayden had aligned himself briefly with an offshoot of SDS known as Weatherman, which planned to organize Chicago street gangs and launch hit-and-run attacks in the city's business district supposedly in protest against the war. They managed to bring several hundred participants to the effort, which turned out to be little more than well-publicized vandalism on the city's swanky Gold Coast that was decisively put down by the police. Weatherman moved on to bank robberies and a series of bombings and appeared to be the dismal lingering residue of a dying movement.

Yet others from the New Left moved toward institutional politics. As the liberal center broke apart in 1968, a solid portion of the Democratic Party, symbolized best perhaps by the antiwar senator from South Dakota, George McGovern, moved guardedly to the left and made it possible, therefore, for many politically minded radicals to find common ground with party progressives. If there was any lasting legacy of the New Left in American politics, it came together here in what was called the "New Politics" of the late 1960s and 1970s. The New Politics institutionalized the various concerns, as well as the diverse constituencies, that had been associated with the left wing through the Sixties. To join in the New Politics coalition, members of these constituencies had to temper their radicalism in exchange for securing power and influencing national policy. Black nationalists moving into the Democratic Party had to discard their black-power berets, but their efforts helped solidify support for what became long-standing, constitutionally protected affirmative action policies. Feminists, gay-rights activists, environmentalists, and consumer-rights groups all made similar compromises.

This partial victory for the New Left came to bear in a very specific way. Because of the battles over the Mississippi Freedom Democratic Party in 1964 and the platform fight in 1968, the Democrats agreed to establish a committee to rewrite their rules for choosing convention delegates, among other things. George McGovern chaired the committee, which met as the Commission on Party Structure and Delegate Selection beginning in fall 1969. The McGovern commission, as it has come to be known, completely disassembled the old system of delegate selection that had managed to keep the Democrats the majority party since 1932. Henceforth, state parties had to abide by the decisions of the party's national committee, which established racial, ethnic, and gender quotes for all delegations. No longer would state parties be permitted to stack conventions with *ex officio* or at-large delegates. Put simply, the McGovern commission destroyed the old-boy, white male dominance in the Democratic Party.

Whether this "quiet revolution," as the political scientist Byron Shafer has called it, has been good or bad depends on whether one is seeking ideological purity or political victories. The party apparatus certainly became more reflective of America's racial diversity, but that achievement came at the cost of support from the nation's white majority. What is indisputable is that the triumph of the New Politics in the Democratic Party was thorough by 1972. That year's presidential convention showed how thoroughly routed the old constituencies were. As historian Fred Siegel has noted, the Iowa delegation contained no farmers; the New York delegation, supposedly representing the nation's most unionized state, had nine gay-rights activists but only three unionists. No wonder none other than George McGovern was chosen as the party's presidential candidate. No wonder McGovern lost in a landslide to Richard Nixon.

The influence of the New Left on the Democratic Party was apparent in ways beyond this sea change in representation. The 1972 party platform included planks on the rights of the poor, on disabled people, on Native Americans—a litany of the marginalized people with whom the early New Left identified. But it ignored working-class whites; the party would not be bound, apparently, to that musty old "labor metaphysics" after all. The McGovern people seemed to think that the party had achieved something pretty close to participatory democracy. And nothing spoke more clearly to the influence of the New Left than the platform statement against social conformity, which declared it a fundamental right "to be different, to maintain a cultural or ethnic heritage or lifestyle, without being forced into a compelled homogeneity."[41]

THE NEW LEFT AND ASSAULT ON LIBERAL CULTURAL AUTHORITY

Cast in such a way, the New Politics was as much a matter of culture as of governance and policymaking. It is thus a fitting testament to the Sixties. For while there is never a direct line between politics and that constellation of beliefs and behaviors we lump together under the term "culture," Sixties radicalism cannot be appreciated without reference to the era's cultural changes. It is too simple to say, as many people believed at the time, that antiwar protesters were long-haired, pot-smoking hippies who rejected America's bedrock values. Yet most radicals saw themselves as part of a seismic shake-up of American life that cut much deeper than politics. If their political activities consumed their energies, those activities went hand-in-hand with a broad set of beliefs about personal morality, social institutions, art and expression, all of which they considered alternatives to the prevailing mores of liberal society. Political activists were hardly the only people rethinking those prevailing mores. Artists, intellectuals, and everyday folks, especially young people, insisted on a greater range of individual freedoms. Cultural radicals imagined that they were repudiating institutional authority almost across the board, from the university to the established churches to the nuclear family. They challenged taboos, especially sexual ones. And they refused to abide by restrictions, either legal or customary, on their right to express their opposition to mainstream culture. Hence the term "counter-culture."

The Sixties culture war began like the period's political strife, not as a rebellion against an oppressive society but against a liberalizing one. Cultural radicals argued that, along with its militarism and racism, America was hung up on sexual repressiveness, social conformity, and money grubbing. It is quite true that until Vietnam and the later Watergate scandals created deep public cynicism, Americans fundamentally trusted their institutional leaders, whether those leaders were in government, the media, churches, or business. In his sensitive memoir of growing up in a conservative Catholic family through the 1950s and 1960s, James Carroll describes a society that was utterly credulous about its leaders; that the "feds," presidents, military chiefs, and Catholic clergy who loomed large in young Carroll's life always told the truth and were always right was taken as a matter of unquestioned faith. Carroll, whose father was with the FBI, recalls his image of bureau agents "as men of such competence and integrity, such selflessness, that one could think of them as modern-day Knights Templars. In my mind, the image of the agent would blur into that of the priest."[42] Television programming testified to and certainly reinforced that faith. In the Fifties the three television networks churned out regular depictions of the happy nuclear family; in the Sixties such family fare went along with shows extolling the exploits of American soldiers in the World War II dramas *Twelve O' Clock High* and *Combat*. While in reality the FBI was under the dictatorial control of J. Edgar Hoover, whose power was so vast that he intimidated presidents, in TV land the Bureau was depicted as incorruptible in a weekly drama that aired in a crucial Sunday evening time slot. Reality and television fantasy did meet on the grounds of national politics: the show's star, Efram Zimbalist, Jr., was an ardent supporter of the Republican presidential candidate, Barry Goldwater, in 1964.

According to Sixties cultural radicals, sexual prudery was one of the main underpinnings of the status quo. Hollywood, for instance, continued to produce under a system of censorship that had been put in place in the 1930s in the form of the Motion Picture Production Code. The Code was a product of intersecting local and state regulations, pressure from private groups such as the Catholic Legion of Decency, and self-censorship of the major film studios, all of which combined to keep a range of subjects and activities out of American movies. Nudity was simply out of the question, as was foul language, however mild. Romance was fine, but anything more than a kiss crossed the line. Common vulgarities were never considered; movie characters never puked or farted. Deviant behavior, such as drug use or drunkenness, was invariably depicted as self-destructive. Even films that challenged accepted authority were frowned on.

Meanwhile, social authorities policed sexuality in countless other ways. Birth control, for instance, was strictly regulated; indeed in several states it was illegal for doctors to discuss birth control with their female patients, much less prescribe it. Customs recognized across the nation put severe social sanction against out-of-wedlock sex. Unmarried couples simply did not live together; pregnant teens were sent away from their families to have their babies with distant relatives. Homosexuality, the greatest taboo, was life-ruining for someone whose orientation became public knowledge; even the relatively liberal American Psychological Association regarded homosexuality as a mental illness.

Nonetheless, there were indications throughout the postwar years that the cultural underpinnings of this institutional authority were beginning to crumble, and that process began not with a burst of radicalism but with a liberalization of values and mores. Beneath the facade of public placidity, for example, the intimate sphere of family and sexuality was quite complex. The famous Kinsey Reports on human sexuality, published in 1948 and 1953, revealed that Americans' sexual behavior was anything but conventional;

indeed the Reports were cultural landmarks for having introduced, under the guise of science, a frank public discussion of sexuality. As iconic as the nuclear family was in the 1950s, there were strains there: marriage rates were very high, but so were divorce rates. Doctor Benjamin Spock's child-care manual, which reigned as the bible of popular advice, discouraged corporal punishment in favor of positive reinforcement and exemplified what some later considered a new liberal permissiveness.

As historian Beth Bailey has demonstrated, 1960 was less a moment when repression gave way to freedom than a kind of tipping point at which the relative balance of sexual latitude and expression in American life began to tilt toward the latter. The forces of liberation had been gathering since at least World War II, she argues, when the upheaval and mobility of the war reshaped the landscape of social authority in America. Competition in the mass-media marketplace pushed the cultural boundaries. When *Playboy* first appeared in 1953, it set off a flood of imitations, and even publications that did not stoop to nudity increasingly flirted with the salacious through seductive cover photos and alluring headlines. Respectable middlebrow reading included Norman Mailer's *The Naked and the Dead* and Henry Miller's *Tropic of Cancer*, both sexually charged books. After a 1948 Supreme Court ruling forced the Hollywood studios to liquidate their control of national theater chains (to that point they controlled both production and retail in the industry) intensified competition at the box office steadily eroded the Production Code. Starlets such as Jane Russell and Marilyn Monroe flaunted their voluptuousness; themes of seduction became overt in films such as *A Street Car Named Desire* (1951) and *From Here to Eternity* (1953).

These challenges to prudery represented the liberal wave of the postwar sexual revolution. At its core were two basic elements: first, the conviction that the frank depiction or discussion of sex was fundamental to free expression; and, second, the assumption that the "sex" in question was straight and of a sort that played principally to the interests of heterosexual men. It was sex as *Playboy* cast it: suave, sophisticated, with the knowing wink of the martini set. It laid claim to a mature, adult awareness of sexual desire, but overwhelmingly it was a male claim delivered with male pleasure in mind. This mentality only slightly altered the age-old double standard that excused male philandering. Male desires were cast as natural, and therefore necessary, while women were regarded as needy and easily had but naturally, and therefore safely, monogamous.

By 1960, American mass culture was full of examples of this sort of man: *Playboy's* founder Hugh Hefner; Elvis Presley; James Bond; or any of the dozens of men depicted in Scotch whiskey or cigarette ads. No one better captured the spirit of the liberal wave of the sexual revolution better than John F. Kennedy himself. Youngish, very wealthy, and urbane, Kennedy exuded not the charisma of a classical leader but the sex appeal of modern American mass media—he was more rock star than Caesar—"superman at the supermarket," as the novelist Norman Mailer once wrote of him. Kennedy avidly read contemporary writers, Mailer among them, and, more to the point, Ian Fleming, whose James Bond novels made much of liberalized sexual values. Proud to show off his glamorous wife in public, Kennedy ran through a series of affairs of various lengths with a list of women that included Marilyn Monroe and mob gal Judith Exner. His sexual exploits were open secrets in Washington, and it was in keeping with the character of the liberal stage of the sexual revolution that while many knew of Kennedy's activities, no one in the almost exclusively male club of the national media exposed them.

The Supreme Court consistently protected this liberalizing trend. Its famous 1957 decision in *Roth v. United States* upheld censorship's constitutionality but did so in such a vague way that the decision was a practical victory for free expression. In *Roth*, the Court defined obscenity as anything that violated community standards, which, needless to say, were difficult to define during this chaotic period. Subsequent decisions constantly narrowed the authority of censors by defining obscenity as only that which was intended solely to titillate and which was completely without artistic merit. When community standards came under frontal assault after 1960, movie and magazine producers could argue that virtually everything had some artistic merit. By the end of the Sixties, pretty much anything was permissible.

These liberalizing trends undermined culturally conservative values, yet set off a rebellion against the cultural establishment that assumed a distinctly antiliberal sensibility, particularly when reinforced by the politics of the Sixties. In many respects, cultural radicals focused less on America's harsh repressiveness than on its liberal permissiveness. They railed not against oppressive values, of which so few remained, but against the hypocrisy of liberal values that preached individual freedom while circumscribing that freedom with demands for "reasonableness." The conventional portrait that emerged by the latter Sixties was that the parental generation, the liberal establishment, had indeed discarded many traditional values. But because that generation had been reared during depression and war, they still clung to the old injunctions about hard work, dedication to task, obedience to the system—values appropriate, many radical theorists said at the time, to the bygone age of scarcity, rather than the present age of affluence. Liberals were halfway to cultural liberation and incapable, if not entirely unwilling, completing that journey. They had undermined the legitimacy of many ditional beliefs yet had not bothered to create meaningful new values.

Without new values appropriate to the age of affluence, cultural radi argued, the baby boom generation was condemned to alienated lives as bu reaucrats and corporate drones. Theodore Roszak, for one, captured this fracture of the generations well in his sympathetic account of the great cultural rebellion, *The Making of a Counter Culture* (1969). Roszak noted with pointed irony that the period's "troublesome children" were the creations of parents who had put before them no stirring purpose in life. The "counter culture," he maintained, had emerged among "disaffected" middle-class kids "stranded between a permissive childhood and an obnoxiously conformist adulthood, experimenting desperately with new ways of growing up self-respectfully into a world they despise." Having never known economic insecurity, the baby boomers saw no reason to "kowtow to the organizations" that had dehumanized their parents. Affluence was all they knew, "and on it they build a new, uncompromised personality, flawed perhaps by irresponsible ease, but also touched with some outspoken spirit."[43] Herbert Marcuse, who briefly became one of the philosophical gurus of the New Left in the late Sixties, argued more aggressively that the permissive society coopted the innate human drive for instinctual freedom, particularly sexual freedom, and thus made true freedom impossible. This amounted, Marcuse insisted, to a system of "repressive tolerance."

As this defense of cultural rebellion suggests, the counterculture took on a distinct feel of a generational war, a society-wide rebellion of the child against the parents. Abbie Hoffman's famous dictum, "Don't Trust Anyone Over Thirty," certainly caught that essence. It is no surprise that the college campuses became settings for cultural rebellion. College administrators were symbolic targets. An overwhelmingly liberal-minded group, they nonetheless presided over booming bureaucratic organizations that created an array of deeply vested interests. They maintained a hierarchical system of education in which professors, in their suits and ties, remained aloof in every sense from their students. College administrators continued to exercise *in loco parentis*, the doctrine that gave them legal responsibility for the students given to their care. That meant dorms segregated by gender and often by race, and particularly strict rules for women, including curfews and constraints on male visits to the women's dorms.

One of the pivotal events in the development of the Sixties student revolt, the Free Speech Movement (FSM), reflected how political and cultural strains came together in condensed and crystalline form. The FSM convened at the University of California, Berkeley, early in the 1964 academic year, when the University tried to extend a long-standing rule that prohibited political activity on campus to the adjacent city sidewalks. The almost immediate result was a contentious student movement dedicated to demanding free speech that included not just radicals like FSM leader Mario Savio but conservative students and some fraternity and sorority students. After nearly two months of negotiations with the students, University of California President Clark Kerr decided to discipline FSM leaders. In response, over one thousand students occupied Sproul Hall, the administration building, in reply—the first large campus demonstration of the period.

While the point at issue—free speech—seems straightforward, the confrontation contained many of the boiling ingredients of the day. The University of California system under Kerr was the very epitome of the "multi-versity"—enormous, complex, and deeply involved in Cold War defense programs. This was the sort of system that Kerr wanted, not because he was a conservative but because he was a true-to-the-bone liberal technocrat. He had opposed the imposition of faculty loyalty oaths in the early 1950s, when he was a professor in industrial relations; his own political leanings became clear when he invited John F. Kennedy to give the 1962 Commencement address. Yet as he was building his own ideal of the university, the New Left was emerging beneath him. A left-wing student group had been challenging for campus leadership since 1957; some fifty Berkeley students, including Mario Savio, had gone south for Freedom Summer. They returned to a campus where a revived sense of activism mixed with the common experience of alienation under bureaucratic control. The Berkeley campus newspaper summed up the sense of student alienation by explaining that "the incoming freshman has much to learn—perhaps lesson number one is not to fold, spindle, or mutilate his IBM card."[44]

Mario Savio became the New Left's first celebrity during the Free Speech Movement. Tall, attractive, and charismatic, the son of reportedly devout Roman Catholic parents, Savio had a gift for capturing and articulating the inchoate feelings of his peers. Denouncing the practice of *in loco parentis*, he insisted that the university tried to isolate students from the ugly realities of racism and war. "The reason why liberals don't understand us," he wrote, "is because they don't realize there is evil in the world." His renowned speech on the Sproul Hall steps remains perhaps the single most stirring evocation of the sense of confinement within an unyielding, impersonal system. President Kerr had explained his reluctance to confront the university Board of Regents over the student suspensions by comparing his position to that of a corporate head who could not buck his corporate board. This analogy sent Savio into a frothing rage. It was the predictable answer from "a well-meaning liberal," he declared. Kerr implied not just that the university was the same as any big business, but that "the faculty are a bunch of employees, and we're the raw material!" Savio called on his peers to resist that dehumanization, to fight being reduced to a product to be "bought by some clients of the University, be they the government, be they industry, be they organized labor, be they anyone! We're human beings!" He then rose to his most passionate call:

There is a time when the operation of the machine becomes so odious, makes you so sick at heart, that you can't take part; you can't even passively take part, and you've got to put your bodies upon the gears and upon the wheels, upon the levers, upon all the apparatus, and you've got to make it stop. And you've got to indicate to the people who run it, to the people who own it, that unless you're free, the machine will be prevented from working at all![45]

The FSM was an explosion waiting to happen, and it hardly died just because the police routed the demonstrators out of Sproul Hall in December 1964. Soon after, the university settled on much-loosened rules for campus political activity and a new campus administration that gave the FSM an unvarnished victory. Yet for FSM leader Art Goldberg, the new rules on political activity were not enough. When a student was arrested in spring 1965 for carrying a placard that read "F-U-C-K," Goldberg tried to revive the student outrage of the previous fall. At a March rally, Goldberg unleashed a tirade of the "f" word precisely in order to challenge the university's prohibition on obscenity; his main point was that university administrators should not have the privilege of defining what was permissible speech for students. Thus what had begun in fall term as a demand for freedom of political expression ended in spring term with demands that anything go. As many saw it, the Free Speech Movement degenerated into the Filthy Speech movement.

The rapid mutation of a political issue into a cultural one in the Free Speech Movement indicated that, as the New Left opened up its critique of the liberal establishment, a new, radicalized stage of the sexual revolution would emerge as well. Just as the Sixties opened at liberal high tide but closed amidst the enflamed outbursts of the New Left, so the sexual revolution blew through the liberal stage and into a period in which a minority of mostly young Americans strained to knock over any remaining barriers to sexual freedom. The *Playboy* ethic and the gains in free speech opened up ground for the more radical denunciation of sexual taboos, which by mid-decade included a reaction against what sexual radicals believed were the phony, unnatural *Playboy* values. Those values, the radicals charged, were exclusively heterosexual and fundamentally exploitative. The second, radical phase of the sexual revolution, accordingly, rejected such values in favor of "polymorphous perversity," an ideal that called for the sexual instincts to be unhinged entirely from any restraints so that a person could enjoy sex with anyone, anywhere, in any way.

Cast as the key to wider revolution, sexual expression and revolt not surprisingly became a weapon, as Beth Bailey has ably argued, a ready-to-use, easy-to-hand weapon for repudiating whatever authority one wanted. Hence the artist used sex to flout aesthetic conventions. The antiwar movement used it to defy governmental authority (a widely distributed MOBE poster depicted a young man burning his draft card beneath the heading "Fuck the Draft") and as a hip form of recruiting (perhaps the most famous antiwar poster showed three fetching young women on a couch beneath the slogan, "Girls Say Yes to Boys Who Say No"). By the late Sixties, radical feminists put sex to the service of political emasculation by insisting on the "myth of the vaginal orgasm." Black Nationalists deployed sex in a similar way when they ridiculed white men as effeminate and impotent. And hippies, those iconic figures of the New Culture, used sex to embody their vision of a society committed totally to individual pleasure.

Two specific developments, radical feminism and the gay-rights movement, brought the use of sexuality as a weapon to its most radical. For women, the first phase of the sexual revolution was no revolution at all. Still, one development of the early Sixties was indisputably important: the reliable birth control pill. Brought out in 1960, the Pill made it possible for women to secure independent control over reproduction—at least once physicians began prescribing it regularly. The Pill was a good example of how the affluent society furthered human mastery of nature, which, as New Culture advocates liked to think, made the pursuit of individual pleasure easier than ever. And as such it was something of the sociological backdrop to the assertion of other forms of independence among young women.

By the late 1960s, young women activists, many of whom had participated in civil rights protests, the antiwar movement, or both, had become deeply disillusioned with the male dominance of both those movements and the cavalier, not to say exploitative, treatment of women activists. Tired of being relegated to roles as secretaries or maids, women radicals began to think that the real problem with America lay deeper than racism and imperialism. Indeed, these injustices might only be embellishments on the most ancient form of oppression, that of men over women. The problem with America, whether in the national political parties or the New Left, was, in a word, men. Not only did this position mark radical women off from the New Left, it also distinguished them from the liberal women of the National Organization of Women (NOW), which had been organized only in 1965 primarily to defend women against discrimination in hiring and employment. The radicals, who began to split formally from SDS in 1967, argued instead that nothing short of a full-scale revolution in gender relations could emancipate women and transform society as a whole in the process. Famously declaring that the "personal was political," the radicals argued that women had to begin their revolution by resisting their relentless dehumanization into sexual playthings or mere housewives. Many agreed with Robin Morgan, one of the radical pioneers, who argued that the exploitation of women in mass culture as well as the nuclear family meant essentially that women's bodies were colonized territory that had to be taken back. The radicals borrowed heavily from New Left rhetoric even as they broke ranks. As they summed up their position in the 1969 Redstocking Manifesto, women, they claimed, were "an oppressed class. Our oppression is total. . . . We are exploited as sex objects, breeders, domestic servants, and cheap labor."[46]

To mainstream feminists such as Betty Friedan, the younger radicals were making all the same mistakes as their male counterparts in SDS or in black-power groups. They were isolating themselves into a self-imposed marginalization, essentially defining themselves out of the social order rather than demanding an equal role within it. The new emphasis on "consciousness raising" with sexual issues at its core struck Friedan as so much hot air. Friedan and her colleagues at NOW continued to push for straightforward gender equality through political and legislative change; while the radicals denounced all men, mainstream feminists pushed a new constitutional amendment, the Equal Rights Amendment (ERA), that would prohibit all forms of gender discrimination. In general, radical feminists did not oppose the ERA, but that had the ironic effect of allowing conservatives to brand the amendment as the creation of man-hating, antifamily, and anti-American radicals.

The momentum of sexual revolution carried over to the most marginalized group, gays and lesbians. A frank lesbianism took hold within the most radical feminist circles by the end of the decade and really defined the difference between a mere "women's libber" and a radical.

To the extent that the split in feminist ranks was related to the sexual revolution, it was carried by a dynamic somewhat different from that which pushed along the splits between the black-power bloc and King, or between SDS and liberal Democrats. Their emergence was linked less to these primarily political splits than to the transformation of public attitudes towards sexuality, which encouraged gay men to assert themselves as well. A muted homosexual advocacy had sounded around the far edges of the early sexual revolution in so-called homophile groups as the Mattachine Society in New York or the Janus Society in Philadelphia, which were committed principally to ending official harassment of gays and lesbians. Still, just as radical women applied the logic of the civil rights movement to their own situation, so gays applied the logic of the later New Left and the second stage of the sexual revolution to theirs. Gay liberationists argued not so much that they had a constitutional right to love whomever they wished but, rather, that the repressive society had imposed straight sex as an unnatural denial of instincts. Like the other liberation movements, gay liberationists proclaimed their cause part of the worldwide upheaval of colonized and oppressed people. The gay liberation movement had its coming-out in New York in 1969 when the patrons of the Stonewall Inn, a gay club in Greenwich Village, successfully fought off a police raid, and in so doing spontaneously launched the public crusade for gay rights.

It was a long way from Hugh Hefner to the Red Stocking Manifesto and Stonewall. It was also a long way from the Scotch-swilling world of establishment liberalism to the infamous drug use of the Sixties. At least in its most celebrated forms, drug use during the Sixties was never aimed at just getting loaded or high, Bob Dylan's woozy "Everybody must get stoned" notwithstanding. Rather, it was supposed to be purposeful and directed toward intensifying experience or aiding in the effort to "turn on and tune in." The choice of drugs was telling. Marijuana and LSD induced psychedelic highs and were in sharp contrast to the establishment's drugs of choice, alcohol and sleeping pills. As the Sixties radicals saw the matter, the deadening effect of booze and barbiturates could hardly even be called a "high"; the older generation leaned on these drugs because they wanted to escape. By contrast, the psychedelics were alleged to generate ecstatic states that carried the user into direct contact with the cosmos. Far from an escape, Sixties drugs were supposed to reconnect people with their genuine selves. Timothy Leary, the one-time Harvard professor who became the foremost advocate of LSD, insisted that the drug "does not produce the transcendent experience. It merely acts as the chemical key—it opens the mind, frees the nervous system of its ordinary patterns and structures." Chemically detached from those "ordinary patterns," voyagers into transcendental experience could be liberated from their egos and escape the dreadful habits of game playing; they ascended into an ecstatic condition of "complete transcendence—beyond words, beyond space-time, beyond self. There are no visions, no sense of self, no thoughts."[47]

Even more than sex and psychedelic drugs, rock and roll distinguished the New Culture as a rebellion of the young. This rebellion too had been in the works since the 1950s, when the Cleveland disc jockey Alan Freed began to play "race music," that is, early rhythm and blues associated with urbanizing blacks, for his young white radio audience. During the mid-decade, a collection of white musicians, many of whom were southern and working out of Memphis, began to popularize this new "rock-and-roll" through exhaustive touring. By the time Elvis Presley exploded on the music market, the sound had caught on nationwide, even if against the disapproval of the cultural guardians. By 1960, this musical form had established several important trends: rock and roll had expropriated black musical forms, above all a technically simple sensuality, for the enjoyment of white teenagers; and it had created a distinct and powerful generational consumer niche among those white teenagers.

Still, as the Sixties began, there was very little indication of popular music's subversive edge. Much of popular music remained lovey-dovey teenaged stuff; the Beach Boys, with their surfing sound, might have been the most innovative group in the early decade. When the Beatles exploded on the scene in 1964, they showed how combustible the music scene could be, but only because they drove young girls into a frenzy with their mop-top hair cuts and bouncy tunes like "I Want to Hold Your Hand!" and "She Loves You." In public, they were insouciant, rather than threatening; they were silly and playful rather than confrontational. Within three years, the Beatles went from a teenybopper phenomenon to a deeply influential group exploring psychedelic imagery in such albums as *Sgt. Pepper's Lonely Hearts Club Band* and *Abbey Road*. Their rapid maturation came from an unleashed musical genius, but even more it seems as though the era swept up the Fab Four and carried them with it. By 1967, they were dabbling in Transcendental Meditation and moving closer to overt political radicalism, which is where John Lennon particularly ended up.

There were always performers who were self-consciously political. Some measure of political consciousness was almost required for the folk musician, since that genre was so directly traced back to the Depression era poet musician Woody Guthrie. Songwriters such as Phil Ochs were very early proponents of the civil rights movement, as were the singers Peter, Paul, and Mary. Mostly coffee house musicians, they were not that interested in entering the world of popular music. Bob Dylan was the exception. Dylan's songwriting skill lay in his ability to catch the mood of the time through allusion and metaphor rather than preachy, self-absorbed pronouncements. True, when he warned the older generation "The Times They Are A-Changin,'" he spoke frankly about the growing divide between the kids and the authorities, but when he sang that the "answer was blowin' in the wind," he evoked the sense of alienation without insisting that he knew the "answer." Just as the changing times carried the Beatles from saccharine sweet popular music to LSD, so they moved Dylan from the coffee house to the rock concert stage and stardom. In 1965, Dylan horrified his purist fans by taking up the electric guitar and recording "Like a Rolling Stone." "Like a Rolling Stone" was like other Dylan songs in that it avoided overt political claims and yet conjured up the mood of aimlessness so characteristic of Sixties youth, and it secured his status as a New Culture prophet.

Rock's most important contribution to the New Culture was not a political one. It served as the most important generational bond, the most pervasive and widely embraced shared experience among the young. It was the generational identifier. It embodied, expressed, and gave daily substance to the essential ideas of the New Culture: the rejection of rationality; the reveling in instinctual pleasures; the chase after intense experience. It was often sexually explicit—more and more so as the Sixties wore on. As the hottest cultural commodity, it had become big business and therefore the epitome of commercial mass culture; and yet much of it was genuine and fresh, the product not of cynical producers but of upstart, often amateur musicians who made up the genre as they went. It was a bottom-up creation.

Nowhere were these qualities all more in evidence than in the emergence of the Bay area music scene after 1965. The home of the Beats, Berkeley, and the Haight-Ashbury bohemia—"Hashbury," the world capital of the drug culture—the Bay area bred a number of path-breaking groups who turned the psychedelic impulses of their neighbors into an entire subgenre of rock. The Jefferson Airplane, Quicksilver, and, above all, the Grateful Dead were rarely political. Nor, for that matter, were they "popular." Grown out of the quirky soil of the Haight, they mostly committed themselves to playing loud, hard, and long. Instead of chasing fat recording contracts, they accepted sponsorship from cultural guru Ken Kesey and drug entrepreneur Augustus Owsley Stanley, the chemist son of a former Virginia senator who set up a lab in Berkeley and churned out much of the high-quality LSD that was sold in the area. They also fell in with an older promoter, Frank Graham, who figured out there was money to be made by putting on huge shows in some of the area's older theaters, where the halls were cheap but large enough to accommodate throngs. It was in places like the famous Fillmore Theater that the Grateful Dead mastered their art of all-night jams and where the idea of the large rock festival was born.

It was appropriate, then, that the archetypical New Culture event was held in San Francisco. In January 1967, the Human Be-In brought the cultural stars, Ginsberg, Leary, and Gary Snyder, the musicians, the area's hippies, and assorted lost souls to Golden Gate Park for no reason other than just "to be." The Hell's Angels motorcycle gang provided security in exchange for beer. Mother Nature, looking kindly on her most colorful children, provided a beautiful day. The musicians played; poets read; and Ginsberg led the crowd in Buddhist chants. A skydiver floated out of nowhere beneath a paisley parachute. Reporters on the scene marveled at the oddity of it all—the bizarre characters, the vibrant colors, and the peacefulness of the whole scene.

On the surface, the Human Be-In was a terrific success. Beyond the tolerant boundaries of Golden Gate Park, however, it pointed toward a many-sided conflict—conflict between cultural and political radicals, and conflict between defenders of the "American way of life" and all those who were trying to change the status quo. It was the first of the famous New Culture celebrations and in its spontaneity, the most genuine. It generated a wave of imitations across the country, including in Washington's Dupont Circle, Philadelphia's Independence Square, and Manhattan's Tompkins Park. As it generated notoriety in the mainstream press and thereby introduced many Americans to the growing phenomenon of the New Culture, the Be-In made the "hippie" a fixture in the national media. For better or worse, the hippie became the media-generated face of cultural radicalism.

Because the hippies made it easy for the defenders of the status quo to debunk all challenges as the products of lunatics, New Left political activists resented them for bringing intensified disfavor on "the movement" while contributing nothing to genuine radical change. More akin to the "nihilism of the 1950s beats" who despaired of changing society than to the New Left activists who were determined to spring a revolution, "the whole hippie contagion," wrote the New Left journalist Jack Newfield, "seems to be a recoil from the idea of politics itself; it is not merely apolitical but anti-political."[48] The typical hippie probably would have agreed with Newfield and been perfectly happy about it. Politics was too much like work; it was for the "uptight," whether the establishment folks in their suits or the ideological kids on campus. Yet, like it or not, cultural radicalism owed its growing magnetism to the simultaneous discrediting of social and political authority across the board, and, like the Beatles and Dylan, it too was being carried along by events. It too was becoming inherently political.

The union of cultural and political radicalism was joined in the partnership of Jerry Rubin and Abbie Hoffman, two media-savvy figures who saw more clearly than anyone the possibilities that a marriage of the two might yield. To them, there was no inherent conflict between the two. They saw the hippies as solid evidence of the collapse of the affluent society. They instinctively understood how incredibly uneasy the hippies made the older generation and appreciated the hippies' latent power to unsettle the status quo. At the same time, they believed that the political system was irredeemable, that it was, in fact, a joke and no longer deserved to be taken seriously. Rubin had been involved in Berkeley politics for several years when he experienced the Be-In and it hit him: Why not use this sort of wackiness to attack the system instead of chanting mantras and proclaiming universal love? The problem with hippies, Hoffman believed, was that they wanted to "drop out" and "just go sit in a closet. But you can't sit there forever." He considered himself not a political radical but a "revolutionary artist" whose "concept of revolution is that it's fun."

So, seeking "revolution for the hell of it," Hoffman and Rubin set off on a series of high jinks as political theater, beginning in 1967 when they showed up at the New York Stock Exchange and showered the trading floor with dollar bills. In summer 1968, they joined with Ed Sanders and Paul Krassner to put culture and politics firmly together by organizing a new "political" party. They called it Yippie, which supposedly stood for Youth International Party, and nominated a pig as their 1968 presidential candidate. The Yippies added inestimably to their reputation by calling on their sympathizers to flood Chicago for the Democratic National Convention. They managed to get the authorities very uptight when they joked about lacing the city's water supply with LSD so that everyone would be tripping when the time came. Yippies staged the "Festival of Life" in Lincoln Park as the opposite to the Democrats' "Convention of Death," and for their troubles brought on the first of the police charges into demonstrators during convention week. Over the course of just a few years, Hoffman was arrested more than thirty times on charges ranging from trying to board a plane with a knife, to "desecrating" the American flag by wearing a stars-and-stripes shirt, to public obscenity for writing the word F-U-C-K backward on his forehead so no photographers would bother him. Rubin and Hoffman were also two of the protest leaders known as the Chicago Eight charged with conspiracy to mayhem for the Chicago convention riots.

As America staggered out of the late 1960s, it groped its way to a new equilibrium that was decidedly more conservative than the nation had been at any time in the twentieth century. A period that began with unquestioned liberal dominance played itself out with the rise of a new conservatism. The great advances against racism remained, of course, but did not erase racial conflict. The liberal reforms of the Great Society did establish permanent programs such as Medicaid and Medicare, but they marked the high point of the welfare state, which was subsequently whittled down under conservative rule. American failure in Vietnam convinced many Americans that liberals were too weak to protect the nation against external threats.

In the long run, however, America's culture was transformed far more than its political or economic systems. New Culture advocates won an almost complete victory against the censors. American popular culture ever since has become intensely sexualized. Even as early as 1968, Abbie Hoffman had to admit that "now I can write FUCK and nobody's prurient interests stir."[49] Public memories about the Sixties are far more likely to involve images of the Woodstock music festival of 1969, without question the most important New Culture spectacle, than they are to collect around New Left activists debating the finer points of Camus. Indeed, it tells us something very important about the nature of the affluent society that the cultural revolution won out even as the political revolution was completely routed. Evidently, the "status quo" was capable of great flexibility when it came to forms of self-expression, so long as the champions of order won when it came to the instruments of social and political power.

NOTES

1. Arthur M. Schlesinger, Jr., "The New Mood in Politics," *Esquire* (January 1960), 44–45, 47–49, 54.

2. Stevenson quoted in Richard Hofstadter, "The Pseudo-Conservative Revolt," in *The Radical Right: The New American Right Abridged and Updated*, ed. Daniel Bell (Garden City, NY: Doubleday, 1963), 76.

3. Alan Brinkley, *Liberalism and Its Discontents* (Cambridge, MA: Harvard University Press, 1998), 47.

4. Allen J. Matusow, *The Unraveling of America: A History of Liberalism in the 1960s* (New York: Harper, 1984), 48.

5. Hofstadter, "Pseudo-Conservative Revolt," 75.

6. Todd Gitlin, *The Sixties: Years of Hope, Days of Rage* (New York: Bantam Books, 1993), 19, 35–36.

7. John Lewis, *Walking with the Wind: A Memoir of the Movement* (New York: Simon & Schuster, 1998), 71.

8. Tom Hayden, *Reunion: A Memoir* (New York: Random House, 1988), 78.

9. C. Wright Mills, "Letter to the New Left," *New Left Review* 1 (September–October 1960), 18–23.

10. Gitlin, *The Sixties*, 21.

11. Hayden, *Reunion*, 80.

12. Kennedy quoted in Taylor Branch, *Parting the Waters: America in the King Years, 1954–69* (New York: Simon & Schuster, 1988), 307.

13. Branch, *Parting the Waters*, 190–91.

14. James Forman, *The Making of Black Revolutionaries: A Personal Account* (New York: Macmillan, 1972), 289.

15. Forman, *The Making of Black Revolutionaries*, 148.

16. "Prelate Objects to Rights Speech," *New York Times*, 29 August 1963; and "Excerpts of Remarks Made at Civil Rights Program," *Washington Post*, 29 August 1963.

17. Quoted in Robert Dallek, *Flawed Giant: Lyndon Johnson and His Times, 1961–1973* (New York: Oxford University Press, 1998), 223.

18. "Dr. King Disputes Negro Separatist," *New York Times*, 28 May 1966.

19. "SNCC Dumps 2 Top Leaders, Names Black Panther Chairman," *Washington Post*, 17 May 1966.

20. Carmichael quoted in Taylor Branch, *At Canaan's Edge: America in the King Years, 1965–68* (New York: Simon & Schuster, 2006), 464.

21. Floyd McKissick address to the National Conference of Black Power, 30 July 1967, printed in *Let Nobody Turn Us Around: Voices of Resistance, Reform, and Renewal*, ed. Manning Marable and Leith Mullings (Lanham, MD: Rowman & Littlefield, 2003), 459–60.

22. John Kenneth Galbraith, *The Affluent Society* (Boston: Houghton Mifflin, 1958), 323.

23. Quoted in Arthur M. Schlesinger, Jr., *Robert Kennedy and His Times* (Boston: Houghton Mifflin, 1978), 411.

24. Quoted in Nicholas Lemann, *The Promised Land: The Great Black Migration and How It Changed America* (New York: Knopf, 1991), 128.

25. Daniel Patrick Moynihan, *Maximum Feasible Misunderstanding: Community Action in the War on Poverty* (New York: Free Press, 1969), 75.

26. Quoted in Lemann, *Promised Land*, 141.

27. "Everything for Everybody," *Chicago Tribune*, 9 January 1964.

28. Quoted in Matusow, *The Unraveling of America*, 125–26.

29. Moynihan, *Maximum Feasible Misunderstanding*, 130.

30. Todd Gitlin and Nancy Hollander, *Uptown: Poor Whites in Chicago* (New York: Harper & Row, 1970), xxii.

31. Quoted in Jennifer Frost, *An Interracial Movement of the Poor: Community Organizing and the New Left in the 1960s* (New York: New York University Press, 2001), 142.

32. Quoted in David Steigerwald, *The Sixties and the End of Modern America* (New York: St. Martin's Press, 1995), 131.

33. Tom Hayden, "Community Organizing and the War on Poverty," *Liberation* 10 (November 1965), 18–19.

34. Richard Flacks, "Is the Great Society Just a Barbecue?" *New Republic* (1966); reprinted in *The New Left: A Documentary History*, ed. Massimo Teodori (Indianapolis: Bobbs-Merrill, 1969), 193–94.

35. Andrew Kopkind, "Soul Power," *New York Review of Books* (24 August 1967), 5.

36. C. Wright Mills, *Listen, Yankee* (New York: McGraw-Hill, 1961), 91–92.

37. I. F. Stone, "Our Air of Injured Innocence Over Cuba," in *The Haunted Fifties* (New York: Random House, 1963), 338–39.

38. A recording of Potter's speech in its entirety can be found at the University of California at Berkeley's Moffitt Library, Media Resource Center, On-line Sixties archive, http://www.lib.berkeley.edu/MRC/pacificaviet/#1965.

39. Carl Oglesby, "Let Us Shape the Future," *Liberation* 10 (January 1966), 11, 14.

40. George Dennison, "Talking with the Troops," *Liberation* 12 (November 1967), 19.

41. Quoted in Thomas and Mary Edsall, *Chain Reaction: The Impact of Race, Rights, and Taxes on American Politics* (New York: Norton, 1992), 95.

42. James Carroll, *An American Requiem: God, My Father, and the War that Came Between Us* (Boston: Houghton Mifflin, 1996), 35.

43. Theodore Roszak, *The Making of a Counter Culture: Reflections on the Technocratic Society and Its Youthful Opposition* (Garden City, NY: Doubleday, 1969), 31, 33.

44. Quoted in W. J. Rorabaugh, *Berkeley at War: The 1960s* (New York: Oxford University Press, 1989), 18.

45. Quoted in Rorabaugh, *Berkeley at War*, 46; for Savio's Sproul Hall speech, see http://www.lib.berkeley.edu/MRC/saviotranscript.html. A film of the speech also can be found at http://www.lib.berkeley.edu/MRC/FSM.html.

46. "Redstockings Manifesto," reprinted in *"Takin' it to the streets": A Sixties Reader*, ed. Alexander Bloom and Wini Brienes, (New York: Oxford University Press, 2003), 407–09.

47. Timothy Leary, Ralph Metzner, and Richard Alpert, *The Psychedelic Experience: A Manual Based on the Tibetan Book of the Dead* (New Hyde Park, NY: University Books, 1964), 11, 13.

48. Jack Newfield, "One Cheer for the Hippies," *Nation* 204 (26 June 1967), 809.

49. Abbie Hoffman, "Yippie!—The Media Myth," in *The Best of Abbie Hoffman*, ed. Daniel Simon and Abbie Hoffman (New York: Four Walls Eight Windows, 1989), 54.

Documents

1

EXCERPTS FROM "THE PORT HURON STATEMENT," STUDENTS FOR A DEMOCRATIC SOCIETY (1962)

INTRODUCTION: AGENDA FOR A GENERATION

We are people of this generation, bred in at least modest comfort, housed now in universities, looking uncomfortably to the world we inherit.

When we were kids the United States was the wealthiest and strongest country in the world: the only one with the atom bomb, the least scarred by modern war, an initiator of the United Nations that we thought would distribute Western influence throughout the world. Freedom and equality for each individual, government of, by, and for the people—these American values we found good, principles by which we could live as men. Many of us began maturing in complacency.

As we grew, however, our comfort was penetrated by events too troubling to dismiss. First, the permeating and victimizing fact of human degradation, symbolized by the Southern struggle against racial bigotry, compelled most of us from silence to activism. Second, the enclosing fact of the Cold War, symbolized by the presence of the Bomb, brought awareness that we ourselves, and our friends, and millions of abstract "others" we knew more directly because of our common peril, might die at any time. We might deliberately ignore, or avoid, or fail to feel all other human problems, but not these two, for these were too immediate and crushing in their impact, too challenging in the demand that we as individuals take the responsibility for encounter and resolution.

While these and other problems either directly oppressed us or rankled our consciences and became our own subjective concerns, we began to see complicated and disturbing paradoxes in our surrounding America. The declaration "all men are created equal . . ." rang hollow before the facts of Negro life in the South and the big cities of the North. The proclaimed peaceful

75

intentions of the United States contradicted its economic and military investments in the Cold War status quo.

We witnessed, and continue to witness, other paradoxes. With nuclear energy whole cities can easily be powered, yet the dominant nation-states seem more likely to unleash destruction greater than that incurred in all wars of human history. Although our own technology is destroying old and creating new forms of social organization, men still tolerate meaningless work and idleness. While two-thirds of mankind suffers undernourishment, our own upper classes revel amidst superfluous abundance. Although world population is expected to double in forty years, the nations still tolerate anarchy as a major principle of international conduct and uncontrolled exploitation governs the sapping of the earth's physical resources. Although mankind desperately needs revolutionary leadership, America rests in national stalemate, its goals ambiguous and tradition-bound instead of informed and clear, its democratic system apathetic and manipulated rather than "of, by, and for the people."

Not only did tarnish appear on our image of American virtue, not only did disillusion occur when the hypocrisy of American ideals was discovered, but we began to sense that what we had originally seen as the American Golden Age was actually the decline of an era. The worldwide outbreak of revolution against colonialism and imperialism, the entrenchment of totalitarian states, the menace of war, overpopulation, international disorder, super-technology—these trends were testing the tenacity of our own commitment to democracy and freedom and our abilities to visualize their application to a world in upheaval.

Our work is guided by the sense that we may be the last generation in the experiment with living. But we are a minority—the vast majority of our people regard the temporary equilibriums of our society and world as eternally-functional parts. In this is perhaps the outstanding paradox: we ourselves are imbued with urgency, yet the message of our society is that there is no viable alternative to the present. Beneath the reassuring tones of the politicians, beneath the common opinion that America will "muddle through", beneath the stagnation of those who have closed their minds to the future, is the pervading feeling that there simply are no alternatives, that our times have witnessed the exhaustion not only of Utopias, but of any new departures as well. Feeling the press of complexity upon the emptiness of life, people are fearful of the thought that at any moment things might thrust out of control. They fear change itself, since change might smash whatever invisible framework seems to hold back chaos for them now. For most Americans, all crusades are suspect, threatening. The fact that each individual sees apathy in his fellows perpetuates the common reluctance to organize for change. The dominant institutions are complex enough to blunt the minds of their potential critics, and entrenched enough to swiftly dissipate or entirely repel the energies of protest and reform, thus limiting human expectancies. Then, too, we are a materially improved society, and by our own improvements we seem to have weakened the case for further change.

Some would have us believe that Americans feel contentment amidst prosperity—but might it not better be called a glaze above deeply felt anxieties about their role in the new world? And if these anxieties produce a developed indifference to human affairs, do they not as well produce a yearning to believe there is an alternative to the present, that something can be done to change circumstances in the school, the workplaces, the bureaucracies, the government? It is to this latter yearning, at once the spark and engine of change, that we direct our present appeal. The search for truly democratic alternatives to the present, and a commitment to social experimentation with them, is a worthy and fulfilling human enterprise, one which moves us and, we hope, others today. On such a basis do we offer this document of our convictions and analysis: as an effort in understanding and changing the conditions of humanity in the late twentieth century, an effort rooted in the ancient, still unfulfilled conception of man attaining determining influence over his circumstances of life. . . .

As a social system we seek the establishment of a democracy of individual participation, governed by two central aims: that the individual share in those social decisions determining the quality and direction of his life; that society be organized to encourage independence in men and provide the media for their common participation.

In a participatory democracy, the political life would be based in several root principles:

that decision-making of basic social consequence be carried on by public groupings;

that politics be seen positively, as the art of collectively creating an acceptable pattern of social relations;

that politics has the function of bringing people out of isolation and into community, thus being a necessary, though not sufficient, means of finding meaning in personal life;

that the political order should serve to clarify problems in a way instrumental to their solution;

it should provide outlets for the expression of personal grievance and aspiration; opposing views should be organized so as to illuminate choices and facilitate the attainment of goals;

channels should be commonly available to related men to knowledge and to power so that private problems—from bad recreation facilities to personal alienation—are formulated as general issues.

2

JOHN F. KENNEDY'S RADIO AND TELEVISION REPORT TO THE AMERICAN PEOPLE ON CIVIL RIGHTS (JUNE 11, 1963)

Good evening, my fellow citizens:

This afternoon, following a series of threats and defiant statements, the presence of Alabama National Guardsmen was required on the University of Alabama to carry out the final and unequivocal order of the United States District Court of the Northern District of Alabama. That order called for the admission of two clearly qualified young Alabama residents who happened to have been born Negro.

That they were admitted peacefully on the campus is due in good measure to the conduct of the students of the University of Alabama, who met their responsibilities in a constructive way.

I hope that every American, regardless of where he lives, will stop and examine his conscience about this and other related incidents. This Nation was founded by men of many nations and backgrounds. It was founded on the principle that all men are created equal, and that the rights of every man are diminished when the rights of one man are threatened.

Today, we are committed to a worldwide struggle to promote and protect the rights of all who wish to be free. And when Americans are sent to Vietnam or West Berlin, we do not ask for whites only. It ought to be possible, therefore, for American students of any color to attend any public institution they select without having to be backed up by troops.

It ought to be possible for American consumers of any color to receive equal service in places of public accommodation, such as hotels and restaurants and theaters and retail stores, without being forced to resort to demonstrations in the street, and it ought to a be possible for American citizens of any color to register and to vote in a free election without interference or fear of reprisal.

It ought to be possible, in short, for every American to enjoy the privileges of being American without regard to his race or his color. In short, every American ought to have the right to be treated as he would wish to be treated, as one would wish his children to be treated. But this is not the case.

The Negro baby born in America today, regardless of the section of the State in which he is born, has about one-half as much chance of completing a high school as a white baby born in the same place on the same day, one-third as much chance of completing college, one-third as much chance of becoming a professional man, twice as much chance of becoming unemployed, about one-seventh as much chance of earning $10,000 a year, a life expectancy which is 7 years shorter, and the prospects of earning only half as much.

This is not a sectional issue. Difficulties over segregation and discrimination exist in every city, in every State of the Union, producing in many cities a rising tide of discontent that threatens the public safety. Nor is this a partisan issue. In a time of domestic crisis men of good will and generosity should be able to unite regardless of party or politics. This is not even a legal or legislative issue alone. It is better to settle these matters in the courts than on the streets, and new laws are needed at every level, but law alone cannot make men see right.

We are confronted primarily with a moral issue. It is as old as the Scriptures and is as clear as the American Constitution.

The heart of the question is whether all Americans are to be afforded equal rights and equal opportunities, whether we are going to treat our fellow Americans as we want to be treated. If an American, because his skin is dark, cannot eat lunch in a restaurant open to the public, if he cannot send his children to the best public school available, if he cannot vote for the public officials who will represent him, if, in short, he cannot enjoy the full and free life which all of us want, then who among us would be content to have the color of his skin changed and stand in his place? Who among us would then be content with the counsels of patience and delay?

One hundred years of delay have passed since President Lincoln freed the slaves, yet their heirs, their grandsons, are not fully free. They are not yet freed from the bonds of injustice. They are not yet freed from social and economic oppression. And this Nation, for all its hopes and all its boasts, will not be fully free until all its citizens are free.

We preach freedom around the world, and we mean it, and we cherish our freedom here at home, but are we to say to the world, and much more importantly, to each other that this is the land of the free except for the Negroes; that we have no second-class citizens except Negroes; that we have no class or caste system, no ghettoes, no master race except with respect to Negroes?

Now the time has come for this Nation to fulfill its promise. The events in Birmingham and elsewhere have so increased the cries for equality that no city or State or legislative body can prudently choose to ignore them. The fires of frustration and discord are burning in every city, North and South, where legal remedies are not at hand. Redress is sought in the streets, in demonstrations, parades, and protests which create tensions and threaten violence and threaten lives.

We face, therefore, a moral crisis as a country and a people. It cannot be met by repressive police action. It cannot be left to increased demonstrations in the streets. It cannot be quieted by token moves or talk. It is a time to act in the Congress, in your State and local legislative body and, above all, in all of our daily lives.

It is not enough to pin the blame on others, to say this a problem of one section of the country or another, or deplore the facts that we face. A great change is at hand, and our task, our obligation, is to make that revolution, that change, peaceful and constructive for all.

Those who do nothing are inviting shame, as well as violence. Those who act boldly are recognizing right, as well as reality.

Next week I shall ask the Congress of the United States to act, to make a commitment it has not fully made in this century to the proposition that race has no place in American life or law. The Federal judiciary has upheld that proposition in a series of forthright cases. The Executive Branch has adopted that proposition in the conduct of its affairs, including the employment of Federal personnel, the use of Federal facilities, and the sale of federally financed housing.

But there are other necessary measures which only the Congress can provide, and they must be provided at this session. The old code of equity law under which we live commands for every wrong a remedy, but in too many communities, in too many parts of the country, wrongs are inflicted on Negro citizens and there are no remedies at law. Unless the Congress acts, their only remedy is the street.

I am, therefore, asking the Congress to enact legislation giving all Americans the right to be served in facilities which are open to the public—hotels, restaurants, theaters, retail stores, and similar establishments.

This seems to me to be an elementary right. Its denial is an arbitrary indignity that no American in 1963 should have to endure, but many do.

I have recently met with scores of business leaders urging them to take voluntary action to end this discrimination, and I have been encouraged by their response, and in the last two weeks over 75 cities have seen progress made in desegregating these kinds of facilities. But many are unwilling to act alone, and for this reason, nationwide legislation is needed if we are to move this problem from the streets to the courts.

I am also asking the Congress to authorize the Federal Government to participate more fully in lawsuits designed to end segregation in public education. We have succeeded in persuading many districts to desegregate voluntarily. Dozens have admitted Negroes without violence. Today, a Negro is attending a State-supported institution in every one of our 50 States, but the pace is very slow.

Too many Negro children entering segregated grade schools at the time of the Supreme Court's decision nine years ago will enter segregated high schools this fall, having suffered a loss which can never be restored. The lack of an adequate education denies the Negro a chance to get a decent job.

The orderly implementation of the Supreme Court decision, therefore, cannot be left solely to those who may not have the economic resources to carry the legal action or who may be subject to harassment.

Other features will be also requested, including greater protection for the right to vote. But legislation, I repeat, cannot solve this problem alone. It must be solved in the homes of every American in every community across our country.

In this respect I want to pay tribute to those citizens North and South who've been working in their communities to make life better for all. They are acting not out of a sense of legal duty but out of a sense of human decency. Like our soldiers and sailors in all parts of the world they are meeting freedom's challenge on the firing line, and I salute them for their honor and their courage.

My fellow Americans, this is a problem which faces us all—in every city of the North as well as the South. Today, there are Negroes unemployed, two or three times as many compared to whites, inadequate education, moving into the large cities, unable to find work, young people particularly out of work without hope, denied equal rights, denied the opportunity to eat at a restaurant or a lunch counter or go to a movie theater, denied the right to a decent education, denied almost today the right to attend a State university even though qualified. It seems to me that these are matters which concern us all, not merely Presidents or Congressmen or Governors, but every citizen of the United States.

This is one country. It has become one country because all of us and all the people who came here had an equal chance to develop their talents.

We cannot say to ten percent of the population that you can't have that right; that your children cannot have the chance to develop whatever talents they have; that the only way that they are going to get their rights is to go in the street and demonstrate. I think we owe them and we owe ourselves a better country than that.

Therefore, I'm asking for your help in making it easier for us to move ahead and to provide the kind of equality of treatment which we would want ourselves; to give a chance for every child to be educated to the limit of his talents.

As I've said before, not every child has an equal talent or an equal ability or equal motivation, but they should have the equal right to develop their talent and their ability and their motivation, to make something of themselves.

We have a right to expect that the Negro community will be responsible, will uphold the law, but they have a right to expect that the law will be fair, that the Constitution will be color blind, as Justice Harlan said at the turn of the century.

This is what we're talking about and this is a matter which concerns this country and what it stands for, and in meeting it I ask the support of all our citizens.

Thank you very much.

3

LYNDON BAINES JOHNSON, "REMARKS ON SIGNING THE ECONOMIC OPPORTUNITY ACT" (AUGUST 20,1964)

My fellow Americans:

On this occasion the American people and our American system are making history.

For so long as man has lived on this earth poverty has been his curse.

On every continent in every age men have sought escape from poverty's oppression.

Today for the first time in all the history of the human race, a great nation is able to make and is willing to make a commitment to eradicate poverty among its people.

Whatever our situation in life, whatever our partisan affiliation, we can be grateful and proud that we are able to pledge ourselves this morning to this historic course. We can be especially proud of the nature of the commitments that we are making.

This is not in any sense a cynical proposal to exploit the poor with a promise of a handout or a dole.

We know—we learned long ago—that answer is no answer.

The measure before me this morning for signature offers the answer that its title implies—the answer of opportunity. For the purpose of the Economic Opportunity Act of 1964 is to offer opportunity, not an opiate.

For the million young men and women who are out of school and who are out of work, this program will permit us to take them off the streets, put them into work training programs, to prepare them for productive lives, not wasted lives.

In this same sound, sensible, and responsible way we will reach into all the pockets of poverty and help our people find their footing for a long climb toward a better way of life.

We will work with them through our communities all over the country to develop comprehensive community action programs—with remedial education, with job training, with retraining, with health and employment counseling, with neighborhood improvement. We will strike at poverty's roots.

This is by no means a program confined just to our cities. Rural America is afflicted deeply by rural poverty, and this program will help poor farmers get back on their feet and help poor farmers stay on their farms.

It will help those small businessmen who live on the borderline of poverty. It will help the unemployed heads of families maintain their skills and learn new skills.

In helping others, all of us will really be helping ourselves. For this bill will permit us to give our young people an opportunity to work here at home in constructive ways as volunteers, going to war against poverty instead of going to war against foreign enemies.

All of this will be done through a program which is prudent and practical, which is consistent with our national ideals.

Every dollar authorized in this bill was contained in the budget request that I sent to the Congress last January. Every dollar spent will result in savings to the country and especially to the local taxpayers in the cost of crime, welfare, of health, and of police protection.

We are not content to accept the endless growth of relief rolls or welfare rolls. We want to offer the forgotten fifth of our people opportunity and not doles.

That is what this measure does for our times.

Our American answer to poverty is not to make the poor more secure in their poverty but to reach down and to help them lift themselves out of the ruts of poverty and move with the large majority along the high road of hope and prosperity.

The days of the dole in our country are numbered. I firmly believe that as of this moment a new day of opportunity is dawning and a new era of progress is opening for us all.

And to you men and women in the Congress who fought so long, so hard to help bring about this legislation, to you private citizens in labor and in business who lent us a helping hand, to Sargent Shriver and that band of loyal men and women who made up this task force that brings our dream into a reality today, we say "Thank you" for all the American people. In the days and years to come those who have an opportunity to participate in this program will vindicate your thinking and vindicate your action.

Thank you very much.

4

CARL WITTMAN AND TOM HAYDEN,
"AN INTERRACIAL MOVEMENT
OF THE POOR?" (1963)

Increasingly today we hear the call for a movement of the American poor. The call is exciting to anyone who cares about democratic improvements in our way of life, and who remembers with nostalgia and some bitterness the achievements and failures of the populist and labor movements of earlier times. But under the excitement is a sense of vast difficulty, and an historical knowledge of the tragic conflicts between groups of the same class situation which have prevented more constructive conflicts between truly opposed classes. Our comments here are meant to be incomplete and unpolished—a set of working notes for those in SDS and elsewhere who wonder about these problems as they work on them. . . .

We are aware that the estrangement between the races can continue indefinitely, as it has in the South for a century. . . . But we remain convinced so far that permanent alienation can be avoided and overcome by a serious movement which fights for the interests of both groups. We know of almost no effort to organize in white communities in the South—and it would be foolish to be either optimistic or pessimistic until actual experiments are further underway. . . . We need to know much more about rank-and-file feelings within the white working class; we need to make contact with whatever radical individuals there are within the Southern union bureaucracy. . . .

Economic deprivation is not an experience peculiar to the Negro in America. It is a class experience which cannot be overcome by a single race. Thus any potential allies of an economically oriented Negro movement will be the class affected by this phenomenon. The essential class unity of a group must not be overlooked: Any united movement must stress this, the only common ground which all members of the group share. Their common consciousness of poverty and economic superfluousness will ultimately have to bring them together. . . .

There is good reason to question whether objective conditions . . . permit effective organization. Some unemployed whites may be more embarrassed than Negroes by their unemployed status, and see their problems as personal or obscure rather than social and clear. Many are not working because the only jobs they can get are not lucrative enough to compete with welfare or the other means of obtaining income. Some are too disillusioned by past disappointments. Others are just momentarily unemployed. . . .

However, these qualifications by no means apply everywhere, and two growing forces could reduce much of their significance. The first is the expanding rate of unemployment which could become a chronic problem for whites unless drastically new ameliorative policies are enacted. The second is the growing visibility of the unemployment problem and the consequent incentive to see it as an issue on which action legitimately can be taken. Together these trends are likely to create a far greater consciousness and movement by the unemployed themselves. . . .

In summary, there are various open possibilities for organizing among the 50 million or more "non-Negroes" who now are in a state of poverty or economic insecurity. What we know does not point towards anti-Negro or fascist attitudes throughout these groups of the poor, contrary to what some premature defeatists declare. We find a diverse series of situations, but most of them are characterized by:

1. The impact of growing economic insecurity.
2. A widespread feeling of alienation and a discouragement with existing economic policies.

Now with an official "war on poverty," there is a chance that the poor will feel a greater common consciousness of the legitimacy of their problems and the inadequacy of government programs. In addition, it is striking to observe that almost no attempts are being made to organize the poor for social change—and no verdict can be reached until a long-term attempt is made.

5

LYNDON BAINES JOHNSON, "PEACE WITHOUT CONQUEST" (APRIL 7, 1965)

Mr. Garland, Senator Brewster, Senator Tydings, Members of the congressional delegation, members of the faculty of Johns Hopkins, student body, my fellow Americans:

Last week 17 nations sent their views to some two dozen countries having an interest in southeast Asia. We are joining those 17 countries and stating our American policy tonight which we believe will contribute toward peace in this area of the world.

I have come here to review once again with my own people the views of the American Government.

Tonight Americans and Asians are dying for a world where each people may choose its own path to change.

This is the principle for which our ancestors fought in the valleys of Pennsylvania. It is the principle for which our sons fight tonight in the jungles of Viet-Nam.

Viet-Nam is far away from this quiet campus. We have no territory there, nor do we seek any. The war is dirty and brutal and difficult. And some 400 young men, born into an America that is bursting with opportunity and promise, have ended their lives on Viet-Nam's steaming soil.

Why must we take this painful road?

Why must this Nation hazard its ease, and its interest, and its power for the sake of a people so far away?

We fight because we must fight if we are to live in a world where every country can shape its own destiny. And only in such a world will our own freedom be finally secure.

This kind of world will never be built by bombs or bullets. Yet the infirmities of man are such that force must often precede reason, and the waste of war, the works of peace.

We wish that this were not so. But we must deal with the world as it is, if it is ever to be as we wish.

The world as it is in Asia is not a serene or peaceful place.

The first reality is that North Viet-Nam has attacked the independent nation of South Viet-Nam. Its object is total conquest.

Of course, some of the people of South Viet-Nam are participating in attack on their own government. But trained men and supplies, orders and arms, flow in a constant stream from north to south.

This support is the heartbeat of the war.

And it is a war of unparalleled brutality. Simple farmers are the targets of assassination and kidnapping. Women and children are strangled in the night because their men are loyal to their government. And helpless villages are ravaged by sneak attacks. Large-scale raids are conducted on towns, and terror strikes in the heart of cities.

The confused nature of this conflict cannot mask the fact that it is the new face of an old enemy.

Over this war—and all Asia—is another reality: the deepening shadow of Communist China. The rulers in Hanoi are urged on by Peking. This is a regime which has destroyed freedom in Tibet, which has attacked India, and has been condemned by the United Nations for aggression in Korea. It is a nation which is helping the forces of violence in almost every continent. The contest in Viet-Nam is part of a wider pattern of aggressive purposes.

Why are these realities our concern? Why are we in South Viet-Nam?

We are there because we have a promise to keep. Since 1954 every American President has offered support to the people of South Viet-Nam. We have helped to build, and we have helped to defend. Thus, over many years, we have made a national pledge to help South Viet-Nam defend its independence.

And I intend to keep that promise.

To dishonor that pledge, to abandon this small and brave nation to its enemies, and to the terror that must follow, would be an unforgivable wrong.

We are also there to strengthen world order. Around the globe, from Berlin to Thailand, are people whose well-being rests, in part, on the belief that they can count on us if they are attacked. To leave Viet-Nam to its fate would shake the confidence of all these people in the value of an American commitment and in the value of America's word. The result would be increased unrest and instability, and even wider war.

We are also there because there are great stakes in the balance. Let no one think for a moment that retreat from Viet-Nam would bring an end to conflict. The battle would be renewed in one country and then another. The central lesson of our time is that the appetite of aggression is never satisfied. To withdraw from one battlefield means only to prepare for the next. We must say in southeast Asia—as we did in Europe—in the words of the Bible: "Hitherto shalt thou come, but no further."

There are those who say that all our effort there will be futile—that China's power is such that it is bound to dominate all southeast Asia. But there is no end to that argument until all of the nations of Asia are swallowed up.

There are those who wonder why we have a responsibility there. Well, we have it there for the same reason that we have a responsibility for the defense of Europe. World War II was fought in both Europe and Asia, and when it ended we found ourselves with continued responsibility for the defense of freedom.

Our objective is the independence of South Viet-Nam, and its freedom from attack. We want nothing for ourselves—only that the people of South Viet-Nam be allowed to guide their own country in their own way.

We will do everything necessary to reach that objective. And we will do only what is absolutely necessary. . . .

This war, like most wars, is filled with terrible irony. For what do the people of North Viet-Nam want? They want what their neighbors also desire: food for their hunger; health for their bodies; a chance to learn; progress for their country; and an end to the bondage of material misery. And they would find all these things far more readily in peaceful association with others than in the endless course of battle.

These countries of Southeast Asia are homes for millions of impoverished people. Each day these people rise at dawn and struggle through until the night to wrestle existence from the soil. They are often wracked by disease, plagued by hunger, and death comes at the early age of 40.

Stability and peace do not come easily in such a land. Neither independence nor human dignity will ever be won, though, by arms alone. It also requires the work of peace. The American people have helped generously in times past in these works. Now there must be a much more massive effort to improve the life of man in that conflict-torn corner of our world.

The first step is for the countries of southeast Asia to associate themselves in a greatly expanded cooperative effort for development. We would hope that North Viet-Nam would take its place in the common effort just as soon as peaceful cooperation is possible.

The United Nations is already actively engaged in development in this area. As far back as 1961 I conferred with our authorities in Viet-Nam in connection with their work there. And I would hope tonight that the Secretary General of the United Nations could use the prestige of his great office, and his deep knowledge of Asia, to initiate, as soon as possible, with the countries of that area, a plan for cooperation in increased development.

For our part I will ask the Congress to join in a billion dollar American investment in this effort as soon as it is underway.

And I would hope that all other industrialized countries, including the Soviet Union, will join in this effort to replace despair with hope, and terror with progress.

The task is nothing less than to enrich the hopes and the existence of more than a hundred million people. And there is much to be done.

The vast Mekong River can provide food and water and power on a scale to dwarf even our own TVA.

The wonders of modern medicine can be spread through villages where thousands die every year from lack of care.

Schools can be established to train people in the skills that are needed to manage the process of development.

And these objectives, and more, are within the reach of a cooperative and determined effort.

I also intend to expand and speed up a program to make available our farm surpluses to assist in feeding and clothing the needy in Asia. We should not allow people to go hungry and wear rags while our own warehouses overflow with an abundance of wheat and corn, rice and cotton.

So I will very shortly name a special team of outstanding, patriotic, distinguished Americans to inaugurate our participation in these programs. This team will be headed by Mr. Eugene Black, the very able former President of the World Bank. . . .

We will do this because our own security is at stake.

But there is more to it than that. For our generation has a dream. It is a very old dream. But we have the power and now we have the opportunity to make that dream come true.

For centuries nations have struggled among each other. But we dream of a world where disputes are settled by law and reason. And we will try to make it so.

For most of history men have hated and killed one another in battle. But we dream of an end to war. And we will try to make it so.

For all existence most men have lived in poverty, threatened by hunger. But we dream of a world where all are fed and charged with hope. And we will help to make it so.

The ordinary men and women of North Viet-Nam and South Viet-Nam—of China and India—of Russia and America—are brave people. They are filled with the same proportions of hate and fear, of love and hope. Most of them want the same things for themselves and their families. Most of them do not want their sons to ever die in battle, or to see their homes, or the homes of others, destroyed.

Well, this can be their world yet. Man now has the knowledge—always before denied—to make this planet serve the real needs of the people who live on it.

I know this will not be easy. I know how difficult it is for reason to guide passion, and love to master hate. The complexities of this world do not bow easily to pure and consistent answers.

But the simple truths are there just the same. We must all try to follow them as best we can.

We often say how impressive power is. But I do not find it impressive at all. The guns and the bombs, the rockets and the warships, are all symbols of human failure. They are necessary symbols. They protect what we cherish. But they are witness to human folly.

A dam built across a great river is impressive.

In the countryside where I was born, and where I live, I have seen the night illuminated, and the kitchens warmed, and the homes heated, where once the cheerless night and the ceaseless cold held sway. And all this happened because electricity came to our area along the humming wires of the REA. Electrification of the countryside—yes, that, too, is impressive.

A rich harvest in a hungry land is impressive.

The sight of healthy children in a classroom is impressive.

These—not mighty arms—are the achievements which the American Nation believes to be impressive.

And, if we are steadfast, the time may come when all other nations will also find it so.

Every night before I turn out the lights to sleep I ask myself this question: Have I done everything that I can do to unite this country? Have I done everything I can to help unite the world, to try to bring peace and hope to all the peoples of the world? Have I done enough?

Ask yourselves that question in your homes—and in this hall tonight. Have we, each of us, all done all we could? Have we done enough?

We may well be living in the time foretold many years ago when it was said: "I call heaven and earth to record this day against you, that I have set before you life and death, blessing and cursing: therefore choose life, that both thou and thy seed may live."

This generation of the world must choose: destroy or build, kill or aid, hate or understand.

We can do all these things on a scale never dreamed of before.

Well, we will choose life. In so doing we will prevail over the enemies within man, and over the natural enemies of all mankind.

To Dr. Eisenhower and Mr. Garland, and this great institution, Johns Hopkins, I thank you for this opportunity to convey my thoughts to you and to the American people.

Good night.

6

PAUL POTTER, "NAME THE SYSTEM!" (APRIL 17, 1965)

Most of us grew up thinking that the United States was a strong but humble nation, that involved itself in world affairs only reluctantly, that respected the integrity of other nations and other systems, and that engaged in wars only as a last resort. This was a nation with no large standing army, with no design for external conquest, that sought primarily the opportunity to develop its own resources and its own mode of living. If at some point we began to hear vague and disturbing things about what this country had done in Latin America, China, Spain and other places, we somehow remained confident about the basic integrity of this nation's foreign policy. The Cold War with all of its neat categories and black and white descriptions did much to assure us that what we had been taught to believe was true.

But in recent years, the withdrawal from the hysteria of the Cold War era and the development of a more aggressive, activist foreign policy have done much to force many of us to rethink attitudes that were deep and basic sentiments about our country. The incredible war in Vietnam has provided the razor, the terrifying sharp cutting edge that has finally severed the last vestige of illusion that morality and democracy are the guiding principles of American foreign policy. The saccharine, self-righteous moralism that promises the Vietnamese a billion dollars of economic aid at the very moment we are delivering billions for economic and social destruction and political repression is rapidly losing what power it might ever have had to reassure us about the decency of our foreign policy. The further we explore the reality of what this country is doing and planning in Vietnam the more we are driven toward the conclusion of Senator Morse that the United States may well be the greatest threat to peace in the world today. That is a terrible and bitter insight for people who grew up as we did—and our revulsion at that insight, our refusal to accept it as inevitable or necessary, is one of the reasons that so many people have come here today.

The President says that we are defending freedom in Vietnam. Whose freedom? Not the freedom of the Vietnamese. The first act of the first dictator, Diem, the United States installed in Vietnam, was to systematically begin the persecution of all political opposition, non-Communist as well as Communist. The first American military supplies were not used to fight Communist insurgents; they were used to control, imprison or kill any who sought something better for Vietnam than the personal aggrandizement, political corruption and the profiteering of the Diem regime. The elite of the forces that we have trained and equipped are still used to control political unrest in Saigon and defend the latest dictator from the people.

And yet in a world where dictatorships are so commonplace and popular control of government so rare, people become callous to the misery that is implied by dictatorial power. The rationalizations that are used to defend political despotism have been drummed into us so long that we have somehow become numb to the possibility that something else might exist. And it is only the kind of terror we see now in Vietnam that awakens conscience and reminds us that there is something deep in us that cries out against dictatorial suppression.

The pattern of repression and destruction that we have developed and justified in the war is so thorough that it can only be called cultural genocide. I am not simply talking about napalm or gas or crop destruction or torture, hurled indiscriminately on women and children, insurgent and neutral, upon the first suspicion of rebel activity. That in itself is horrendous and incredible beyond belief. But it is only part of a larger pattern of destruction to the very fabric of the country. We have uprooted the people from the land and imprisoned them in concentration camps called "sunrise villages." Through conscription and direct political intervention and control, we have destroyed local customs and traditions, trampled upon those things of value which give dignity and purpose to life.

What is left to the people of Vietnam after 20 years of war? What part of themselves and their own lives will those who survive be able to salvage from the wreckage of their country or build on the "peace" and "security" our Great Society offers them in reward for their allegiance? How can anyone be surprised that people who have had total war waged on themselves and their culture rebel in increasing numbers against that tyranny? What other course is available? And still our only response to rebellion is more vigorous repression, more merciless opposition to the social and cultural institutions which sustain dignity and the will to resist.

Not even the President can say that this is a war to defend the freedom of the Vietnamese people. Perhaps what the President means when he speaks of freedom is the freedom of the American people.

What in fact has the war done for freedom in America? It has led to even more vigorous governmental efforts to control information, manipulate the press and pressure and persuade the public through distorted or downright dishonest documents such as the White Paper on Vietnam. It has led to the confiscation of films and other anti-war material and the vigorous harassment by the FBI of some of the people who have been most outspokenly active in their criticism of the war. As the war escalates and the administration seeks more actively to gain support for any initiative it may choose to take, there has been the beginnings of a war psychology unlike anything that has burdened this country since the 1950s. How much more of Mr. Johnson's freedom can we stand? How much freedom will be left in this country if there is a major war in Asia? By what weird logic can it be said that the freedom of one people can only be maintained by crushing another?

In many ways this is an unusual march because the large majority of people here are not involved in a peace movement as their primary basis of concern. What is exciting about the participants in this march is that so many of us view ourselves consciously as participants as well in a movement to build a more decent society. There are students here who have been involved in protests over the quality and kind of education they are receiving in growingly bureaucratized, depersonalized institutions called universities; there are Negroes from Mississippi and Alabama who are struggling against the tyranny and repression of those states; there are poor people here—Negro and white—from Northern urban areas who are attempting to build movements that abolish poverty and secure democracy; there are faculty who are beginning to question the relevance of their institutions to the critical problems facing the society. Where will these people and the movements they are a part of be if the President is allowed to expand the war in Asia? What happens to the hopeful beginnings of expressed discontent that are trying to shift American attention to long-neglected internal priorities of shared abundance, democracy and decency at home when those priorities have to compete with the all-consuming priorities and psychology of a war against an enemy thousands of miles away?

The President mocks freedom if he insists that the war in Vietnam is a defense of American freedom. Perhaps the only freedom that this war protects is the freedom of the warhawks in the Pentagon and the State Department to experiment with counter-insurgency and guerilla warfare in Vietnam. . . .

Thus far the war in Vietnam has only dramatized the demand of ordinary people to have some opportunity to make their own lives, and of their unwillingness, even under incredible odds, to give up the struggle against external domination. We are told, however, that the struggle can be legitimately suppressed since it might lead to the development of a Communist system, and before that ultimate menace all criticism is supposed to melt. . . .

But the war goes on; the freedom to conduct that war depends on the dehumanization not only of Vietnamese people but of Americans as well; it depends on the construction of a system of premises and thinking that insulates the President and his advisors thoroughly and completely from the human consequences of the decisions they make. I do not believe that the President or Mr. Rusk or Mr. McNamara or even McGeorge Bundy are particularly evil men. If asked to throw napalm on the back of a ten-year-old child they would shrink in horror—but their decisions have led to mutilation and death of thousands and thousands of people.

What kind of system is it that allows good men to make those kinds of decisions? What kind of system is it that justifies the United States or any country seizing the destinies of the Vietnamese people and using them callously for its own purpose? What kind of system is it that disenfranchises people in the South, leaves millions upon millions of people throughout the country impoverished and excluded from the mainstream and promise of American society, that creates faceless and terrible bureaucracies and makes those the place where people spend their lives and do their work, that consistently puts material values before human values—and still persists in calling itself free and still persists in finding itself fit to police the world? What place is there for ordinary men in that system and how are they to control it, make it bend itself to their wills rather than bending them to its?

We must name that system. We must name it, describe it, analyze it, understand it and change it. For it is only when that system is changed and brought under control that there can be any hope for stopping the forces that create a war in Vietnam today or a murder in the South tomorrow or all the incalculable, innumerable more subtle atrocities that are worked on people all over—all the time.

How do you stop a war then? If the war has its roots deep in the institutions of American society, how do you stop it? Do you march to Washington? Is that enough? Who will hear us? How can you make the decision makers hear us, insulated as they are, if they cannot hear the screams of a little girl burnt by napalm?

I believe that the administration is serious about expanding the war in Asia. The question is whether the people here are as serious about ending it. I wonder what it means for each of us to say we want to end the war in Vietnam—whether, if we accept the full meaning of that statement and the gravity of the situation, we can simply leave the march and go back to the routines of a society that acts as if it were not in the midst of a grave crisis. Maybe we, like the President, are insulated from the consequences of our own decision to end the war. Maybe we have yet really to listen to the screams of a burning child and decide that we cannot go back to whatever it is we did before today until that war has ended.

7

EXCERPTS FROM *RIGHTS IN CONFLICT: CHICAGO'S 7 BRUTAL DAYS*, A REPORT SUBMITTED BY DANIEL WALKER, DIRECTOR OF THE CHICAGO STUDY TEAM, TO THE NATIONAL COMMISSION ON THE CAUSES AND PREVENTION OF VIOLENCE, 168–77 (1968)

THE CLASH

Thus, at 7:57 p.m., with two groups of club-wielding police converging simultaneously and independently [at the intersection of Balbo and Michigan in front of Chicago's Conrad Hilton Hotel], the battle was joined. The portions of the throng out of the immediate area of conflict largely stayed put and took up the chant, "The whole world is watching," but the intersection fragmented into a collage of violence.

Re-creating the precise chronology of the next few minutes is impossible. But there is no question that a violent street battle ensued.

People ran for cover and were struck by police as they passed. Clubs were swung indiscriminately.

Two assistant U.S. attorneys who were on the scene characterized the police as "hostile and aggressive." Some witnesses cited particularly dramatic personal stories.

"I saw squadro[n]s of policemen coming from everywhere," a secretary . . . said. "The crowd around me suddenly began to run. Some of us, including myself, were pushed back onto the sidewalk and then all the way up against . . . the Blackstone Hotel along Michigan Avenue. I thought the crowd had panicked. . . .

"As I looked up I was hit for the first time on the head from behind by what must have been a billy club. I was then knocked down and while on my hands and knees, I was hit around the shoulders. I got up again, stumbling and was hit again. As I was falling, I heard words to the effect of 'move, move' and the horrible sound of cracking billy clubs.

"After my second fall, I remember being kicked in the back, and I looked up and noticed that many policemen around me had no badges on. The police kept hitting me on the head."

Eventually she made her way to an alley behind the Blackstone and finally, "bleeding badly from my head wound," was driven by a friend to a hospital emergency room. Her treatment included the placing of 12 stitches.

Another young woman, who had been among those who sat down in the intersection, ran south on Michigan, a "Yippie flag" in her hand, when she saw the police. "I fell in the center of the intersection," she says. "Two policemen ran up on me, stopped and hit me on the shoulder, arm and leg about five or six times, severely. They were swearing and one of them broke my flag over his knee." By fleeing into Grant Park, she managed eventually to escape.

Another witness said: "To my left, the police caught a man, beat him to the ground and smashed their clubs on the back of his unprotected head. I stopped to help him. He was elderly, somewhere in his mid-50's. He was kneeling and holding his bleeding head. As I stopped to help him, the police turned on me. 'Get that cock sucker out of here!' This command was accompanied by four blows from clubs—one on the middle of my back, one on the bottom of my back, one on my left buttock, and one on the back of my leg. No attempt was made to arrest me or anybody else in the vicinity. All the blows that I saw inflicted by the police were on the backs of heads, arms, legs, etc. It was the most slow and confused, and the least experienced people who got caught and beaten.

"The police were angry. Their anger was neither disinterested nor instrumental. It was deep, expressive and personal. 'Get out of here you cock suckers' seemed to be their most common cry."

One demonstrator said that several policemen were coming toward a group in which he was standing when one of the officers yelled, "Hey, there's a nigger over there we can get." They then said to have veered off and grabbed a middle-aged Negro man, whom they beat. . . .

In balance, there is no doubt that police discipline broke during the melee. The deputy superintendent of police states that—although this was the only time he saw discipline collapse—when he ordered his men to stand fast, some did not respond and began to sally through the crowd, clubbing people they came upon. An inspector-observer from the Los Angeles Police Department, stated that during this week, "The restraint of the police both as individual members and as an organization, was beyond reason. . . ."

While violence was exploding in the street, the crowd, wedged behind the police sawhorses along the northeast of the Hilton, was experiencing a terror all its own. Early in the evening, this group had consisted in large part of curious bystanders. But following the police surges into the demonstrators clogging the intersection, protestors had crowded the ranks behind the horses in their flight from the police.

From force of numbers, the sidewalk crowd of 150 to 200 persons was pushing down toward the Hilton's front entrance. Policemen whose orders were to keep the entrance clear were pushing with sawhorses. Other police and fleeing demonstrators were pushing from the north in the effort to clear the intersection. Thus, the crowd was wedged against the hotel, with the hotel itself on the west, sawhorses on the southeast and police on the northeast. . . .

"The cops just waded into the crowd," says a law student. "There was a great deal of clubbing. People were screaming, 'Help!'"

As a result, a part of the crowd was trapped in front of the Conrad Hilton and pressed hard against a big plate glass window of the Haymarket Lounge. A reporter who was sitting inside said, "Frightened men and women banged . . . against the window. A captain of the fire department inside told us to get back from the window, that it might get knocked in. As I backed away a few feet I could see a smudge of blood on the glass outside."

With a sickening crack, the window shattered, and screaming men and women tumbled through, some cut badly by jagged glass. The police came after them.

"I was pushed through by the force of large numbers of people," one victim said. "I got a deep cut on my right leg, diagnosed later by Eugene McCarthy's doctor as a severed artery. . . . I fell to the floor of the bar. There were ten to 20 people who had come through. . . . I could not stand on the leg. It was bleeding profusely.

"A squad of policemen burst into the bar, clubbing all those who looked to them like demonstrators, at the same time screaming over and over, 'We've got to clear this area.' The police acted like mad dogs looking for objects to attack.

"A patrolman ran up to where I was sitting. I protested that I was injured and could not walk, attempting to show him my leg. He screamed that he would show me I could walk. He grabbed me by the shoulder and literally hurled me through the door of the bar into the lobby. . . .

"I stumbled out into what seemed to be a main lobby. The young lady I was with and I were both immediately set upon by what I can only presume were plainclothes police. . . . We were cursed by these individuals and thrown through another door into an outer lobby." Eventually a McCarthy aide took him to the 15th floor.

In the heat of all this, probably few were aware of the Haymarket's advertising slogan: "A place where good guys take good girls to dine in the lusty, rollicking atmosphere of fabulous Old Chicago."

THE LIBERAL-CONSERVATIVE DEBATES OF THE 1960s

Michael W. Flamm

In January 1961, less than a week before the inauguration of John Kennedy, a founding editor at *National Review*, the flagship publication of the conservative movement, hailed a development unnoticed by most Americans. For Frank S. Meyer, "the revival of conservative thought in the United States that has taken place over the last half decade" far outweighed the political disappointment of the recent election, in which a liberal Democrat had succeeded a moderate Republican. "For the first time in modern America," he wrote, "the rising influence among intellectuals is the influence of conservatism."[1] Six months later, a student journalist with a very different ideology published a warning to liberals in a very different publication—*Mademoiselle*. For Tom Hayden, a University of Michigan undergraduate who later became famous as the radical author of the Port Huron Statement of 1962 and the passionate leader of Students for a Democratic Society (SDS), the main organization of the New Left, what was noteworthy in August 1961 was that the "new conservatives are not disinterested kids who maintain the status quo by political immobility. . . . What is new about the new conservatives is their militant mood, their appearance on picket lines."[2]

Taken together, these two complementary observations by distinctly different individuals suggest an alternative view of the 1960s. The older interpretation emphasized how liberal, even radical, the decade was. It was, after all, the age of powerful social movements on behalf of civil rights and women's rights. It was also an era when the counterculture challenged many of the values and beliefs held by morally traditional Americans. And it was a time when mass protests against the Vietnam War erupted in the streets and on the campuses, where revolts against authority in all forms were commonplace. Finally, it was a period when the most visible and vocal debates usually took place between liberals and radicals, uneasy allies and frequent rivals on the left.

But a newer interpretation stresses how truly polarized the 1960s were, how radicals, liberals, *and* conservatives repeatedly clashed in ideological combat for the hearts and minds of American voters. Millions in the center and on the right contested the counterculture, defended the Vietnam War, opposed the Great Society, and resisted the civil rights movement. During the decade, the New Left received the most attention, but the most powerful political force to emerge from the 1960s was the conservative movement, which in the 1970s became known as the New Right. The triumph of Ronald Reagan in 1980 surprised many commentators at the time, but it was the culmination of years of preparation.

The rise of the conservative movement in the 1960s was largely unexpected. At the dawn of the decade most scholars and commentators had assumed that the center would hold—that either moderate liberals (Democrats in the mold of Franklin Roosevelt) or moderate conservatives (Republicans in the mold of Dwight Eisenhower) would remain in power and continue to accept the broad parameters of the New Deal. But in the 1960s the advent of a more activist liberal orthodoxy altered the political equation. And then the appearance of a more purist conservative movement defied the conventional wisdom. First, it achieved an ideological unity (albeit tenuous) between libertarian, traditionalist, and anticommunist conservatives. Second, it developed older institutions, such as *National Review*, and newer organizations, such as the Young Americans for Freedom (YAF) and the John Birch Society (JBS). Third, the movement began to shed the extremist label which liberals and moderates were quick to affix to conservatives. Finally, it captured the Republican presidential nomination in 1964.

The emergence of the conservative movement began with ideology. The mantra was "ideas matter"—and they did. In the 1940s and 1950s, the right was divided and dispirited. It was unclear how best to combat the menace of communism and the appeal of government programs like Social Security. Moderates wanted to limit or contain the growth of the New Deal. Conservatives wanted to shrink it initially and dismantle it eventually.

By contrast, liberals wanted to expand the New Deal into new fields like health care and public education. In the aftermath of World War II, they were confident, even arrogant. "In the United States at this time liberalism is not only the dominant but even the sole intellectual tradition," commented Lionel Trilling, a Columbia University literary critic, in 1950. " This does not mean, of course, that there is no impulse to conservatism or to reaction. But the conservative impulse and the reactionary impulse do not, with some isolated and some ecclesiastical exceptions, express themselves in ideas but only in action or in irritable mental gestures which seek to resemble ideas."[3]

In response and opposition, two clusters of purist conservatives emerged. Libertarians stressed that human freedom and economic freedom were inextricably intertwined. The more government intervened in the economy, the less control individuals would have over their lives. The libertarian "Bible" was *The Road to Serfdom* (1944) by Friedrich von Hayek, an émigré economist from Austria who warned that communism, fascism, and liberalism would all lead to the same end—totalitarianism and collectivism. Any interference with property rights or the free market would place American society on the slippery slope to a socialist state. Yet many libertarians who supported the principle of limited government made an exception when it came to military spending and national security.

Traditionalists, the second cluster of purist conservatives, stressed that freedom was impossible in a society without stability, which in turn was impossible without authority whose legitimacy derived from history and morality. Respect for the past dictated resistance in the present to social engineering. Liberal reforms, even those with the best of intentions, would ultimately backfire and threaten the social order, which rested on family, church, and community. Among the traditionalist "Bibles" was *The Conservative Mind* (1953) by Russell Kirk, an intellectual historian who wrote that a "divine intent rules society as well as conscience," which meant that "political problems, at bottom, are religious and moral problems."[4] Yet religious differences often divided the traditionalist camp, which overwhelmingly consisted of conservative Catholics and Protestants.

In the 1960s, the emergence of issues like school prayer and birth control revealed tensions within the alliance. Many religious traditionalists were outraged when the Supreme Court ruled in *Engel v. Vitale* (1962) that the First Amendment banned even nondenominational prayer in the public schools. But others held their fire, some because of their acceptance of the separation of church and state, some because of their allegiance to parochial schools. Likewise, most conservative Catholics were outraged when the Supreme Court ruled in *Griswold v. Connecticut* (1965) that individuals had a constitutional right to privacy, and that therefore the state could not prohibit the purchase or use of contraceptives by adults, whether married or not. But many conservative Protestants had few moral objections to birth control. It was not until the 1970s, when the right to privacy became the cornerstone of *Roe v. Wade* (1973), which legalized abortion, that evangelical Fundamentalists mobilized in large numbers and reentered the political fray. By the 1980s, they had formed the Christian Right and were a powerful force in the New Right.

In theory, the ideas of the libertarians and traditionalists were incompatible, given the innovative but destructive role of capitalism. What if the free market, left unregulated as the libertarians demanded, fostered the development of products and the pursuit of activities which eroded the moral beliefs and communal values held dear by traditionalists? In practice, common ground on economic issues like high taxes enabled conservatives to sidestep, temporarily, this dilemma. Two common enemies also helped bridge the divide. The first was communism, which promoted atheism (the bane of traditionalists) and opposed capitalism (the mainstay of libertarians). The second was liberalism, which advocated economic regulation (anathema to libertarians) and social engineering (anathema to traditionalists) by an activist and interventionist federal government.

Thus shared opposition to communism and liberalism was in large part what united, uneasily, the diffuse and diverse conservatives under the banner of "fusionism," of which Meyer was the founding father. But at the same time the movement needed a meeting place where conservatives of all varieties could exchange ideas and develop strategies. Enter William F. Buckley, who at the age of thirty founded *National Review* in 1955. One of ten children, the son of a wealthy entrepreneur who was a staunch anticommunist and conservative Catholic, and a former CIA officer in Mexico, Buckley was already famous thanks to his bestseller, *God and Man at Yale* (1951), which criticized the liberal faculty at his alma mater. He was also controversial thanks to his spirited defense of Republican Senator Joseph McCarthy, the anticommunist crusader whose investigative methods challenged civil liberties and inspired liberal loathing. It is difficult to exaggerate the influence and significance of Buckley, who was the intellectual godfather for a new generation of conservative activists.

Under Buckley's leadership, *National Review* became to conservatives what *The New Republic* was to liberals. In his first "Publisher's Statement," he wrote that the magazine "stands athwart history, yelling Stop at a time when no one is inclined to do so." On a political level, announced Buckley, *National Review* would fight big government and communist aggression. It would also oppose labor unions, world government, and the "cultural menace" of liberal artists. In general, the magazine favored states' rights over civil rights and warned that social welfare would disrupt the social order.[5]

On a philosophical level, Buckley drew a sharp distinction between conservatives and liberals. The former stressed human imperfection, limited government, eternal truths based on Christian values, and the unintended consequences of social policies. The latter tended, he wrote, "to believe that the human being is perfectible, and social progress predictable, and that the instrument for effecting the two is reason, that truths are transitory and empirically determined, that equality is desirable and attainable through the action of state power . . . that all peoples and societies should strive to organize themselves upon a rationalist and scientific paradigm."[6] It was a fair assessment of modern liberalism, written in the erudite style for which Buckley was known.

The three hallmarks of modern liberalism, which Buckley had identified, were secular rationalism, social pluralism, and moral relativism. Individuals were capable of improvement, if not perfection, when guided by impartial experts who relied upon reason rather than religion. Communities were capable of progress when directed by enlightened bureaucrats who believed in the power and purpose of government. And morality was in the eyes of the beholder, which meant that tolerance of alternative lifestyles and values was imperative in a diverse world of cultural differences. On all three counts, Buckley strongly objected.

In September 1960, almost two years before Hayden and a group of young radicals gathered in Port Huron to form SDS, Buckley hosted a conference of young conservatives at his estate in Sharon, Connecticut. Most were East Coast college students from religious families. They would form the core of YAF, which by 1964 had more than 350 chapters and thirty thousand members across the country. Like their SDS counterparts, the YAF delegates were tired of liberal complacency and believed in the potential of campus activism based on political principle. Unlike the radicals, who felt that structural change in American society was necessary, the conservatives believed that ideological change—first and foremost in the Republican Party—was sufficient. They would also, for the most part, confine their activism to the classroom, unlike SDS, which later took to the streets. "But what is so striking about the students who met at Sharon," observed Buckley with enthusiasm, "is their appetite for power. . . . They talk about *affecting* history; we have talked about *educating* people to want to affect history."[7]

"In this time of moral and political crises," the Sharon Statement began, "it is the responsibility of the youth of America to affirm certain eternal truths." The principal author was M. Stanton Evans, a twenty-six-year-old Yale graduate who was a friend of Buckley's and already the chief editorial writer for the *Indianapolis News*. The "eternal truths" included individual freedom and limited government beyond "the preservation of internal order [and] the provision of national defense." The brief manifesto also hailed the free market as the greatest strength of the United States and warned that international communism was the greatest threat to the United States. But left unmentioned were the complicated relationship between states' rights and civil rights and the tenuous balance between libertarians and traditionalists. In short, the Sharon Statement expressed in concise form the fusionist faith of the conservative credo. (See document 1.)

The goal of YAF was to cultivate the next generation of conservative leaders. But other organizations were also determined to educate, organize, and mobilize grass-roots conservatives. Of these, the most influential was the JBS, founded in 1958 by Robert Welch, a retired candy manufacturer. The organization was named after a Baptist missionary and intelligence agent who supposedly became the first casualty of the Cold War when he was killed by Chinese Communists ten days after World War II had ended. The JBS was opposed to social welfare, world government, the liberal chief justice of the Supreme Court ("Impeach Earl Warren" was a popular bumper sticker), and civil rights, which it saw as a communist plot to destroy American society. In fact, the JBS tended to see communist conspiracies everywhere and was determined to foil them. As it declared:

> We believe that communism is as utterly incompatible with all religion as it is contemptuous of all morality and destructive of all freedom. It is intrinsically evil. It must be opposed, therefore, with equal firmness, on religious grounds, moral grounds, and political grounds. We believe that the continued coexistence of communism and a Christian-style civilization on one planet is impossible. The struggle between them must end with one completely triumphant and the other completely destroyed. We intend to do our part, therefore, to halt, weaken, rout, and eventually to bury, the whole international Communist conspiracy. (See document 2.)

Alarmist rhetoric and conspiracy theories aside, the JBS was usually not engaged in extremist behavior. It had a membership estimated at more than sixty thousand by 1961, making it the largest grass-roots conservative organization. The typical JBS member was a white suburban Protestant, who was middle class and well educated in a technical field. In local chapters, members spent most of their time reading and discussing materials sent to them by the national office, then orchestrating letter-writing campaigns and joining local organizations like the PTA and the School Board. The JBS recruited activists for the conservative cause and offered conservative leaders a way to reach their followers. And it made other conservatives appear more mainstream in comparison.

But therein lay the rub—the existence of the JBS also enabled liberals to tar the entire conservative movement as extremist. It was, in a sense, guilt by association, although Welch bore much of the blame. In 1954, he had written a manuscript, *The Politician*, in which he had called Dwight Eisenhower, war hero and moderate Republican, a "conscious agent" of the communist conspiracy. Once revealed, the claim brought ridicule to the JBS and embarrassment to conservatives like Buckley, who in 1962 publicly disavowed Welch, a supporter of *National Review* from the start. The movement, Buckley knew, could not hope to attract Eisenhower Republicans if it continued to promote the more extreme ideas of the JBS. Conservatives, he wrote, had to "expand by bringing into our ranks those people who are . . . on our immediate left—the moderate, wishy-washy conservatives" who would never "join a movement whose leadership believes the drivel of Robert Welch."[8] The action was controversial—many readers of *National Review* were sharply critical of Buckley—but it was critical to the bid for political respectability by conservatives, who by then were also engaged in a battle for the ideological soul of the Republican Party.

In 1960, the movement faced a dilemma—to support or oppose Richard Nixon, a moderate Republican whom most conservatives distrusted. "Who likes Nixon's Republicanism?" asked *National Review*. "We don't."[9] But John Kennedy, a liberal Democrat, seemed worse. And so conservatives held their noses and voted for the Republican, hoping that they could push him and the party to adopt their positions in the future. Then Nixon lost by a narrow margin and the question became what to do to regain the White House. Moderates argued that the Republicans should remain in the middle and compete with the Democrats for the "vital center" of the American electorate. Conservatives argued that a large but silent majority shared their views. Therefore the time had come to move to the right and purify the principles for which the party stood—or should stand.

For conservatives, the man of the moment was Arizona Senator Barry Goldwater. A square-jawed and rough-hewn Westerner, he would lead the rebellion against the eastern elites, the moderate Republicans who had run the party since the 1940s. In fast-growing, middle-class suburbs across the Sunbelt, from California to Texas, Georgia to Florida, Goldwater aroused passionate support among white residents. The supposed author of *The Conscience of a Conservative* (1960), a blunt tract which sold three million copies, he was opposed to the welfare state, forced racial integration, and any policy which promised anything less than victory over communism. For young conservatives, Goldwater was their first true political love. As one YAF member recalled, he was "the knight on the white horse . . . riding out to do battle with evil, a rugged individualist evoking the great West's heroes who eschewed cant and guile and spoke their minds simply and to the point, a man who rose above the phoniness of the unprincipled politico and the fraud of the backroom bosses."[10] In a sense, Goldwater was the counterpart to Buckley—he was the political godfather of the conservative movement.

In 1964, Goldwater won the Republican nomination thanks to the coordinated efforts of a small group of dedicated conservatives and an unprecedented grass-roots mobilization endorsed by *National Review* and led by the JBS and YAF. At the Republican Convention, he thrilled the delegates by lambasting the Democratic record of retreat and failure. Then he made it clear that the Republican Party now belonged to the conservatives, who would pursue principle first and power later. Those who disagreed were free to leave. Finally, he uttered the words that would become famous: "I would remind you that extremism in the defense of liberty is no vice! And let me remind you also that moderation in the pursuit of justice is no virtue!" (See document 5.) The convention exploded.

The campaign, however, fizzled. To his credit, Goldwater refused in 1964 to run a campaign based on racial demagoguery or compromise his positions on the issues. He wanted to offer the voters, as he put it, "a choice, not an echo." But to his detriment, Goldwater often seemed determined to alienate them. His strident criticism of Social Security and agricultural programs angered the elderly and farmers. His casual comments about nuclear weapons scared many others. Republicans claimed that "In Your Heart You Know He's Right." In response, Democrats joked that "In Your Guts You Know He's Nuts" and exploited the fear evoked by Goldwater in a controversial commercial. The political ad, which featured the image of a young girl picking the petals off a daisy and then morphing into a mushroom cloud as a countdown climaxed, aired only once but tens of millions of Americans eventually watched it on news programs, which repeated it often.[11] Lyndon Johnson, who promised to uphold Kennedy's legacy and seemed like the voice of reason in comparison to Goldwater, was far ahead from the start and won in a landslide.

Conservatives were deeply disappointed in the outcome of the election and extremely angry with those Republican moderates who had abandoned the nominee. But the conservatives were not discouraged. They had lost the battle in 1964, but the war for America would continue, with ordinary citizens now enlisted in the antiliberal crusade inspired by elite intellectuals. As former Democrat and actor Ronald Reagan, who gave the single most effective speech on behalf of Goldwater (see document 6), put it, "We represent the forgotten American—that simple soul who goes to work, bucks for a raise, takes out insurance, pays for his kids' schooling, contributes to his church and charity and knows there 'just ain't no such thing as a free lunch.'"[12] Four years later, after immense turmoil and trauma, Nixon would avenge the 1960 election and win the White House by appealing directly to the "forgotten Americans" of whom Reagan had spoken. (See document 7.)

How similar was the conservative movement of the early 1960s to the conservative movement of the late 1960s? Scholars disagree on this question. Some stress the continuity between the movements. They claim that the right consistently promoted anticommunism at home and abroad while opposing the expansion of the welfare state and federal power (except in regard to national security). Other scholars focus on the changes between the movements. They contend that for the right the external threat posed by communist aggression receded in the mid-1960s, replaced by the internal threat posed by street crime, racial unrest, cultural conflict, and political protests, now seen as the logical outgrowth of liberal policies, not the direct product of communist subversion. Demands for a restoration of social order soon facilitated the rise of a more populist and traditionalist conservative movement, which was substantially different from the older and more elitist movement of anticommunists and libertarians.[13]

Regardless, conservatives were poised and prepared despite their divisions to take advantage of events in the 1960s. Once organized and mobilized, they challenged liberals in every major policy area, from the Great Society and foreign relations to civil rights and social order. The movement was also ready and able to exploit the weakness of liberals, whose strength was never as great as it seemed except on the Supreme Court. Conservatives were, for example, in effective control of Congress during most of the decade save for the period from 1964 to 1966, when the legislative foundations of the Great Society were laid.

By the end of the 1960s, an embattled minority had become a confident majority and transformed American politics. For one young conservative, "the '60s were the decade not of Kennedy but Goldwater, not SDS but YAF, not *The New Republic* but *National Review*, not [radical philosopher] Herbert Marcuse but Russell Kirk . . . not Lyndon Johnson's Great Society but Ronald Reagan's Creative Society, not a 'meaningless' civil war in Vietnam but an important battle in the protracted conflict against communism."[14] He was not alone.

GREAT SOCIETY

In January 1964, Lyndon Johnson vowed to continue the work of John Kennedy, his martyred predecessor. In his State of the Union address, the new president declared a War on Poverty. He inherited the liberal idea from Kennedy, whose tragic death in November 1963 gave the issue political traction and momentum. Johnson also held the liberal assumption that the poor had mainstream values and middle-class aspirations but lacked the means or skills to achieve them. Therefore it was incumbent upon government to provide them with the tools to take advantage of opportunities for advancement. Finally, Johnson shared the liberal confidence that the United States could fight and win a War on Poverty, the first step in the eventual creation of a Great Society.

This confidence had three main sources. First and foremost was the belief that the United States could afford a War on Poverty. Economic prosperity made it possible to help everyone—and no one would have to earn less or pay more in taxes. As Johnson declared, "I'm sick of all the people who talk about all the things we can't do. Hell, we're the richest and most powerful country in the world. We can do anything."[15] Second was the rediscovery of poverty amidst plenty. In 1962, *The Other America* by Michael Harrington revealed that as many as forty to fifty million Americans, 25 percent of the population, were poor even if they were largely invisible to the rest of society because they lived in rural isolation or urban slums. The book's findings impressed Kennedy and his advisers, who were excited by the challenge. It also embarrassed the administration, which was eager to counter Soviet propaganda about the superiority of communism to capitalism. Third was the faith most Americans had in experts and government—a faith not yet eroded by Vietnam or Watergate.

The War on Poverty was a dream for Johnson. Part of his motivation was compassion. As a young teacher in a one-room schoolhouse on the Texas-Mexico border, he had seen firsthand the impact of poverty on his students. Another part of Johnson's motivation was ambition. As a young politician, his idol was Franklin Roosevelt, whose New Deal had eased the mass suffering of the Great Depression. Now Johnson had the opportunity to surpass his role model and become the greatest president in U.S. history. And of course politics was part of his motivation. The Great Society, he hoped, would cement the loyalty of a new generation of American voters to the Democratic Party in the 1960s as the New Deal had in the 1930s.

The War on Poverty was also a dream for liberals. At last the United States could meet the basic needs and improve the quality of life of all. It had the material resources—America was, by many measures, the wealthiest nation in the history of the world. It had the intellectual capital—liberal policymakers now believed they understood both the problem of poverty and the solution to it. And the country had the political will—both Kennedy and Johnson had lent their prestige and power to the War on Poverty. Liberals saw it as a moral imperative—in a society of abundance, the persistence of deprivation was intolerable. They also saw ending poverty as an economic issue—increasing the purchasing power of the less fortunate would boost consumer spending and strengthen the American economy.

For conservatives the War on Poverty was a nightmare. They feared it would lead to an enormous bureaucracy and higher taxes at the expense of individual initiative and economic growth, the only paths to lasting and universal prosperity via private-sector job creation. The antipoverty program would, claimed Reagan, "trade our freedom for the soup kitchen of the welfare state." (See document 6.) Conservatives also contended that it ignored how living standards had risen since the 1920s. By the 1960s, many of the poor had indoor plumbing and owned televisions as well as cars—luxuries unimaginable to previous generations. To be sure, the poor often experienced a sense of relative deprivation thanks to television, but that was no reason to raise taxes or increase welfare.

Moreover, conservatives believed that poverty resulted not from a lack of opportunity but from a lack of character. Social programs would aggravate rather than alleviate social problems by encouraging personal dependence and discouraging personal responsibility. Conservatives especially objected that the War on Poverty made no distinction between the "deserving" and "undeserving" poor. Those who were in need of assistance through no fault of their own—widows, orphans, or individuals with legitimate disabilities, mental or physical—deserved support. Those who were able-bodied but unmotivated or unskilled deserved their fate. Most low-income individuals worked hard and managed to make ends meet. Therefore government would only strengthen the culture of poverty if it provided aid to drunks and deadbeats, "welfare queens" and drug addicts.

Finally, conservatives harbored deep doubts about whether it was possible or desirable to eliminate poverty. In their view it was in the nature of society for some to succeed and others to struggle. Protestant fundamentalist ministers reinforced the traditionalist perspective by removing any guilt some rich Christians might feel. "You have a God-ordained right to be wealthy," wrote the popular televangelist Robert Schuller in *God's Way to the Good Life* in 1963. "You're a steward of the goods, the gold, the gifts, [which] God has allowed to come into your hands. Having riches is no sin, wealth is no crime."[16] Presumably, poverty was a sign of God's disfavor.

In February 1964, Johnson asked R. Sargent Shriver, the head of the Peace Corps and a brother-in-law of Kennedy, to draft a bill. Both men wanted to limit welfare spending. Both wanted to foster individual responsibility, not dependency. And both wanted to avoid tax increases, wealth redistribution, or large-scale jobs programs, which were costly and controversial. The goal was a "hand up"—through educational programs and job training—not a "hand out." Johnson and Shriver were, observed historian James Patterson, "optimists who reflected the confidence of most contemporary American liberal thought. Unlike radicals, they thought that most poor people needed only a helping hand to rise in life. Unlike conservatives, they had great faith that government could and should extend that hand."[17]

In May 1964, Johnson demonstrated that optimism. In a commencement address at the University of Michigan, he described a world in which everyone would enjoy rich and satisfying lives in every respect:

> The Great Society is a place where every child can find knowledge to enrich his mind and to enlarge his talents. . . . It is a place where the city of man serves not only the needs of the body and the demands of commerce but the desire for beauty and the hunger for community. It is a place where man can renew contact with nature. . . . It is a place where men are more concerned with the quality of their goals than the quantity of their goods. (See document 4.)

Conservatives reacted with scorn. "The quality of life has heretofore depended on the quality of the human beings who gave tone to that life," commented Buckley, "and they were its priests and poets, not its bureaucrats."[18] Government intervention could not ensure personal happiness or end human misery. The Great Society, conservatives feared, would ultimately infringe upon individual freedom and community control of local affairs. Utopias were chimeras.

Passage of the poverty bill was never in serious doubt, despite conservative opposition to the centralized power the poverty "czar" would have. But events in the spring and summer of 1964 added to the sense of urgency among liberals. During the Republican primaries, Arizona Senator Barry Goldwater blamed the rising tide of urban violence on the welfare state. "Government seeks to be parent, teacher, leader, doctor, and even minister," he charged. "And its failures are strewn about us in the rubble of rising crime rates . . . " These and many other confrontational statements made Goldwater a hero to conservatives, who rewarded him with the Republican nomination.

In July 1964, hours before Goldwater accepted the nomination, an off-duty New York police officer in plainclothes shot and killed a black teenager armed with a knife. Two days later, a rally in Harlem to protest the Mississippi murders of three civil rights workers turned into a march on a precinct police station, where officers and demonstrators clashed. For the next week, street rallies in New York led to violent confrontations as police battled protesters hurling bricks and bottles. Arson and looting followed, with scores of injuries. In the symbolic and historic heart of black America, a new dynamic in the racial politics of the nation had begun.

The violence sent shock waves through the White House. In public, Johnson remained calm. In private, he was concerned—even alarmed—by the Harlem Riot, which he speculated was orchestrated by conservatives determined to deny him the election. "One of my political analysts tells me that every time one occurs, it costs me 90,000 votes," he complained to his FBI liaison. The next day the president called FBI Director J. Edgar Hoover. "We're getting floods of wires and telegrams," Johnson told him. "Here's one. [reads aloud:] 'I'm a working girl. . . . I'm afraid to leave my house. . . . I feel the Negro revolution will reach Queens. . . . Please send troops immediately to Harlem.'" Ultimately, he chose not to send the U.S. Army to New York. But three months later he would make an equally fateful decision.

In August 1964, Congress easily passed the poverty bill. It established a number of agencies, including Volunteers in Service to America (VISTA), a domestic counterpart to the Peace Corps; Head Start, an early education program for disadvantaged children; and the Job Corps, whose mission was to provide training to the poor. To oversee these programs, the bill created an Office of Economic Opportunity (OEO). The title illustrated how central the idea of opportunity was to liberals. The bill also endorsed "community action" and encouraged the "maximum feasible participation" of the poor. This language would cause considerable controversy in the years to come, especially when the needs and demands of the poor conflicted with the interests of politicians in their cities and states.

In October 1964, with the presidential campaign in full swing, Johnson uttered the words that would haunt his administration in the years to come.

At the ceremony to swear in Shriver as chief of OEO, the president pledged to abolish poverty. Engaging in rhetorical oversell, he damaged his personal credibility as well as public faith in liberal reforms. In addition, Johnson promised that the War on Poverty would constitute a war on crime and disorder. Without mentioning Goldwater by name, the president said, "There is something mighty wrong when a candidate for the highest public office bemoans violence in the streets but votes against the War on Poverty, votes against the Civil Rights Act, and votes against major educational bills that have come before him as a legislator. The thing to do is not to talk about crime; the thing to do is to fight and work and vote against crime." In so doing, Johnson expressed the liberal conviction that it was vital to combat the "root causes" of street crime. The president also blunted Goldwater's claim that the White House had no plan to reduce urban violence. But by bonding the War on Poverty to a war on crime, Johnson had made each war more vulnerable to conservative crossfire.

In November 1964, Johnson won a landslide victory. He received 61 percent of the popular vote and carried every state, with the exception of the Deep South (Mississippi, Alabama, South Carolina, Georgia, and Louisiana) and Arizona (Goldwater's home state). Goldwater had inspired and galvanized a new generation of conservative believers. He had also laid the ideological foundations for the movement. But liberals now had majorities in both the House and Senate—and many of the new members knew they owed their election to Johnson's triumph. The future of conservatism was uncertain. The future of liberalism seemed bright and limitless, although the president, ever the consummate politician, knew all too well that mandates in American politics are fleeting.

In January 1965, Johnson began his race against time. In the next six months, he compiled a legislative record unsurpassed since the New Deal. The Clean Air Act and the National Wilderness Act helped launch the modern environmental movement. The Immigration Act ended the quota system of the 1920s and opened the doors to mass immigration from the Caribbean, Latin America, and Asia, with unforeseen and unintended consequences that promise to transform American politics and society in the twenty-first century. The National Endowments for the Arts and Humanities made the federal government a major player in the cultural world. The middle class welcomed many of the measures. Liberals enthusiastically cheered. Conservatives glumly objected. "Trouble ahead," warned *National Review*, which in an overall appraisal of the Great Society worried that "doctrinaire collectivism," held in check since the New Deal, was again on the march.[19]

Beyond the War on Poverty, two other measures marked the Great Society. The first was federal aid to elementary and secondary education. Liberals believed that education was the path from poverty and that billions for compensatory education would give disadvantaged students from low-income families greater and more equal opportunities. Conservatives were skeptical. It was not clear that more money was needed for teacher training or school construction, since the peak of the school-age baby boom had passed by the 1960s. Nor was it clear that districts would spend the funds for compensatory education wisely or efficiently, especially when it came to helping students from deprived backgrounds. Conservatives also warned that federal dollars invariably and inevitably came with federal strings attached, leading to the erosion of local control and the imposition of national standards as well as racial equality.

The second measure was Medicare, which provided all Americans over sixty-five with subsidized health care and medical insurance. The measure fulfilled a liberal objective dating back to the 1940s, which both Truman and Kennedy had promised but failed to achieve. It was also a legislative priority of Johnson, who knew that more than half of all elderly Americans lacked health insurance and that they voted in large numbers. To overcome opposition from the American Medical Association (AMA), he agreed to permit doctors who treated Medicare patients to practice privately and charge their normal fees, which the government paid. To build support with the public, especially the middle class, the president made Medicare benefits, linked to Social Security, available to all Americans regardless of need. For liberals, it was not comprehensive or universal national health insurance, which remained the ultimate dream even after Medicaid extended federal assistance to welfare recipients and poor people of all ages. Nevertheless, Medicare and Medicaid brought the miracle of modern medicine to millions and were large steps in the right direction.

For conservatives, they were large steps in the wrong direction of "socialized medicine." Medicare and Medicaid, they argued, would raise the cost and lower the quality of health care. In addition, the programs would depersonalize the doctor-patient relationship by wrapping it in red tape. Many doctors might leave the profession while others might never enter. Medicare would also expand the federal bureaucracy and drain the federal budget because it was an entitlement program with no means test—everyone was eligible for assistance. Conservatives further objected to funding the program through involuntary payroll taxes, which reminded them of Social Security, a compulsory program many like Goldwater hoped to make voluntary.

While Medicare rapidly became popular, the War on Poverty quickly became controversial. "Poverty War Out of Hand?" asked *U.S. News & World Report* in 1965. It maintained that Head Start salaries were too high and that OEO had "administrative chaos, bureaucratic bungling, waste, extravagance, costly duplication of existing services, internal squabbling." Accompanying the article was a photo of black workers lounging at a Job Corps center.[20] In New York and Los Angeles, Chicago and Philadelphia, the mayors vehemently objected to Shriver's decision to send assistance directly to programs administered by activists without local oversight or control. As a result, OEO had to withhold funds from those cities because their community action programs failed to provide the poor with maximum feasible participation.

By the summer of 1967, civil unrest and urban violence had shredded liberal confidence in the War on Poverty. In Newark, the beating of a black cabdriver by white officers led to a riot which required the deployment of the New Jersey National Guard. In Detroit, hundreds of millions of dollars in federal antipoverty aid were unable to prevent—and may have encouraged—a riot which resulted in dozens of deaths and which the city police, National Guard, and state police were unable to suppress. Eventually, the president had to do what he would not do in Harlem in 1964—deploy the U.S. Army to restore the peace. But even as the soldiers patrolled the streets of Detroit, the Johnson administration was tabulating telegrams to see if the public blamed the War on Poverty. Shriver was informed that OEO could send no assistance to the beleaguered city without prior authorization from the White House.

The riots in Newark and Detroit rocked the nation and divided liberals. Outside the administration, the popular belief was that the War on Poverty was too little too late. Despite progress, blacks remained victims of "relative deprivation," with high unemployment rates and low income levels in comparison to whites. Inside the administration, the preferred explanation was that the War on Poverty was a victim of its own success, however limited. It had engendered "rising expectations" that were beyond immediate realization. Meanwhile, most liberals tried to suppress the gnawing fear that the social programs had somehow contributed to rather than calmed the social unrest.

For conservatives, the riots were largely the result of liberals who had falsely conflated race and disorder. "There is indeed a problem of the slums," conceded *National Review*. "And there is the problem of rioting and civil disobedience. But the two are not the same problem, and it is distinctively liberal fatuity to suppose that they are."[21] If the riots had a root cause, conservatives charged, it was not poverty since the American economy was in robust health. On the contrary, the real cause was the War on Poverty, which had fostered dependency and irresponsibility among the disadvantaged, many of whom were now angry and frustrated, without the individual initiative and moral integrity to make progress on their own.

More aid now, conservatives continued, would only make matters worse by feeding the frustration. It was time to dismantle the War on Poverty. Administered by distant bureaucrats with little regard for local traditions or values, it had rewarded the rioters, pandered to criminals, and squandered the hard-earned tax dollars of hard-working Americans. To add injury to insult, liberals had failed even to protect law-abiding citizens, black and white, from the violence that threatened to engulf them. The War on Poverty had reaped what it had supposedly sowed—urban destruction rather than renewal. Now, in the aftermath of Detroit, and Newark, conservatives charged that civil unrest represented the ultimate breakdown of civil society and the ultimate bankruptcy of modern liberalism, whose social programs had apparently backfired.

In 1968, the crescendo of criticism mounted. Bumper stickers appeared with slogans like "I Fight Poverty: I work" and "Join the Great Society: Go on Welfare."[22] At the Republican Convention, presidential nominee Richard Nixon stated that Americans had poured billions of dollars into "programs for the unemployed, programs for the cities, programs for the poor, and we have reaped from these programs an ugly harvest of frustration, violence and failure across the land." (See document 7.) Once elected, he shifted the Job Corps to the Department of Labor and Head Start to the Department of Health, Education, and Welfare. He also increased welfare expenditures, a source of dismay to conservatives. But in 1973, Nixon symbolically terminated OEO, the flagship of the antipoverty program in 1965 but by then a shell of what it once was.

Was the War on Poverty a success or failure? This is a difficult and controversial question to answer. On the one hand, the poverty rate fell significantly in the 1960s, to an all-time low in 1973, especially among the elderly whose life expectancy continued to rise significantly. The black middle class also expanded dramatically. On the other hand, the decline in the poverty rate was due primarily to economic growth, not social programs, as OEO routinely received less than 1 percent of the federal budget. Similarly, the rise in life expectancy was due primarily to long-term trends like better diets, not medical intervention made possible by Medicare spending.

From the outset the War on Poverty, like the war in Vietnam, was at best a limited conflict. Programs like Head Start were never fully funded, in part because of conservative opposition, in part because Johnson wanted to balance the budget, and in part because the Vietnam War demanded ever-larger sums. The money that was spent went mostly to administrators and contractors, few of whom were poor. The tactics employed by OEO were also limited. The reliance on education and training meant that few permanent jobs were created and few disadvantaged individuals were given meaningful opportunities.

Nevertheless, the Great Society left a large and enduring legacy. The environmental legislation championed by Johnson markedly improved the air and water quality enjoyed by millions of Americans. The Immigration Act literally changed the face of America by opening the doors to millions of Asians, Africans, and Latinos. Medicare helped transform the elderly from the poorest to the wealthiest segment of American society. More fundamentally, the Great Society substantially redirected federal spending from national defense to entitlement programs like Social Security, which today dominate the federal budget and dwarf what the United States devotes to welfare assistance and foreign aid.

But in the end, the War on Poverty in the 1960s led to great disappointment and disenchantment, for both liberals and conservatives. Fairly or not, it also came to symbolize the Great Society as a whole in the eyes of many Americans. Johnson had promised more than he could deliver, although perhaps he had little choice, given the political realities of his brief mandate. In any event, his unconditional and uncompromising rhetoric had raised expectations to unsustainable levels. And then the urban unrest of the mid-1960s had dashed those expectations and contributed to the popular sense that the War on Poverty was a lost cause and that, by extension, the Great Society was a great mistake, doomed from the start and destined to disillusion both supporters and opponents. It was a sobering conclusion to a great crusade inspired by confidence and optimism, both of which were in short supply by the 1970s.

FOREIGN RELATIONS

In 1960, Democratic nominee John Kennedy charged that the Eisenhower administration had permitted the Soviet Union to develop a dangerous advantage in nuclear weapons. This "missile gap," claimed Kennedy, symbolized national complacency and jeopardized national security. In fact, there was no missile gap, as he soon discovered after becoming president. But in a close election, the issue may have swayed a significant number of voters. It also demonstrated how during the Cold War conservatives and liberals saw the conflict with the Soviets in similar terms. Both agreed on the desired end—the downfall of communism—but disagreed on the best means to achieve it.

At the start of the decade, both liberals and conservatives were firmly opposed to Soviet expansion and aggression. Both also saw communism as monolithic. That is, there were no major differences between Russian, Chinese, Cuban, or Vietnamese communists—all were working together to overthrow democracy and destroy capitalism. Both liberals and conservatives also accepted the logic of the domino theory, which assumed that the fall of a single small nation to the communists would threaten an entire region and, eventually, the United States and the world. Every nation therefore had to choose sides—to stand with us (the anticommunists) or them (the communists). Neutrality or nonalignment was in general not a viable or acceptable option.

But within that broad consensus, important differences existed. Liberals wished to prevent the expansion of communism. In essence, they accepted the premise that the Soviet Union, if contained, would ultimately crumble from internal weakness—the economic system would fail to meet the needs and desires of ordinary citizens. Liberals also supported the idea that peaceful coexistence was possible and mutual disarmament was desirable. Moreover, they favored foreign aid and cultural exchange programs. The Peace Corps and the Alliance for Progress in Latin America were important tools in the war of ideas. Finally, liberals were in general supportive of third-world nationalism and advocated multilateral action through the United Nations (UN), which could resolve conflict through mediation.

Kennedy voiced many of these themes in his famous inaugural address, which focused exclusively on foreign affairs. On the one hand, he used uncompromising and unconditional language in describing the threat and defining how the United States would respond. "Let every nation know," he declared, "whether it wishes us well or ill, that we shall pay any price, bear any burden, meet any hardship, support any friend, oppose any foe to assure the survival and the success of liberty." On the other, he expressed a willingness to negotiate with the Communists under the right circumstances. "Let us never negotiate out of fear," he said, noting that the United States would have to maintain a position of strength and verify all agreements. "But let us never fear to negotiate." Finally, he expressed careful sympathy toward the nationalist aspirations of the Third World.

Conservatives disagreed strongly with Kennedy on most points. They wished to "roll back"—not contain—communism. In their view peaceful coexistence was impossible. Negotiation and accommodation were, according to Reagan, akin to appeasement, which had failed with Hitler and left "no choice between peace and war, only between fight and surrender." (See document 6.) Mutual disarmament was unacceptable—the communists were not trustworthy and arms control would threaten U.S. superiority in nuclear weapons. Therefore, as conservative activist Phyllis Schlafly put it, "Our goal must be victory—not containment, coexistence, disengagement, or stalemate."[23] Conservatives, moreover, were suspicious of nonmilitary foreign aid and cultural exchange programs. Intentionally or not, they might buttress rather than counter the influence of communists. Finally, conservatives often saw third-world nationalism as a cover for communism, especially in Latin America and Southeast Asia.

Conservatives were also distrustful and disdainful of the UN, which they saw as an ineffectual debating society where the alleged sins of the free world received far more attention than the actual sins of the communist world. "The UN," wrote *National Review* in 1968, "is impotent, a crumbling monument to the internationalist aspirations of liberalism, a gathering-place for Afro-Asian minipowers to rally against the remnants of nineteenth-century European colonialism while twentieth-century Soviet colonialism consolidates its grip upon Europe itself and African tribes, in the name of independence and nationhood, claw each other in genocidal wars."[24] In contrast to liberals, who espoused multilateral action with UN support, conservatives argued that unilateral action with or without UN sanction was often necessary and always appropriate when in defense of vital interests and national security.

Cuba was the first battleground of the decade. In 1959, the communist leader Fidel Castro marched into Havana and took control of the country. The Eisenhower administration responded by imposing an economic embargo and severing diplomatic relations with Cuba, which established close relations with the Soviet Union. The CIA also began to train and arm Cuban expatriates. The plan was to invade the island and overthrow the Castro regime with the enthusiastic support of the Cuban people. When Kennedy became president, he inherited the plan, about which he had serious doubts. But in April 1961 he approved the operation and 1,400 armed exiles landed at the Bay of Pigs. They expected American air cover, which Kennedy had promised but later withdrew for fear it would provoke the Soviets. The spontaneous uprising also failed to materialize, and Castro easily crushed the invasion. "How could I have been so stupid?" Kennedy asked aides.[25]

Conservatives had answers. "The failure," opined *National Review*, "was a failure of will."[26] Kennedy should not have lost his nerve—he should have provided direct U.S. military support. Goldwater even met with the president during the operation. Kennedy asked him what he would do. "I'd do whatever is necessary to make this invasion a success," the Arizona Republican replied. Kennedy then asked about world opinion and his public pledge on the eve of the invasion not to commit U.S. forces. "I said," recalled Goldwater, that "the American people didn't give a damn about world opinion, that our friends around the world would applaud him, and that he would be a hero in the eyes of American voters." He regretted that Kennedy had opted not to follow his advice, which might have prevented future crises.[27]

Following the Bay of Pigs fiasco, Kennedy journeyed to Vienna in June 1961 to meet with the Soviet leader Nikita Khrushchev, who was singularly unimpressed with the young president. During the summit, Khrushchev attempted to browbeat and bully Kennedy, who at times seemed almost in shock at such behavior. Then in August the Soviet Union directed East Germany to construct a wall between East and West Berlin so that Germans could no longer emigrate to the free world and embarrass the communist world. Those who tried to escape would now face guards with orders to shoot to kill. Kennedy sent troops to West Berlin to protect the city and traveled there to denounce the Berlin Wall, which became the most powerful symbol of the Cold War. But he would not go to war over the wall.

Conservatives again were livid. The president had once more used words rather than action. In March 1962, YAF held a mass rally at Madison Square Garden in New York, where L. Brent Bozell, Buckley's brother-in-law, gave perhaps the most dramatic speech of the evening. Before a crowd of thousands, he offered the following instructions: "To the Joint Chiefs of Staff: Make the Necessary Preparations for landing in Havana. To our commander in Berlin: Tear Down the Wall. . . . To the chairman of the Atomic Energy Commission: Schedule testing of every nuclear weapon that could conceivably serve the military purpose of the West. To the chief of the CIA: You are to encourage liberation movements in every nation of the world under Communist domination, including the Soviet Union itself."[28] Here in brief was the conservative agenda, assertively articulated.

In September 1962, the specter of Castro reappeared. According to conservatives, Kennedy's pledge that the United States would not allow Cuba to export rebellion throughout Latin America proved only that the policy of containment was bankrupt, morally and militarily. "The United States," asserted *National Review*, "is now flat on its face, its limbs flailing the air, before a small, underdeveloped island run by a strutting, drunken bandit!" The United States had to remove Castro from power before Khrushchev could threaten it with missiles fired from a base ninety miles off the coast of Florida.[29]

In October 1962, that potential threat became a reality. Aerial photographs revealed that the Soviets were constructing launch sites for nuclear missiles in Cuba. The measure was primarily defensive—it was intended to deter future aggression and counter American missiles stationed in Turkey. Nevertheless, Kennedy had promised back in April 1961 that he would never permit offensive weapons in Cuba. Now he had to act. He had to secure the removal of the missiles at all costs. It was the most dangerous moment of the Cold War.

On October 22, after tense deliberations in the White House, Kennedy announced on national television that he had imposed a naval and air quarantine of the island. For the moment, he rejected calls from the Joint Chiefs of Staff to authorize air strikes or launch a full invasion. But Soviet technicians in Cuba continued to race to make the sites operational. On October 26, Kennedy received a message from Khrushchev stating that he would remove the missiles in return for a U.S. pledge not to invade Cuba. The president publicly accepted the terms and privately agreed, in response to a second, stronger message from Moscow, that the United States would also accelerate the already planned withdrawal of missiles from Turkey. The crisis was over. But it had brought the United States and the U.S.S.R. to the brink of nuclear war.

For liberals, the Cuban Missile Crisis was a great triumph, for the nation and for Kennedy, who had faced the Soviet threat with coolness and firmness. He had successfully avoided national humiliation and defended national security. He had averted war, but not at the price of surrender. And he had done so by crafting a face-saving solution, which allowed both the Americans and the Soviets to back down with their prestige intact. It was, in short, a masterful performance, proof that Kennedy had matured in office.

For conservatives, the Cuban Missile Crisis was a significant setback, proof that Kennedy was incapable of waging or winning the Cold War. The no-invasion pledge was a major victory for Castro, who could now spread revolution throughout the region. It was also a repudiation of the Monroe

Doctrine, which conservatives believed gave the United States the right to police the Western Hemisphere. Finally, the decision to trade missiles in Turkey for missiles in Cuba meant, in effect, that the United States had yielded to nuclear blackmail.

In the aftermath of the crisis, relations improved between the United States and the U.S.S.R. A "hotline" was established between Moscow and Washington so that the two leaders could communicate directly. The two nations also agreed on a Test Ban Treaty in 1963 that halted the atmospheric testing of nuclear weapons. It was the first significant arms control agreement of the Cold War. The treaty was not comprehensive—it imposed, for example, no limitations on underground or undersea testing—but according to Kennedy it would reduce the threat of nuclear proliferation and was "an important first step, a step toward peace, a step toward reason, a step away from war." Above all, it was recognition that the Americans and the Soviets shared a common humanity, that "in the final analysis . . . we all inhabit this small planet, we all breathe the same air, we all cherish our children's futures, and we are all mortal." (See document 3.)

Liberals celebrated the Test Ban Treaty, but conservatives were critical and skeptical for two reasons. First, the treaty implied that peaceful coexistence with the Soviet Union was possible, a premise they utterly rejected. Second, conservatives saw no way for the United States to verify Soviet compliance, rendering the treaty both useless and dangerous because it could lull the United States into a false sense of complacency. "President Kennedy is right that this treaty is a first step," warned YAF President Robert Bauman. "But it is a first step toward ultimate surrender, or war on terms most disadvantageous to us."[30]

In fact, the Soviet Union would begin a massive buildup of conventional and nuclear weapons in 1964, when Leonid Brezhnev replaced Khrushchev as leader. Among the reasons for Khrushchev's downfall was the sense in Moscow that he had capitulated in Cuba after the crisis had revealed how inferior the Soviets were militarily compared to the Americans. The arms race launched by the Soviet Union would last for two more decades. But it came as no surprise to conservatives, who had long warned that the communists remained committed to world domination.

That was the bad news. The good news for conservatives was that the United States could and would win the arms race. Given the overwhelming strength of the capitalist system, argued *National Review* associate editor and CIA consultant James Burnham, it was "probably the most effective form of political-economic warfare we can conduct against our enemy."[31] Eventually the Soviet system would buckle under the strain, leading to economic crisis and political discontent. Thus an arms race was not a necessary evil—it was a positive good which would contribute to the collapse of communism. In essence, this logic also underlay the Reagan administration's military buildup in the 1980s, which pressured Soviet leader Mikhail Gorbachev to undertake major reforms in a futile effort to save the Communist system.

By contrast, liberals saw an arms race as unwinnable. Neither the United States nor the U.S.S.R. could afford it, not when both had glaring social problems at home. Liberals also believed that it would raise tensions to the point where war became inevitable. Finally, they refused to accept the idea that the Communists were committed to global conquest. "I do not believe that the Soviets desire to dominate the world as the Germans did," said Arkansas Senator William Fulbright. "Russia, like America, is a nation of many races; and I can see no reason why we cannot get along peaceably."[32] Accordingly, he and other liberals supported arms negotiations.

Conservatives saw such individuals as fools or traitors. In their view arms control was fatally flawed because it assumed that weapons were the problem, whereas the real threat was the Cold War. Win it and there was no need for an arms race. In other words, preparation for wars triggered the race for weapons, not vice versa. What conservatives wanted was nuclear superiority, not "sufficiency" or parity. Peace through strength was their motto. Force was the only language the Communists understood. Accordingly, conservatives wanted to build more missiles and develop new weapons like the land-based anti-ballistic missile (ABM) system, which the Nixon administration believed would enable the United States to destroy incoming missiles. The Reagan administration later had similar hopes for the Strategic Defense Initiative (SDI), essentially a space-based ABM system.

Conservatives also opposed negotiations because these presumed faith in Communist leaders, who by definition were untrustworthy. Even if a real reformer appeared, which was doubtful, what assurances would the United States have that he had the power to make—or, more importantly, keep— any agreements he negotiated? And what would happen when he was eliminated or removed from power? Was Brezhnev likely to respect or comply with any treaties Khrushchev had signed? The answer to conservatives seemed obvious and dangerous, which was why so many would view with deep distrust Nixon's overtures to the Soviet Union and Communist China in the early 1970s.

During the 1960s, the arms race led to a nuclear stalemate. Both the United States and the U.S.S.R. now had the means to destroy the world many times over. Liberals tended to accept this development as a hopeful sign on the uphill road to normal relations with the Soviet Union, now seen increasingly as a positive counterbalance to Communist China. Conservatives viewed the nuclear paralysis in negative terms. Removing the threat from the United States of nuclear war, they argued, enabled the Communists to wage revolutionary war by any means necessary or desirable—political, economic, cultural, or psychological.

It was in this context that economic and cultural exchanges with the Soviet Union and Eastern Europe became controversial. Liberals tended to see both in positive terms, as bridges to peace. Cultural exchanges lowered cultural barriers and promoted mutual understanding, whether it was the Moscow Ballet coming to the United States or Count Basie bringing jazz to the U.S.S.R. Economic exchanges led to mutual profit, especially if American corporations and farmers had a surplus of industrial products and agricultural commodities that the Russians needed. Make trade not war was a liberal motto in the 1960s.

By contrast, interaction with the communists on any level anywhere was anathema to conservatives. Programs like the Peace Corps, they feared, were infiltrated by liberals, who would encourage anti-Americanism. And trade with the communists, whether in Havana or Warsaw or Moscow, made no sense because it helped to perpetuate repressive regimes. Either they were the enemy or they were not. Moreover, by shipping supplies to Eastern Europe and the Soviet Union, the United States was indirectly assisting North Vietnam, which received communist aid it might otherwise have not. The economic bridges the United States had built were not bridges to peace, argued *National Review*, they were "bridges of death for thousands of American soldiers and South Vietnamese."[33]

In a similar vein, YAF protested against Chase making loans to the Soviets or Ford building a plant in Siberia. After all, trucks were a major export to North Vietnam, which used them to transport supplies on the Ho Chi Minh Trail. "A lot of young conservatives as I did thought," recalled a demonstrator, "'why are we fighting communism in Vietnam and losing all these young American lives in order that the major American corporations can make billions of dollars on the blood of young Americans?'"[34] Here it is interesting to note that both young radicals and conservatives often distrusted large corporations, but for different reasons—the former because they objected to capitalism and the latter because they objected to communism.

The belief that the Soviets had "mellowed" or become more flexible took a hard blow in 1968. In April, the new leader of the Czech Communist Party promoted a series of political reforms. For a brief time, Czechs were able to enjoy free speech and a free press—even listen to rock music. But in August, Soviet soldiers and tanks invaded the capital and put an end to the "Prague Spring." Students and workers tried in vain to resist with civil disobedience, guerrilla warfare, and general strikes. The silence from the United States was deafening, in part because the nation was consumed by the dramatic developments of the presidential election. But it was also because of significant events happening in South Vietnam, where the war had reached a critical point.

The U.S. commitment to South Vietnam began in 1945, when Democratic President Harry Truman enabled the French to reclaim control of their former colony. Then Republican President Dwight Eisenhower provided the

French with economic and military assistance. When the French army suffered a devastating defeat at the hands of Communist forces at Dien Bien Phu in 1954, the United States became the main supporter and supplier of arms and aid to South Vietnam, whose Catholic prime minister, Ngo Dinh Diem, was popular with liberals and conservatives. Thus a broad bipartisan consensus existed at the start of the 1960s. No one wanted to see the country fall to the Communists. Everyone believed that U.S. credibility was on the line and that if South Vietnam fell, so too would the rest of Southeast Asia as the domino theory predicted.

By the end of the 1960s, the consensus had shattered. Liberalism was deeply divided. Older Cold War liberals remained convinced that the cause of preserving an independent, anticommunist South Vietnam was important and just. Younger antiwar liberals had come to believe the war was a strategic mistake and moral catastrophe. But conservatives too found that the formula of "fusionism" no longer held. Most traditionalists and anticommunists remained steadfast in their support of South Vietnam and their calls for victory over North Vietnam, but many libertarians now believed that the war and the draft had curtailed civil liberties and promoted big government.

As in Cuba, Kennedy inherited a mess that was not of his making. But by 1963 the situation in South Vietnam was deteriorating rapidly despite his decision to deploy thousands of U.S. advisors. By day the security forces in theory were in control of the villages and countryside; by night the Vietcong (communist guerrillas) in fact were in charge. Even in the cities the Diem regime grew more unpopular as its repression of Buddhists grew more severe. Was he the wrong man in the wrong place at the wrong time, as many liberals now believed? Or was he the man of the moment, America's best hope, as most conservatives believed?

In September 1963, Kennedy sent Diem a clear message. In a press conference, the president publicly declared that the United States would not withdraw from South Vietnam because the stakes were too high. But he added that the prime minister had to act more wisely and take more responsibility for the ultimate success or failure of his government. Privately, Kennedy in October gave a "green light" via the CIA to a group of South Vietnamese generals who were plotting a coup against Diem.

Meanwhile, conservatives lambasted Kennedy for attempting to turn Diem into a scapegoat. The media, they argued, had exaggerated the corruption in his regime and the persecution of the Buddhists. Reporters also failed to document Communist atrocities. "Diem is the best that has been available in South Vietnam," maintained Burnham, "and a damn sight better than we had any reason to expect." The real problems, he explained, were the U.S. unwillingness to escalate the conflict and willingness to accommodate the Soviets despite their support of North Vietnam.[35]

In November 1963, the coup took place. Diem was deposed and then, despite explicit U.S. instructions to the contrary, executed with his brother in the back of an armored personnel carrier. Few liberals mourned him, but conservatives expressed regret. "He was a relentless, undeviating, active, fighting anti-communist," wrote *National Review* of Diem. "That is the besetting sin of our time, and few can survive it. . . . In international politics, a strong and purposive friendship for this country tends to lead to what one might call the American Way of Death."[36] Kennedy had hoped that Diem's death would open the door for a more effective leader. But three weeks later, an assassin's bullet claimed Kennedy's life. In the years to follow, political instability remained rampant in South Vietnam, as coup followed coup and questionable elections led to shaky governments. In the end, the search for a reliable and popular partner in the fight against communism would prove futile.

In August 1964, with the presidential campaign in high gear, the White House reported that North Vietnamese gunboats had twice fired upon U.S. naval vessels on routine patrol in international waters in the Gulf of Tonkin. In fact, they were reconnaissance ships and the second attack probably never took place. But the Johnson administration seized upon this dubious pretext to request authorization from Congress to respond with military force. Congress complied, issuing a resolution that gave Johnson the power to take "all necessary measures" to defend U.S. personnel against Communist aggression. The vote in the House was 416–0; in the Senate it was 88–2. Liberals and conservatives cheered. The consensus held.

During the election, Goldwater was the so-called war candidate. He was determined to defend South Vietnam at all costs. He wanted the United States to use air and sea power without restriction to force North Vietnam to surrender or sue for peace. He even proposed using low-grade nuclear weapons to defoliate the jungles and deprive the Communists of cover. If the United States was not prepared to pursue victory, if it was not ready to wage war effectively and aggressively, it should withdraw. Above all, if the United States committed troops it should first declare war so that the American people were prepared and willing to make sacrifices.

In the fall of 1964, Lyndon Johnson was the so-called peace candidate. He wanted to concentrate on domestic issues, to wage a War on Poverty and build a Great Society for all. But he also knew that he had to show he had the resolve to defend national security. Otherwise conservatives would assert that he was weak on communism, a death sentence in American politics. The Gulf of Tonkin Resolution insulated Johnson from that charge and helped him defeat Goldwater easily. But what he would do in Vietnam remained unclear.

After the election, Johnson continued to have deep misgivings about Vietnam. On the one hand, he correctly feared that Vietnam would ultimately destroy his Great Society by draining the federal budget of needed dollars. On the other, he was certain that his ambitious domestic agenda would never have a chance in Congress unless he placated conservatives. Accordingly, Johnson in the spring of 1965 made the fateful decision to send U.S. troops to South Vietnam so that it would not fall to communism on his watch. But the objective was not victory because a wider or larger war might lead to intervention by China, as it had in Korea. Instead, the United States would pursue a limited war with limited means and ends—a negotiated settlement with North Vietnam that left in place an independent, anticommunist South Vietnam.

Conservatives objected to both the policies and the premises. Containment in Southeast Asia, warned Burnham, was a reactive strategy doomed to failure unless the United States seized the initiative through a proactive "policy of liberation" and forced the Communists to fight where they were at a disadvantage. "You cannot win by negotiation what you have lost in the field," he warned.[37] A student newspaper at Penn State made a similar point: "South Vietnam is the present battlefield of the Cold War. Korea, Laos, and Cuba are former battlefields. America has never had a decisive victory over Communism on any of the battlefields because of self-restraint. It is time for the U.S. to show its strength to the world by turning South Vietnam into a place of victory."[38]

For the next three years, Johnson gradually but inexorably increased the U.S. commitment until half a million American soldiers were stationed in South Vietnam. On the ground, they conducted "search and destroy" missions in an effort to make contact with the Vietcong. In the air, the United States escalated the bombing campaign (including the widespread use of napalm and Agent Orange, a toxic defoliant) in an effort to weaken the will of the North Vietnamese and drive them to the bargaining table. In public, U.S. officials repeatedly expressed confidence and optimism about the war. They saw steady progress and claimed to see the "light at the end of the tunnel." Soon the Communists would concede and agree to a negotiated peace. In private, the White House knew the war was going poorly, as the Pentagon Papers would later reveal.

In general, conservatives supported Johnson. Some wanted the president to take more aggressive measures, to bomb Hanoi and blockade or invade North Vietnam. Others wanted less civilian control and more military emphasis on the air war, which nevertheless managed to kill hundreds of thousands of Vietnamese and eventually exceed the total tonnage of bombs dropped by every nation in World War II combined. But what was most important was that the president had not chosen to retreat or withdraw. He had not yielded to the "appeasers," a term favored by *National Review*. "Essentially this battle has nothing to do with a particular geographic area," it warned in 1965. "The stake at issue is simple: *Have we the will to resist the advance of communism* [original italics]?"[39] For conservatives, Vietnam was only one front in a larger and more vital struggle.

As the Vietnam War escalated, organized opposition arose. At first the protests took the form of teach-ins on college campuses. In 1966, the antiwar movement received a political boost when Arkansas Democrat William Fulbright, chair of the Senate Foreign Relations Committee, held televised hearings on the war and gave a powerful platform to respectable critics like George Kennan, the architect of containment. In 1967, mass protests began. In the spring, an estimated 150,000 demonstrators took to the streets of New York to protest the war and burn draft cards. In the fall, tens of thousands participated in a March on the Pentagon.

Antiwar liberals defended the demonstrators. The protests were patriotic and in the democratic tradition of American dissent. The protesters were upholding American values and principles. "Our youth are showing that they still believe in the American dream," said Fulbright in August 1967, "and their protests attest to its continuing vitality." The younger generation, he added, had by necessity assumed the mantle of moral leadership from the older generation, which supported a war that was "poisoning and brutalizing our domestic life." The Great Society, he concluded, was becoming a sick society because the war abroad was causing division and discord at home.[40]

Conservatives by contrast decried the demonstrators as unpatriotic defeatists who had no sense of what was at stake in Vietnam or the scope of the communist threat. Nor had they learned the lesson of history—that appeasement always failed with dictators like Adolf Hitler or Ho Chi Minh, the Communist leader of North Vietnam. Some protesters were "congenital soreheads, who will revolt against anything and anyone, anytime"; others were either deliberate traitors or misguided souls.[41] Regardless, the antiwar activists had chosen to give aid and comfort to the enemy by encouraging him to believe that America's will to fight would soon crumble.

Class resentment often underlay opposition both to the Vietnam War and the antiwar movement, which was dominated by college students. By the end of 1967 it was apparent that the children of the working class were fighting and dying in disproportionate numbers while the children of the middle class were evading military service thanks to medical exemptions and student deferments, which were available only to those who were in school full-time. The class bias of the draft system increasingly enraged ordinary Americans, even those who supported the war. A firefighter who lost his son in Vietnam put it bluntly:

I'm bitter. You bet your goddamn dollar I'm bitter. It's people like us who give up our sons for the country. The business people, they run the country and make money from it. The college types, the professors, they go to Washington and tell the government what to do. . . . But their sons, they don't end up in the swamps over there, in Vietnam. No sir. They're deferred, because they're in school. Or they get sent to safe places. Or they get out with all those letters they have from their doctors. . . . Let's face it: if you have a lot of money, or if you have the right connections, you don't end up on a firing line in the jungle over there, not unless you *want* to. [My son] had no choice.[42]

In January 1968, North Vietnam launched the Tet Offensive, which was named for the Chinese New Year and intended to undermine public support for the war at the start of the election year. In coordinated assaults across South Vietnam, the Vietcong took advantage of a declared ceasefire and caught the U.S. forces by surprise. A suicide squad even managed to penetrate the courtyard of the U.S. Embassy in Saigon, the symbolic heart of the American presence in South Vietnam. Broadcast images of the event filled living rooms across the country and shocked many Americans, who had assumed the war was going well because Johnson, Secretary of Defense Robert McNamara, and General William Westmoreland, the U.S. commander in Vietnam, had told them so. Eventually, the U.S. Army regrouped and regained control of the cities. But the fighting, especially in Saigon and Hue, was bloody and brutal, as troops had to battle the Vietcong house by house, street by street.

Tet cracked the consensus. It now became a question of when, not if, the United States would withdraw from Vietnam. Antiwar liberals openly challenged the war and the Cold War liberals in the White House who had led America into it. CBS anchorman Walter Cronkite traveled to Vietnam and, when he returned, expressed deep misgivings about U.S. policy on the air. In March 1968, Senator Eugene McCarthy almost won the New Hampshire Democratic primary on an antiwar platform. Then Senator Robert Kennedy entered the presidential race, promising that he would change the leaders and policies responsible for Vietnam. At the end of the month, Johnson stunned the nation by announcing that he would not seek reelection. The conflict was, if not immoral, at the very least a strategic blunder in the eyes of antiwar liberals. It was time to find a way out of the quagmire.

Conservatives rejected this analysis. In their view Tet was a military victory, not a defeat, regardless of how the media chose to report it. Once the Vietcong had chosen to fight in the open, the U.S. Army was able to inflict punishing casualties. Moreover, the South Vietnamese army had fought well and the civilians had chosen, for the most part, not to cast their lot with the communists. The enemy had tried but failed to break their will. "Far from an allied setback, morally or materially," wrote Colonel James Graham from Saigon in February 1968, Tet was "possibly the longest step forward we have taken in this war."[43] It was time, conservatives believed, to pursue a strategy that would lead to victory.

But in November 1968, Republican Richard Nixon was elected on a platform of "peace with honor." Like Johnson, he would seek a negotiated settlement—not total victory. Unlike Johnson, who had "Americanized" the war, Nixon would seek to return primary responsibility to South Vietnam. His strategy of "Vietnamization" was to withdraw U.S. troops and escalate the bombing campaign, which would compensate for the force reductions and reassure the South Vietnamese. The White House also believed that American airpower would demonstrate American willpower and pressure the North Vietnamese into accepting a division of the country along the 17th Parallel, similar to the division of Korea along the 38th Parallel. Left unstated was the assumption that air raids would at least postpone the fall of South Vietnam to the Communists until Nixon had won reelection, left office, and a "decent interval" had passed.

Initially, Nixon's strategy had support, albeit grudging, from many antiwar liberals and most conservatives. Liberals opposed to the U.S. mission in Vietnam saw the troop withdrawals as a positive first step and were pleased to see the casualty count decline. Campus protests declined significantly because students believed the war was coming to a close and the lottery had replaced the draft. Conservatives had doubts about the means employed by Nixon, although many recognized that he was probably doing all that public opinion would accept. Incremental escalation, they feared, would not intimidate or coerce the North Vietnamese into making diplomatic concessions. What was needed was an all-out air campaign using every weapon in the U.S. arsenal short of nuclear weapons (which some extreme conservatives wanted to use).[44] But mainstream conservatives largely accepted the end sought by Nixon.

Two events threatened the fragile accord Nixon had achieved. The first was the revelation in 1969 that U.S. soldiers under the command of Lieutenant William Calley had earlier massacred hundreds of Vietnamese civilians, including old women and young children, near a hamlet known as My Lai. The troops had also committed numerous rapes of younger women, some of whom were pregnant. The subsequent trial and court-martial of Calley caused a firestorm of protest. Antiwar liberals maintained that My Lai was not an isolated incident and was a war crime. More importantly, it was a crime in which all Americans were implicated. "We sense—all of us—that our best instincts are deserting us," wrote the *New Yorker*, "and we are oppressed by a dim feeling that beneath our words and phrases, almost beneath our consciousness, we are quietly choking on the blood of innocents."[45]

Conservatives denied that My Lai was a permanent stain on the nation's conscience and morality. They condemned what *National Review* described as the "uncontrollable impulse not to blame the particular criminal, but rather to vilify America generally."[46] Conservatives maintained that My Lai was an isolated incident and not a war crime. It was also the tragic but predictable outcome of an ambiguous war in which communist guerrillas deliberately chose to operate among innocent peasants. Above all, conservatives objected to how the liberal media had rushed to judgment, exaggerated the event, and failed to report countless Vietcong atrocities.

The second event, which shattered the tentative liberal-conservative unity, was the invasion of Cambodia in 1970. Nixon contended that it was necessary to destroy the sanctuaries which the Communists used as bases for operations in South Vietnam. By his logic he had widened the war in order to shorten it. Most liberals were outraged. In their view the president had betrayed his promise to end the war. The campuses exploded in protest—a quarter of all college students participated in strikes and demonstrations. At Kent State, the Ohio National Guard shot and killed four white students; at Jackson State, Mississippi police officers shot and killed two black students. Suddenly, it was 1968 again, with chaos on the campuses and violence in the streets.

Conservatives were outraged by the protests. At Kent State, the demonstrators had provoked the police and received what they deserved. The Cambodian invasion was in line with the president's policy of "Vietnamization"— he was merely doing what he could to ensure that the South Vietnamese could effectively combat communist aggression. Moreover, the reaction was all out of proportion to the operation, which was modest in scale. "From the hysteria in the Senate, the media and the campuses," observed *National Review*, "one would have imagined that the president had ordered, at the very least, the H-bombing of half of Asia, the conscription of all persons from eighteen to sixty, and the defoliation of the redwoods."[47] In fact, conservatives argued, the Communists had provoked the invasion, and the temporary occupation of "neutral" Cambodia was only a small part of a larger strategy, which most Americans had previously accepted without question.

In January 1973, after four years of difficult negotiations, the United States and North Vietnam signed a peace treaty in Paris. The agreement called for an immediate ceasefire, which both sides knew would not last. North Vietnam promised to release all American prisoners of war and permit the president of South Vietnam to remain in power for now. North Vietnam also stated that the United States could continue to provide military assistance to South Vietnam if it wished. The United States agreed to allow North Vietnamese army units to remain in South Vietnam—a major concession—and pledged reparations to rebuild North Vietnam. The United States also agreed to remove all remaining troops from South Vietnam, which eventually fell to the Communists in 1975.

Few liberals or conservatives saw the outcome as "peace with honor." Some liberals reacted with relief, but most were skeptical. By 1973 the Watergate scandal had erupted and they had no love and little trust for Nixon. Many antiwar liberals believed that he could have negotiated a similar deal years earlier, saving hundreds of thousands of lives and billions of dollars, but that he had delayed until after he had won reelection in 1972. Few thought the agreement would bring lasting peace to Southeast Asia. On the contrary, most liberals by then felt that the war was a violation of moral principles and had brought lasting shame to the United States.

Conservatives were equally critical. The United States had betrayed and abandoned a loyal ally. The agreement treated North Vietnam as both the victor (it was not required to relinquish any land it had conquered) and the victim (it would receive substantial reparations). It also set the stage for a Communist victory, which would lead to a bloodbath throughout the region and damage the credibility of the United States around the world. Some conservatives like Buckley later conceded that it was probably the best deal possible under the circumstances. But most saw it as a "dishonorable peace preparing the way for renewed aggression in Southeast Asia."[48]

Vietnam was a bitter and divisive war. It shattered the containment consensus shared by liberals and conservatives since the end of World War II. It also divided conservatives. On the margins, for example, the JBS at first opposed the war on the grounds that it was a ploy to convince the American public that Johnson was a firm anticommunist. Moreover, antiwar protests would trigger a police crackdown, increasing the possibility of the United States becoming a police state and distracting law enforcement from the real threat—communist subversion. Later the JBS would seek to rejoin the conservative mainstream by supporting the war but asserting that the failure of the United States to achieve victory in Vietnam was proof of Johnson's closet communist sympathies.

More significantly, the war weakened the "fusionist" coalition of libertarians, traditionalists, and anticommunists. Most conservatives opposed the draft, which they saw as a form of involuntary servitude. But many libertarians also objected increasingly to the war itself, which had widened the scope and scale of government. In 1967, YAF took a position against the draft. In 1969, the tensions exploded into confrontation at the national convention, where chants of "kill the commies" alternated with "power to the people." The anticommunists and traditionalists, who continued to support the war, then purged the libertarians from leadership positions in YAF.[49]

Other conservatives saw the libertarians as ideologues who would, like the communists, "replace God's creation of this multifarious, complex world in which we live and substitute for it their own creation, simple, neat and inhuman. " Tradition was the essence of civilization and libertarianism would discard it. "In its opposition to the maintenance of defenses against Communism, its puerile sympathy with the rampaging mobs of campus and ghetto, its contempt for the humdrum wisdom of the great producing majority," Frank Meyer wrote, "it is directed towards the destruction of the civilizational order which is the only real foundation in a real world for the freedom it espouses."[50]

The war may have hurt conservatism somewhat in the short run. But in the long run it fractured liberalism along ideological and generational lines. In the years to come, Cold War and antiwar liberals would often seek common ground in vain. The war also damaged liberal credibility with the American people on the critical issue of national security, with important and lasting consequences. More fundamentally, Vietnam deeply eroded popular faith in government and trust in leaders. Both beliefs were critical to an ideology premised on the conviction that government could and should provide effective solutions to major problems. Yet both were casualties of the war. In the words of YAF leader and Nixon speechwriter Patrick Buchanan: "Vietnam was liberalism's last great adventure, and greatest debacle."[51]

Whether that is fair is debatable. Certainly most conservatives had pressed for intervention, supported the war, and shared some responsibility for the outcome. And Nixon was in some ways one of their own, even if few conservatives wanted to claim him in the wake of Watergate. But the sense of loss and regret was perhaps greater among liberals. As activist and scholar Todd Gitlin later put it, "Imagine the sixties without the acceleration of the Vietnam War in 1965, and you can imagine an enduring era of reform. You can imagine a reasonably successful wave of racial integration, a modestly successful War on Poverty, a weakened black power strain."[52] Without Vietnam, liberals might have remained in control and conservatives might have remained on the margins of power. Imagine—it isn't hard to do, as ex-Beatle John Lennon sang. But it cannot alter how events unfolded in the 1960s.

CIVIL RIGHTS

In 1988, conservative commentator Patrick Buchanan paid liberals a large, if belated, compliment. "In retrospect, the civil rights movement was liberalism's finest hour," he wrote in his memoirs. "The liberals paid a heavy price for having championed civil rights in the '50s and early '60s, for preaching and advancing the ideal of equality and justice under the law. If they have stumbled and blundered terribly since, they knew what they were doing then, and what they were doing was right."[53]

The political price was indeed heavy. The issue of race fractured the already unstable New Deal coalition of ethnic workers, northern liberals, black Americans, and white Southerners which had dominated presidential politics since the 1930s. Prior to the 1960s, the "Solid South" was decisively Democratic. Since then it has become reliably Republican—an outcome Lyndon Johnson privately predicted when he signed into law the landmark Civil Rights Act of 1964. In the rise of the modern conservative movement, the "white backlash" to civil rights was an important factor.

But in general liberals had little choice, although the issue of tactics divided them. Many older liberals, who came of age in the 1950s, were suspicious of mass movements, a legacy of the fight against fascism, and preferred legal action to direct action, a reflection of their view that racial segregation was primarily a southern problem which would disappear eventually. Many younger liberals, who joined the cause in the 1960s, were impatient and saw no good alternative to mass protest and nonviolent civil disobedience. In their hearts, they believed that racial equality was a moral imperative as well as a matter of simple justice. In their minds, they thought the time had come, at last, to provide equal rights for all Americans, black and white. Otherwise the promise of the Declaration of Independence—"all men are created equal"—and the potential of the United States would remain unfulfilled. The nation also could not hope to win the ideological confrontation at the core of the Cold War. In the global propaganda battle for the hearts and minds of Asians and Africans, democracy could not defeat communism unless the fruits of freedom were available to all at home.

By contrast, conservatives after World War II saw communism—not racism—as the most important issue facing the United States. Externally, the U.S.S.R. and China posed an immediate threat. Internally, communists posed an eventual threat. By infiltrating the civil rights movement, they hoped, claimed conservatives, to sow strife and discord, weakening the nation and paving the path to revolution. The chaos would also erode constitutional principles and social traditions. In the late 1950s and early 1960s, some conservatives even believed that the racial inferiority of black Americans justified white supremacy in the South, a stronghold of moral traditionalism.

By the mid-1960s, most conservatives had shifted their focus to a constitutional defense of states' rights and property rights. Promoting civil rights, they contended, would foster the unrestrained growth of federal power, which would infringe upon the rights reserved to the states under the 10th Amendment. It would also deny individuals the right to dispose of their property as they saw fit, which was the foundation of freedom. In addition, conservatives chose to portray street crime and urban violence as the negative by-products of civil disobedience. Finally, in the late 1960s they opposed affirmative action and forced busing, the liberal solutions for racial inequality in the workplace and public schools.

Civil rights divided a new generation of college activists. For liberal white students, it was the great crusade, which inspired the New Left and other rights-based groups such as the women's movement and the gay movement. Older liberals praised their courage and commitment to the cause, if not their tactics. Older conservatives were skeptical of their "noble" intentions and "critical" impact. Cornell Professor Allan Bloom noted that the demonstrations often coincided with exams and that students usually participated "with the confident expectation that they would not be penalized by their professors for missing assignments while they were off doing important deeds, in places where they had never been and to which they would never return, and where, therefore, they did not have to pay any price for their stand, as did those who had to stay and live there."⁵⁴

For conservative white students, the civil rights movement was of little personal or political significance. The Sharon Statement, for example, contained no direct references to the freedom struggle. Lee Edwards was one of the few YAF members who attended the March on Washington in August 1963. "I was deeply moved by the spirit of brotherhood and . . . love that permeated the great throng," he recalled. "But I could not accept their solution. Most blacks looked to the federal government to solve their problems. Conservatives saw the federal government as the problem. In truth, we spoke two very different languages, and there were few interpreters on either side."⁵⁵

The conflict between liberals and conservatives over civil rights escalated in the 1950s. In 1954, the Supreme Court ruled in *Brown v. Board of Education* that segregated schools violated the equal protection clause of the 14th Amendment largely because of the psychological harm they inflicted on black students. The unanimous decision overturned the legal precedent set in 1896 by *Plessy v. Ferguson*, which had deemed separate but equal public facilities constitutional. The *Brown* decision was limited in the sense that it failed to specify when or how school districts were to integrate (a year later, *Brown II* merely required integration "with all deliberate speed"). But it led to a firestorm of criticism across the South. Whites immediately mounted a campaign of "massive resistance" to what they saw as a direct threat to their way of life, which rested on a system of segregation known as Jim Crow.

In 1955, a courageous black woman named Rosa Parks confronted Jim Crow when she refused to give up her seat to a white rider on a city bus in Montgomery, Alabama. In response to the arrest of Parks, a respected seamstress and activist, the black community organized a bus boycott. It also filed a federal lawsuit and selected as movement leader a twenty-six-year-old minister named Dr. Martin Luther King, Jr., who unveiled his tactic of nonviolent civil disobedience and catapulted to national prominence. Eventually, a combination of economic and legal pressure—the boycott hurt downtown businesses and the Supreme Court ruled in 1956 that racial segregation in public transportation was a violation of the equal protection clause of the 14th Amendment—forced Montgomery to capitulate.

Liberals celebrated these developments. The *Chicago Defender*, a prominent black newspaper, even called the *Brown* decision a "second emancipation proclamation."⁵⁶ The victory in Montgomery emboldened younger liberals, who now had a promising leader and tactic. Nonviolent civil disobedience gave the movement the moral high ground, dispelled the stereotype of the angry black man, and generated positive publicity. It ensured that violent resistance by white Southerners would generate more sympathy and support for civil rights, especially among northern liberals and moderates.

But conservatives were critical of the *Brown* decision and the Montgomery protest. The boycott, they conceded, was legal and legitimate, "a
classic and wholly defensible instrument of voluntary protest."[57] The
Supreme Court was, however, acting in a dictatorial manner. Granting power
to southern blacks prematurely would also anger southern whites, who were
already making slow but steady voluntary progress toward racial equality
without federal intrusion. Finally, some conservatives claimed that the racial
inferiority of blacks entitled whites to govern with a free hand in the South,
an important bastion of traditional moral and cultural values. In 1957,
Buckley wrote that white rule was justified "because, for the time being, it is
the advanced race. . . . It is more important for any community anywhere in
the world, to affirm and live by civilized standards, than to bow to the demands of the numerical majority."[58]

In 1962, a federal judge ruled that James Meredith, a black Air Force vet-
eran, might enroll at the all-white University of Mississippi. But Governor Ross
Barnett vowed that he would defend states' rights and prevent forced integration as long as he was in office. After lengthy negotiations, the Kennedy administration believed that it had made a deal with Barnett to admit Meredith
and maintain order on campus. But when he tried to register for classes, an angry mob confronted him and the Mississippi Highway Patrol withdrew, leaving only lightly armed and badly outnumbered federal marshals to protect
him. Later a riot erupted in which two were killed and more than one hundred
and fifty were injured. Peace was restored only when five thousand U.S. Army
paratroopers arrived on the campus.

By then, almost all conservatives had abandoned the argument that black
inferiority justified white rule. But they remained steadfast in their opposition
to federal enforcement of civil rights and forced integration. The court order at
the University of Mississippi, claimed *National Review*, was a "judicial usurpa-
tion" of states' rights, part of a pattern of judicial activism and federal intrusion
dating back to the *Brown* case. The magazine also implied that the Kennedy administration's decision to send troops to enforce the order was motivated at
least in part by the upcoming midterm elections in which the black vote in
northern cities might well prove critical.[59] The conservative contention that
northern Democrats promoted civil rights for political gain would reappear in
election years for the rest of the decade.

In 1963, the debate reached a new crescendo. In April, King began a
campaign of nonviolent civil disobedience in Birmingham, Alabama, re-
putedly the most segregated city in the South. Soon he and hundreds of his
adult followers were in prison. There King wrote his famous "Letter from a
Birmingham Jail," in which he outlined and explained his political beliefs.
Peaceful protest, he asserted, was a moral imperative when a majority imposed unjust laws upon a minority denied basic political rights. After he was

released, King helped organize a protest march by the black children of Birmingham. In response, public safety commissioner "Bull" Connor unleashed water cannons and police dogs on the children, many of whom were under the age of twelve. The events were captured on film and broadcast on television to the nation. Liberals, northern and southern, young and old, were sickened and outraged.

Even Kennedy, heretofore a reluctant supporter of civil rights who feared it would harm his popularity with southern whites and jeopardize his reelection chances, was moved to take action. Worried that the events in Birmingham would bolster communist propaganda and damage the U.S. reputation in the world, the president introduced a civil rights bill in Congress and addressed the nation in support of it. Calling racial equality a "moral issue" as "old as the Scriptures and as clear as the Constitution," he eloquently articulated the liberal consensus: "The heart of the question is whether all Americans are to be afforded equal rights and equal opportunities. . . . If an American, because his skin is dark . . . cannot enjoy the full and free life which all of us want, then who among us would be content to have the color of his skin changed and stand in his place?"

Conservatives too were troubled by the events in Birmingham, but they objected primarily to King's use of civil disobedience. He maintained that the time had come when resistance to human law and recourse to a "Higher Law" was justified. Not so replied Buckley, who contended that the demonstrators had provoked the police into violence. "The right to peaceable assembly," he wrote, "does not rank above the need for public order."[60] Other conservatives feared civil disobedience would mean the end of constitutional democracy, the only political system capable in their view of producing a lasting solution to racial strife. Many also saw King's defense of civil disobedience as a recipe for anarchy or "mobocracy" (a common conservative term for mob rule). After all, who would determine what laws were unjust, when to break them, and which "Higher Law" to follow? "Strange as it may seem to Dr. King," wrote conservative Catholic Will Herberg, "the very purpose of government is to make us obey laws of which we do not approve."[61]

The threat of "mobocracy" soon seemed serious to conservatives. In August 1963, more than 250,000 Americans, black and white, gathered in Washington to demand passage of the civil rights bill proposed by Kennedy but stalled in Congress as southern Democrats voiced objections and prepared a filibuster. Behind the scenes, it was a tense time as conflict erupted between the White House and civil rights leaders over the length of the demonstration, the tone of the speeches, the role of whites, even the dress of the participants. But in the end, the March on Washington was to most Americans a triumph of the human spirit and an historic occasion when racial reconciliation at last seemed like a realistic possibility.

short run, the effort to pressure Congress through mass protest would, they feared, impede careful deliberation and damage the credibility of whatever legislation was enacted. In the long run, the political institutions of a free society would, they predicted, suffer irreparable harm from this dangerous precedent. "What society, at any time in history," wondered *National Review*, "was free, and just, and civilized, and ruled by the mob?"[63]

By the spring of 1964, the most controversial issue in American politics was the civil rights bill, which Kennedy had introduced in Congress a year earlier, prior to his assassination in November 1963. The bill banned racial discrimination in privately operated public accommodations, such as hotels and restaurants, movie theaters and gas stations. It authorized the U.S. Attorney General to investigate and eliminate *de jure* (legal) segregation in public places, such as schools, hospitals, and museums. And it stated that public schools and institutions which continued to segregate would face a loss of federal funds. The bill said nothing about racial discrimination in the workplace. It was also silent on the issue of *de facto* (actual) segregation in schools and housing. Nevertheless, it was a sweeping measure which reflected the liberal consensus in favor of equal rights and would, if enacted, end Jim Crow in the South and transform the racial landscape across the nation.

But would Congress pass the bill? The new president, Lyndon Johnson, was determined that it would. He put every ounce of his political muscle and legislative smarts behind it. He knew that his political future (1964 was an election year) and historical reputation rested on it. But opposition inside the Senate from Southerners, almost all of whom were Democrats, was strong. For three months, an all-time record, they filibustered against the bill. Meanwhile, conservatives outside Congress mustered every argument they could in opposition, claiming the legislation jeopardized private property, individual freedom, and constitutional democracy.

In Virginia, a thirty-one-year-old minister named Jerry Falwell gave a sermon in which he announced that the foremost duty of Christians was to spread the word of Christ. Politics was for politicians. "If as much effort could be put into winning people to Jesus Christ across the land as is being exerted in the present civil rights movement," he preached, "America would be turned upside down for God. . . . I feel that we need to get off the streets and back into the pulpits and into the prayer room." In a subsequent interview, he called the civil rights bill "a terrible violation of human and private property rights. It should be considered civil wrongs rather than civil rights."[64] The statement made Falwell both famous and notorious—he was branded a bigot and racist by many. In later years, it was also a source of regret for the minister, who in 1979 would form the Moral Majority, an important organization in the Christian Right.

In Alabama, another critic of civil rights was Governor George Wallace, a candidate for president who had promised segregation forever to his constituents. "We are faced with the astounding spectacle, for the first time in a civilized nation, of high officials calling for the passage of a so-called civil rights bill for fear of threat of mob violence," he declared, couching conservative themes in inflammatory rhetoric. " This bill takes a long step toward transferring private property to public domain under a central government. . . . Under any name, it will create a dictatorship the likes of which we or our fathers have not witnessed. . . . If victory for freedom is impossible, then surrender to communism is inevitable and we can begin fitting the yokes of slavery to the necks of our children even now as the riots and mobs lap at the streets of these United States."[65]

In June 1964, a northern coalition of Democrats and Republicans broke the filibuster and overwhelmed southern resistance in the Senate. The final vote was 73–27. More Republicans than Democrats voted for the measure, which Johnson signed into law in July. In the end, only six Republicans voted against the Civil Rights Act. One of them was Barry Goldwater and, like Wallace, he was a candidate for president.

Goldwater was not a racist. He was a member of the National Association for the Advancement of Colored People (NAACP) in his hometown of Phoenix. He was also a believer in voluntary integration—he had even led a fight to integrate his Air Force reserve unit. But in his 1960 bestseller, *Conscience of a Conservative*, he had made it clear that he opposed involuntary integration, supported local control, and was not willing to impose his views on "the people of Mississippi or South Carolina. . . . That is their business and not mine. I believe that the problem of race relations, like all social and cultural problems, is best handled by the people directly concerned." Like other conservatives, Goldwater felt that legislation in general—and laws imposed by Congress in particular—had little chance of changing people's hearts, especially on a matter as fundamental and personal as race.[66]

In Goldwater's heart, he most feared an expansive and intrusive federal government. Inevitably, the United States would become a police state where the executive branch promoted the rights of the minority at the expense of the freedoms of the majority. Property owners would no longer have the right to rent or sell to whomever they wanted. Small businesses would no longer have the right to offer or deny service to whomever they wanted. States would no longer have the right to pass or enforce laws which reflected

local values or c⌐
hire or fire whom⌐
to governmental re⌐
ernment and local con⌐

Goldwater's defeat in t⌐ encouraged liberals who wished to advance the cause of civil rights. In the spring of 1965, King chose as his next campaign a march in Alabama from Selma to Montgomery, the state capital. He sought to provoke Sheriff Jim Clark of Selma, an avowed segregationist who wore a button with the word NEVER printed on it, into violence as King had goaded "Bull" Conner in Birmingham. On March 7 ("Bloody Sunday"), Clark behaved as hoped and feared—he and his officers charged the demonstrators with batons and bullwhips as they tried to cross the Edmund Pettus Bridge. Many were hospitalized.

Once again, a national television audience reacted with horror. Liberals reserved their outrage for Clark and his violent tactics. Conservatives reserved their anger for King and his nonviolent civil disobedience. "It . . . is hypocrisy on a grand scale," wrote Meyer in *National Review*. It could not succeed, he noted, unless and until it provoked violence, making escalation inevitable. Civil disobedience was also "violent in its very essence, relying as it does upon the terror inspired by mobs to destroy the processes of constitutional government." At times, Meyer conceded, it was justified, as in resistance to Nazi genocide or communist oppression. "But against a constitutional order with inbuilt modes for the redress of grievances," he concluded, "there is no such justification."[67]

On March 15, Johnson went to Congress to lobby for a strong new voting rights law. On television that night, he said of the victims in Selma, "Their cause must be our cause, too. Because it is not just Negroes, but really all of us who must overcome the crippling legacy of bigotry and injustice. And, we shall . . . overcome." King was moved to tears. On March 21, the march began again and this time it succeeded. Meanwhile, the voting rights bill cleared the House easily and won overwhelming passage in the Senate after supporters invoked cloture and broke a twenty-five-day southern filibuster.

In August 1965, Johnson signed into law the Voting Rights Act, which protected both the right to vote and the right to register. In particular, it empowered the Justice Department to suspend literacy tests in southern counties where less than 50 percent of eligible voters were registered. Traditionally, white officials had used such tests to deny black voters the right to register. The attorney general could also send federal registrars to oversee the election process in those counties. The law had an immediate and dramatic effect. Within four years, the percentage of blacks registered to vote in the South had risen sharply—in Mississippi alone, it had jumped from less than 10 percent to more than 50 percent.

Reaction to the Voting Rights Act was, predictably, mixed. Liberals saw it as an unmitigated triumph. At last southern whites would have to extend equal voting rights to southern blacks, who could, it was hoped, leverage political power into equal treatment and equal opportunity in other areas. Conservatives saw the Voting Right Act as an unprincipled disaster. It was national legislation with a regional bias—it imposed federal oversight on the South only. It was unconstitutional—the Constitution clearly reserved the right to set voting standards to the states. And it was based on a false premise—that giving illiterates, black and white, the right to vote would constitute positive progress. On the contrary, noted Buckley, "True reform in the South would involve raising the standards for voting—and raising them impartially, for black and white alike."[68] Left unanswered was whether that was politically feasible.

In retrospect, passage of the Voting Rights Act in August 1965 was the last great triumph of the interracial liberal coalition that had powered the civil rights movement. Days after Johnson put pen to paper, a riot erupted in the Watts section of Los Angeles and shattered the liberal dream of a Great Society built on material prosperity and racial harmony. The country had reached a crossroads between the optimism of the early 1960s and the pessimism of the late 1960s. In 1966 and 1967, civil unrest erupted in many cities, most notably Newark and Detroit, spreading death, destruction, and despair. In response, conservatives blamed black leaders for failing to halt the riots and white liberals for promoting programs which seemed to reward the rioters. What most conservatives now wanted, above all, was a restoration of law and order.

What younger blacks wanted was new leadership and new ideas. King, many thought, was tired and irrelevant. The Civil Rights Act and Voting Rights Act were too little too late. Expectations had risen and patience had eroded, but progress was slow or so it seemed (in fact, black Americans had made significant legal and political gains between 1963 and 1966). The time had come for black power, which emphasized racial separation, not integration, and endorsed violence in self-defense, not nonviolence under all circumstances. Whites were also no longer welcome in the civil rights movement, at least not in prominent roles, because blacks needed to pursue self-determination in their own manner and at their own pace. Black power shattered liberal unity within and across racial lines. Many older blacks and whites denounced it as misguided and counterproductive, even reverse racism. Younger whites were divided—some tried to accept black power while most rejected it and refocused their energies on causes such as opposition to the Vietnam War or support for the women's movement.

Conservatives were united in opposition to the urban disorder and black power. Some called for a temporary moratorium on demonstrations and legislation. "The time is at hand," wrote Buckley, "to depoliticize the civil rights movement for the sake of everyone involved." Otherwise, the black minority would risk losing the good will of the white majority, which in turn would risk losing sight of the importance of racial progress. Others were more critical and alarmist. Black power, wrote Meyer, was a revolutionary program of "confiscatory socialism." It aimed to redistribute wealth and abolish inequality by any means necessary, including "blackmail by violence." He blamed liberals for encouraging an alliance of black activists and criminals which, Meyer argued, had created "a climate of terror on a scale never before seen in American society."[69]

In 1968, an act of white violence lifted the climate of terror to new heights. On April 4, James Earl Ray shot and killed King outside his motel room in Memphis, where he had journeyed in support of a strike by sanitation workers. For conservatives, the event was tragic but expected. "We are now witnessing the whirlwind sowed years ago when some preachers and teachers began telling people that each man could be his own judge in his own case," stated Senator Strom Thurmond of South Carolina. For liberals, it was another opportunity to reflect on the rampant violence in American society. It was clear, observed Senator Robert Kennedy of New York, that "violence breeds violence, repression breeds retaliation, and only a cleansing of our whole society can remove this sickness from our souls." But, he added, "there is another kind of violence, slower but just as deadly and destructive as the shot or the bomb in the night. This is the violence of institutions, indifference, inaction and decay. This is the violence that afflicts the poor, that poisons relations between men, because their skin is different colored." As Kennedy spoke, major riots erupted in over sixty major cities, including the nation's capital.

In the wake of the disorders, a fearful Congress passed the Open Housing Act. In theory, the law banned discriminatory practices in most real estate transactions. No longer could property owners choose who to sell or rent to on the basis of race. In practice, the legislation placed the burden of proof on the complainant and contained few enforcement provisions. An essentially symbolic act, it had little or no impact on residential segregation. Liberals were disappointed, although they tended to see the act as a step in the right direction. Conservatives saw it as another infringement upon states' rights and property rights. Since when, they asked, was owning a house a form of interstate commerce, as Congress had claimed? And if it was unconstitutional to allow individuals to handle their property as they saw fit, how could Congress legally exempt small rooming or boarding houses, which it had?

By then new issues and new controversies had emerged. In June 1965, President Johnson had presented the liberal case for affirmative action in a powerful speech at Howard University. "You do not take a person who, for years, has been hobbled by chains and liberate him, bring him up to the starting line of a race and then say, 'you are free to compete with all the others,' and still justly believe that you have been completely fair," he said. "Thus it is not enough just to open the gates of opportunity. All our citizens must have the ability to walk through those gates. This is the next and the more profound stage of the battle for civil rights. We seek . . . not just equality as a right and a theory but equality as a fact and equality as a result." In September, Johnson had issued an executive order which stated that federal contractors must hire and treat employees without regard to race, color, religion, or national origin (sex was added in 1967). In 1968, the Department of Labor required that employers develop general guidelines to ensure equal opportunity for disadvantaged individuals; by 1970, it required that employers set specific goals for minority groups by establishing *de facto* quotas based on race and sex.

Like black power, affirmative action divided white liberals. Many, like Johnson, saw it as necessary and overdue because it was so difficult to prove racial discrimination in the workplace, especially given the backlog of cases at the Equal Employment Opportunity Commission, which was empowered to investigate. But others saw in it the potential for reverse discrimination. Conservatives saw in affirmative action the reality of reverse discrimination. Gone were the principle of meritocracy and the ideal of a color-blind society embedded in the Civil Rights Act of 1964. Gone too was King's dream where the content of one's character was more important than the color of one's skin. In their place was a federal government bent on accumulating power and destroying liberty. It was, in essence, the conservative nightmare.

Equally controversial was court-ordered busing to achieve racial integration in public schools. By the end of the decade, the Supreme Court had lost patience with school districts that continued to resist implementation of *Brown II*. In 1969, it ruled unanimously in *Alexander v. Holmes* that officials had to dismantle "at once" dual systems for black and white students. In the South, the number of integrated schools rose significantly. Then in 1971 in *Swann v. Charlotte-Mecklenburg* the Supreme Court ruled, again unanimously, in favor of a court-ordered plan in Charlotte, North Carolina, which imposed busing on the county as a whole. Liberals in general applauded because they believed that racially separate housing patterns left no alternative to judicial intervention.

But in the North and the South, the public outcry was intense. In Boston, Irish-Americans and Italian-Americans protested vehemently, asserting ethnic pride and, in an ironic twist, borrowing language, tactics, and even songs from the civil rights movement. Polls showed that an overwhelming majority of whites and a narrow majority of blacks opposed forced busing. The Nixon administration took notice and began to do all it could to slow the pace of integration. In 1974, the Supreme Court ruled in *Milliken v. Bradley* that the city of Detroit might not bus students to the suburbs. The margin was 5–4, with all four of Nixon's appointees in the majority. Justice Thurgood Marshall, the first African-American to serve on the

Supreme Court, dissented. "Unless our children begin to learn together," he wrote, "there is little hope that our people will ever learn to live together."[70] For the first time in many years, conservatives applauded the Supreme Court. It had, at last, recognized that busing was a mistake, that integration produced minimal or no educational gains. Conservatives also claimed that busing actively harmed black children by placing them under the dubious influence of government-certified white experts. And they argued that busing represented an unwarranted intrusion by federal officials into the local control of public schools. Here elite conservatives found common ground with grass-roots conservatives, who railed against powerful outsiders determined to correct the ills of society at the expense of powerless communities. In the years to come, this alliance would pay large political dividends for conservative candidates who learned to speak the language of reactionary populism.

In the end, the clash over civil rights revealed and reflected profound differences in how liberals and conservatives perceived the past and the present. Liberals tended to view American history in negative terms by focusing on the nation's record of exploitation and oppression. Contemporary racism, they argued, was in large part the historical legacy of slavery and segregation. Therefore white Americans bore a collective guilt and owed a collective debt to black Americans. Conservatives disagreed on all counts. They tended to view American history in positive terms. Injustices had occurred, they conceded, but on balance the nation had done well in eventually extending freedom and opportunity, albeit unevenly, to all Americans. Therefore white Americans had no reason for collective guilt. As Buchanan, a conservative Catholic, put it, "To us, sin is . . . a matter for personal confession, personal contrition, personal reconciliation with God. Our sense of shame and sense of guilt are about what we have done ourselves."[71] If white Americans had a moral debt to black Americans, conservatives by the 1970s considered it repaid in full, whereas liberals believed it continued to draw interest and demand attention.

SOCIAL ORDER

In July 1964, Arizona Senator Barry Goldwater accepted the Republican Party's presidential nomination in a fiery speech at the Cow Palace in San Francisco. What subsequently attracted the most attention was his memorable aphorism about extremism and liberty, vice and virtue. But at the time it was his invocation of law and order that roused the delegates to a fever pitch. Demanding that social order "not become the license of the mob and of the jungle," the Republican decried the Democrats for allowing "violence in our streets" to flourish. Blending the threats to personal and national security, he declared that "security from domestic violence, no less than from foreign aggression, is the most elementary and fundamental purpose of any government." (See document 5.)

At that moment, a new issue moved from the margins to the mainstream of national politics. Law and order both reflected and reinforced the sense that the country was coming apart, that disorder and disrespect toward authority were rampant at all levels of society from the family home to the White House. In 1964, Goldwater was a flawed messenger—he seemed like an angry prophet and racial extremist to many voters. He was also somewhat premature, as social conditions had not yet reached critical mass. But in the next four years, as street crime, civil unrest, political demonstrations, and cultural change swept across the country, the fear and anxiety felt by tens of millions of Americans crystallized into a demand for law and order. In the 1968 presidential election, the issue enabled conservative Republican Richard Nixon to defeat liberal Democrat Hubert Humphrey by a narrow margin.

Liberals failed to take the need for order seriously until it was too late. As crime skyrocketed—the murder rate alone almost doubled between 1963 and 1968—they maintained that the statistics were faulty. The response was as insufficient as it was insensitive to the victims of crime as well as their friends and family, coworkers and neighbors. Liberals also dismissed those who pleaded for law and order as racists, ignoring blacks who were victimized more often than any other group and insulting Jews who had steadfastly supported the civil rights movement. In addition, liberals consistently defined crime control as a local problem, which constitutionally it was. But the argument seemed disingenuous because they had already defined every other issue, from job training to voting rights, as a federal matter. Finally, liberals insisted with some merit that the best way to fight violent crime was to attack the "root" causes like poverty and unemployment. But the loss of law and order eroded faith in government and complicated efforts to sell more social programs to anxious Americans.

By contrast, conservatives offered a clear and direct critique. They maintained that the breakdown in social order was the result of three developments aided and abetted by liberals. First, both Kennedy and Johnson had supported the King doctrine of civil disobedience, which promoted disrespect for law and authority. Second, the Supreme Court had enhanced the rights of criminal defendants at the expense of law enforcement and public safety in cases like *Miranda*, which in 1966 required that police advise suspects in custody of their rights. Finally, the White House had directly or indirectly rewarded undeserving minorities for their criminal behavior during urban riots.

Conservatives also offered a positive program for the restoration of security and decency. Inverting their traditional stance on federalism, they maintained that the national government should assume a major role in the local fight against violence and disorder. The president should exert moral leadership from Washington, reinforcing respect for the law and encouraging contempt for those who violated it. The Congress should curtail the liberal welfare state, which promoted dependency at the expense of responsibility. And the Supreme Court should reverse rulings like *Miranda* and permit the police to collect evidence and conduct interrogations as they saw fit within broad limits.

At a theoretical level, conservatives presented a dual vision of order. On the one hand, they repudiated the progressive ideal of a planned society administered by distant experts. Reasserting a conservative variant of American populism, they expressed hostility to social engineering as practiced by Supreme Court justices and Great Society bureaucrats in faraway Washington. Defending local institutions and individuals, conservatives praised in particular the neighborhood policeman who protected local values—political, moral, and property. On the other hand, they contended that the community's right to order took precedence over the individual's right to engage in disruptive behavior. Rejecting the liberal claim that public space was where anyone could assert such rights as free speech and free assembly, conservatives maintained that only residents had the right to unrestricted use—and then only if they complied with the legitimate demands of legitimate authority.

At a popular level, law and order resonated both as a social ideal and political slogan because it combined an understandable concern over the rising number of traditional crimes—robberies and rapes, muggings and murders—with implicit and explicit unease about civil rights, civil liberties, and civil unrest as well as antiwar protests, sexual habits, and drug use. Any challenge to authority—in the home, the streets, or the classroom—became fodder for fear, which politicians, pundits, and propagandists across the political spectrum exploited as they turned law and order into a Rorschach test of public anxiety.

What made law and order such a potent weapon for conservatives was that they could use it to represent different concerns to different people at different moments. Liberals could, with justification, note that the issue often rested on racial prejudice. Often civil disobedience was the only recourse left to demonstrators denied fundamental freedoms and confronted by officials who themselves repeatedly defied the law. But conservatives could use law and order to clarify or simplify a troubling world of danger and disorder. The issue identified a cast of villains (protesters, rioters, and criminals), explained the causes of their actions (above all the doctrine of civil disobedience and the paternalism of the welfare state), and offered a solution (limited government, moral leadership, and judicial firmness).

Yet law and order was more than the sum of its parts. Conservatives charged that the loss of security was the most visible sign and symbol of the perceived failure of activist government. In their view the liberal welfare state had squandered the hard-earned taxes of the deserving middle class on wasteful programs for the undeserving poor. It had also failed to ensure the safety of the citizenry, black and white—the primary duty of any government. The charge posed a dilemma for liberals, who could not always differentiate effectively or persuasively between criminal behavior and civil disobedience, lawful demonstrations and unlawful riots, actual crime and irrational fear.

Law and order shattered the fragile New Deal coalition of ethnic workers, northern liberals, black Americans, and white Southerners, which Franklin Roosevelt had assembled in the 1930s. In industrial cities like Detroit and Chicago, white opposition to black neighbors revealed in the 1940s and 1950s how inherently unstable the alliance was. But the demise of the New Deal coalition was not inevitable. Prior to the early 1960s, many white workers in effect split their ballots. They balanced support for conservative local candidates committed to residential segregation with support for liberal national candidates committed to racial integration. By the mid-1960s, however, the balancing act had become untenable in large part because crime and disorder had become the nexus at which local concerns and national policies seemed to intersect. Law and order thus became the vehicle by which urban whites transmitted their fear of racial violence from the municipal to the presidential arena.

In 1964, two individuals placed the issue of law and order on the national agenda. In the Democratic primaries, Alabama Governor George Wallace, an avowed opponent of civil rights and defender of racial segregation, made it the centerpiece of his campaign, which showed surprising strength in unexpected states like Wisconsin, Indiana, and Maryland. In the Republican primaries, Arizona Senator Barry Goldwater used law and order to broaden his appeal, help him wrest control of the party from moderates, and secure the nomination. Both candidates were able to tap into deep reservoirs of fear and anxiety among ordinary voters.

Days after Goldwater accepted the nomination, a riot erupted in Harlem. The stakes were clear to conservatives. "Unless there is order in the streets," warned *National Review,* "unless citizens . . . [are] secure in their persons, property, homes and place of business, we no longer have a nation or society at all; we have returned to anarchy and Hobbes' war of all against all." The editorial also cautioned that the "revolutionaries—not all of them communists—now actively exploiting the civil rights movement understand very well that the undermining of the police force, and of public confidence in the police, is a key part of their task of destroying our society."[72]

To restore public confidence in the police and the administration, Johnson declared war on crime in September 1965. "I will not be satisfied," he announced with ambitious rhetoric that echoed Kennedy's inaugural, "until every woman and child in this Nation can walk any street, enjoy any park, drive on any highway, and live in any community at any time of the day or night without fear of being harmed." By promoting the idea of victory and hailing the policeman as "the frontline soldier in our war against crime," Johnson had risked a great deal of his political credibility. The president had also made a major miscalculation, because the war on crime, like the war in Vietnam, would prove unwinnable.

The speech reflected the confidence that the president and most liberals felt in 1965. But it also reflected the anxiety caused by events a month earlier. On a hot August evening, days after Johnson had signed into law the Voting Rights Act, Watts exploded in violence. Before the National Guard could restore order, thirty-four were dead, hundreds were injured, almost four thousand were arrested, and roughly $35 million in damage was done. The riot highlighted the political danger the White House faced in assuming greater responsibility for social order. In the aftermath, two official investigations also generated more controversy than consensus as liberals and conservatives debated the larger meaning of the riot, which exposed and exacerbated the racial and ideological fissures in the nation.

In Washington, Johnson announced that Attorney General Ramsey Clark would head a federal task force to investigate the causes of the riot. The task force report provided a snapshot in 1965 of liberal thought and optimism at the time. Riots were "manifestations of defects in our development as a democratic society"—but not structural defects, as evidenced by the fact that most residents of Watts were law-abiding. Although the report briefly noted the need for social order, it identified the real causes of the riot as discrimination, unemployment, and poverty. In the long run, the report maintained, the police could not prevent riots because it "is no more possible to suppress rioting where its causes are fermenting than it is to hold the lid on a boiling pot." But the task force was confident that more social programs could and would lower the heat.

The report was, however, never released due to opposition from Johnson. Instead, the president threw his support behind the findings of the McCone Commission, chaired by John McCone, a Los Angeles resident and former CIA director. It identified similar "underlying causes" such as the heavy black migration to Los Angeles and the resultant housing strains. But the commission placed more blame on "aggravating events" such as the false expectations raised by the antipoverty program and the favorable publicity given to unlawful protests by civil rights activists.

Above all, the McCone Commission claimed that the rioters were "riffraff" with "no legal or moral justification for the wounds they inflicted" because Watts was no slum and Los Angeles offered unequaled opportunities for black advancement. "What happened," it concluded, "was an explosion—a formless, quite senseless, all but hopeless violent protest—engaged in by a few but bringing great distress to all." The explosion occurred even though there was no evidence of outside agitators or premeditation. But the commission harshly criticized black leaders who had supposedly failed to take personal responsibility for their community's lack of progress, promoted the careless use of civil disobedience, and, in some cases, issued "brutal exhortations to violence."

The commission's conclusions attracted harsh criticism from all quarters. Liberals condemned the "riffraff theory," asserting that far more blacks than officially estimated had participated in the riot and that they were far more representative of their community than McCone had contended. This assertion in turn had two corollaries. First, it meant that the black leadership was hardly to blame for Watts—not when the crisis of the slum was so systemic and conditions were so oppressive. Second, the widespread support for the riot—and the deliberate decision to leave churches, homes, and libraries untouched—indicated that Watts was a conscious political protest, not the "formless" explosion that the report had contended.

Conservatives also objected to the commission's claim that Watts was not organized and orchestrated with political intent. Behind the riot, they said, undoubtedly lay the insidious actions of activists—possibly communists engaged in a conspiracy to destabilize society—and the invidious appeal of civil disobedience. "If you are looking for those ultimately responsible for the murder, arson, and looting in Los Angeles," wrote a conservative theologian, "look to them: they are the guilty ones, these apostles of 'nonviolence.' They have taught anarchy and chaos by word and deed—and, no doubt, with the best of intentions—they have found apt pupils everywhere, with intentions not of the best."[73]

The core conservative claim was that Watts was the responsibility of individuals, not society. Moral failure was to blame, not social conditions. Most immigrants, argued conservatives, had peacefully and quietly endured far worse poverty and deprivation. Therefore the fault belonged first and foremost to the black rioters themselves and then to their unwitting accomplices, the white liberals who had inculcated a culture of dependency and entitlement. According to conservatives, government planners in remote Washington had imposed confiscatory taxes on hard-working middle-class whites, squandered the funds on undeserving minorities, raised false expectations among them, and constructed an expansive as well as intrusive bureaucracy that trampled on the prerogatives of municipalities and the values of communities.

In 1966, a rising tide of public anxiety over law and order helped sweep incumbent liberals from power and presented insurgent conservatives with new opportunities. The issue enabled conservative leaders to mobilize grassroots conservatives, who in turn received a language of protest and a vocabulary of ideas with which to link troubling changes in their communities to broader developments in American society and culture. The power and potency of law and order seemed limitless. Suddenly, the future of conservatism appeared bright and the future of liberalism appeared dim. Two events in particular signaled this transformation.

In California, former actor Ronald Reagan shocked and surprised the political world when he easily upset two-term incumbent Democrat Pat Brown in the race to become governor of California. Reagan's success was due in large measure to his charm and charisma—in sharp contrast to the angry Goldwater, he was the friendly face of modern conservatism. But it also demonstrated the visceral appeal and volatile force of law and order, whose three touchstones in California were the Watts Riot, the Berkeley protests, and street crime. In a political world increasingly dominated by the televised sound bite, the issue had extraordinary appeal because it was simple and malleable. Politicians could tailor it to specific audiences and situations—or allow listeners to assign whatever meanings they wished to it.

As an activist, Reagan had gained national attention in 1964, when he gave a televised speech on behalf of Goldwater. "A Time for Choosing" made Reagan, a former liberal who had campaigned for Franklin Roosevelt in 1944 and Harry Truman in 1948, a political sensation and household name among conservatives. "You and I are told increasingly that we have to choose between a left or right, but I would like to suggest that there is no such thing as a left or right," he declared. "There is only an up or down— up to a man's age-old dream, the ultimate in individual freedom consistent with law and order—or down to the ant heap of totalitarianism. " (See document 6.)

At Berkeley, the flagship university in the state's system of higher education, student protests in favor of free speech and civil rights had erupted in 1964. The following year, campus activists brought into political discourse such cultural flashpoints as drug use, long hair, and homosexual behavior. Conservative resistance to what seemed like subsidized sinfulness soon reached a boiling point. To exploit this anger, Reagan gave a powerful speech in 1966 at the Cow Palace in San Francisco, where he provided a graphic description of a dance party sponsored by an antiwar group:

> Three rock 'n' roll bands were in the center of the gymnasium playing simultaneously all during the dance, and all during the dance movies were shown on two screens at the opposite ends of the gymnasium. These movies were the only lights in the gym proper. They consisted of color sequences that gave the appearance of different-colored liquid spreading across the screen, followed by shots of men and women[;] on occasion, shots were of the men's and women's nude torsos, and persons twisted and gyrated in provocative and sensual fashion. The young people were seen standing against the walls or lying on the floors and steps in a dazed condition with glazed eyes consistent with the condition of being under the influence of narcotics. Sexual misconduct was blatant.

The breakdown in morality, claimed Reagan, dated from 1964, when the university administration had first permitted student demonstrators to defy the police, the symbol of law and order. Now liberal tolerance had become permissiveness, which jeopardized all standards of decency. How far, Reagan asked, would respectable citizens allow this epidemic of immorality to spread? The question resonated because to many the disorder at Berkeley represented more than an indirect threat to moral values and legitimate authority. It also represented a direct threat to their children's future.

In New York, the politics of law and order centered on the threat to everyone, young and old, posed by street crime and symbolized by the Harlem Riot of 1964. At stake in 1966 was a referendum to abolish civilian review for the New York Police Department (NYPD). Supporters of civilian review contended that it would improve police-minority relations and reduce the likelihood of future riots. Opponents contended that it would handcuff the police and weaken public safety. In the end, the referendum passed easily. In the nation's largest and perhaps most progressive city, a measure promoted as an extension of the civil rights cause and endorsed by every prominent liberal politician and organization had met disastrous defeat. The outcome was a stunning blow to liberalism. It was also a reflection of the growing strength of conservatism.

At the same time, the referendum results revealed how deep and widespread the fear of crime had become. Between 1960 and 1969 the rate of violent crime doubled. At first liberals expressed legitimate doubts about the accuracy of the statistics, which were collected and reported by the police. They also contended that even if impartial experts processed the data, shifts in the public's willingness to report certain crimes (such as rape) and the police's willingness to enforce certain laws (such as drunk driving) would render the statistics of dubious value. When liberals belatedly acknowledged the problem of crime, they tended to argue that it was due to demographics (the unusually large number of single young men) or the availability of guns and popularity of drugs.

Conservatives rejected this analysis. They accepted at face value the crime statistics, using them as proof that lawlessness was rampant. But the main cause of the crime crisis was widespread disrespect for adult authority and traditional morality. Liberals had made matters worse, conservatives continued, by claiming that social conditions, not individual choices, were responsible. "What matters to the average citizen is not so much the abstract of statistical problems or even the sociologists' long-range solution," wrote conservative columnist James J. Kilpatrick. "His concern goes to the mugger, the rapist, the dope-crazed thief, the arrogant young punks who infest his streets. What can be done about them now?" Conservatives also had little reluctance to discuss openly the racial dimension of street crime.

By contrast, the racial factor divided and troubled white liberals, who had to reconcile their political principles with the murder and mayhem on the streets. Intellectually, they knew that most blacks were not muggers. But emotionally they could not ignore the sense that every mugger seemed black. What was the fundamental cause of urban violence—the denial of civil rights, economic opportunity, or racial equality? And what would reduce the rate of crime, whose perpetrators and victims were disproportionately black? At the heart of these questions was race. But racism was not the primary motivation for most whites; rather it was the growing sense that personal safety was now of necessity a political priority. It was also an economic priority, since many urban liberals had to confront the material threat to their life savings and economic security, which were often tied to apartments and homes whose value plummeted when neighborhoods changed.

Conservatives harbored no such doubts. During his unsuccessful bid to become mayor of New York in 1965, Buckley compared the threat to national security in the 1950s with the threat to personal security in the 1960s. In both cases, liberals had provided aid and comfort to the enemy, first the communists and now the criminals, who were active agents of evil, not passive victims of society. Buckley also noted with scorn how liberals endorsed the Supreme Court's expansive view of civil liberties, encouraged cries of police brutality regardless of proof, and excused "political" violence in the name of favored causes. Above all, he accused liberals of exalting the absolute rights of individuals and criminals over the abstract rights of the community and victims.[74] The indictment proved persuasive to many New Yorkers in 1966 and many others in 1968, when the United States seemed on the brink of anarchy.

In March 1968, the Kerner Commission (named after Illinois Governor Otto Kerner, who was the chair) issued a final report. Johnson had convened the commission in the desperate days after the Detroit Riot in July 1967. He had hoped that it would contain the political damage and endorse his social programs. But ultimately the commission dashed his hopes, producing a controversial report that further divided liberals and enraged the president, who ignored it. The assertion that "white racism" was a causal factor in the civil unrest shook the increasingly fragile Democratic coalition of northern workers, white liberals, and urban minorities. And the memorable phrase—"Our nation is moving toward two societies, one black, one white, separate and unequal"—suggested that the liberal commitment to building a Great Society and encouraging racial integration had failed.

Ironically, the report for the most part repeated the conventional liberal wisdom, buttressed by statistics and surveys. It issued a series of predictable suggestions for containing and preventing civil unrest. It showed that the "typical rioter" was not a member of the "riffraff," a theory first advanced by the McCone Commission. And it declared that there was no conspiracy, although militant organizations had created an atmosphere ripe for riots and would undoubtedly seek to exploit future disorders. The report even straddled the issue of whether the civil disorders constituted political protests. On the one hand, it rejected the McCone Commission assertion that the riots were aimless. On the other, it denied that they were revolutionary in intent.

Conservatives strenuously rejected the idea that the cause of the riots was "white racism" and the remedy was more government aid to the inner cities. In *National Review*, Meyer chastised the commission for placing "the blame everywhere but where it belongs, everywhere, that is, except upon the rioters and upon the liberals who, with their abstract ideology, prepared the way for the riots by their contempt for social order and their utopian, egalitarian enticements and incitements."[75] More social programs now would only reward the rioters, he and others argued.

Other events soon overshadowed the debate over the Kerner Commission. In April 1968, student demonstrators at Columbia University seized several buildings as a protest against university policies and the Vietnam War. As clashes erupted on campus between radical and conservative students, liberal efforts to broker a compromise between the administration and the protestors failed. Eventually, Columbia President Grayson Kirk requested the intervention of the NYPD, which cleared the students and their supporters from the buildings with force, leading to hundreds of arrests and injuries.

Liberals were outraged. The decision of the president was unjustified. The actions of the police were unwarranted. The resort to force was unnecessary and out of proportion to the minor threat posed by the student demonstrators who represented majority opinion. Conservatives disagreed on all counts. The protestors, who were a minority, posed a serious threat to the university as a whole. The administration's response was appropriate if overdue. And the NYPD had done what it was trained and supposed to do.

At a deeper level, conservatives blamed the campus turmoil of the late 1960s, which engulfed hundreds of institutions from coast to coast, on a number of factors. First, the universities were too large and too impersonal— they overflowed with students who were incapable of and uninterested in learning. The results were lowered standards and a diluted curriculum— pablum for the masses, who became either bored or enraged. Second, liberal professors had compounded the crisis by promoting permissiveness and "relevance" at the expense of traditional moral education. "What wonder that the campus sank into anarchy?" observed conservative lecturer Russell Kirk. "The wonder really was that violent protest against academic anonymity and academic fraud had not burst forth earlier."[76]

In June 1968, Robert Kennedy was killed shortly after he had won the California primary, which might have given him the momentum to capture the Democratic nomination. In life, Kennedy had personified the liberal hope that new leadership could provide new solutions. In death, he became both a national symbol and trigger point in the debate over disorder. The question of whether America was a "sick society" now generated liberal confusion and conservative contempt.

At first, liberals endured an intense period of hand-wringing and soul-searching. "Has violence become an American way of life?" asked *Time*. Many thought so. "The country does not work any more," lamented a newspaper columnist. "All that money and power have produced has been a bunch of people so filled with fear and hate that when a man tries to tell them they must do more for other men, instead of listening they shoot him in the head." According to many liberals, a culture of death now pervaded American society.

Conservatives condemned the idea that the nation was sick. If social order had declined, it was due to the widespread acceptance of civil disobedience, the root cause of the epidemic of murders, riots, protests, and assassinations. Compounding the crisis was liberal permissiveness. "In a civilized nation it is not expected that public figures should be considered proper targets for casual gunmen," charged *National Review*. "But in civilized nations of the past it has not been customary for parents to allow their children to do what they feel like; for students to seize their schools and smash their equipment; for police to be ordered to stand by while looters empty stores and arsonists burn down buildings. . . . "77

In time more sober thoughts began to prevail among liberals. Johnson noted that a lone and troubled assassin had killed Kennedy, not two hundred million Americans. Others noted that the murder rate was actually lower than in the 1930s. After the death of King in April 1968, Kennedy had proclaimed that "only a cleansing of our whole society can remove this sickness from our souls." But now liberals urged calm. More social programs might not restore social order. But gun control would and so too might an examination of the impact of television, which brought into homes nightly the true horrors of Vietnam and the gratuitous violence of Hollywood films. Henceforth liberals would routinely decry the insidious influence of popular culture—a position that conservatives would eagerly embrace as their own in the 1990s, when school shootings in California and Colorado led to renewed calls for gun control.

In essence, a new liberal agenda had emerged by the summer of 1968. The media exploited violence. Restrictions—like a ratings system for Hollywood films—would reduce the exposure of children. Firearms killed people and destroyed lives. Gun control would help prevent political assassinations and improve riot control. In the end, the Gun Control Act of 1968 was a compromise measure. It placed a ban on inexpensive imports and the interstate mail-order sale of all weapons. But it lacked registration and/or licensing provisions. Nevertheless, it was the first major federal gun control legislation since the 1930s, and it reflected the new liberal consensus that was forming.

Conservatives were contemptuous of gun control. It represented legislation by hysteria and would not deter violence or keep weapons out of the hands of criminals or assassins. On the contrary, it might eventually deprive law-abiding citizens of their constitutional right to hunt animals or protect themselves, which could lead to anarchy or tyranny. In the meantime, the breakdown of law and order made gun ownership more essential than ever. "Self-defense today has become not only a right but a duty," wrote Meyer in *National Review*. He added that improving social conditions (the usual liberal remedy) and restoring moral values (the usual conservative remedy) would do little to improve personal security in the near future.[78]

In August 1968, the crisis of order worsened. In Chicago, site of the Democratic National Convention, thousands of police officers and antiwar demonstrators clashed under the bright lights of television cameras. As the delegates nominated Vice President Hubert Humphrey for president, the convention climaxed with what an official report later termed a "police riot." Exhausted after three days of extended duty and faced with mounting verbal and physical provocation, the officers responded with unrestrained and indiscriminate violence as they attacked demonstrators and onlookers alike.

Liberals took the side of the protestors. They blamed Mayor Richard Daley and the Chicago Police Department for the violent confrontations. "With billy clubs, tear gas, and Mace, the blue-shirted, blue-helmeted cops violated the civil rights of countless innocent citizens and contravened every accepted code of professional police discipline," stated *Time*. Most of the marchers were "idealistic, demonstrably brave, concerned about their country and their fellow men," wrote Tom Wicker in the *New York Times*. "The truth is that these were our children in the streets and the Chicago police beat them up."

Conservatives rushed to defend Daley and the police, who in their view had acted appropriately despite individual acts of police brutality. The demonstrators had provoked the officers, who had given them precisely what they deserved. More seriously, the events in Chicago were the logical expression of the right to riot, which liberals had legitimized through their tolerance of civil disobedience. And that so-called right could lead to the rise of revolution or fascism, as it had in Nazi Germany. The fate of constitutional government ultimately rested, conservatives argued, on the legitimate defense of legitimate order. Otherwise the people would demand action, even if the price was a police state.[79]

Polls soon showed that most Americans, by more than a two-to-one margin, agreed with the conservatives. Contrary to what liberals like Wicker had suggested, it was apparently not their children who were beaten and bloodied in the streets of Chicago. The public reaction illustrated the continuing significance of class and the growing appeal of law and order. But it also underlined three other elements at work in the clash between the working-class police and the middle-class demonstrators.

The first element was the extent to which a sense of localism and distrust of distant authority permeated the conservative viewpoint. In Daley's eyes, he was the defender of his community, which was under siege from "outsiders," from riot agitators, federal judges, government bureaucrats, street criminals, political demonstrators, and Eastern reporters. Conservatives decried the undemocratic power of institutions physically distant from the communities of "real" America. They also decried the disproportionate influence of individuals philosophically distant from the values of "real" Americans.

The second element was competing conceptions of public space. Conservatives saw it as a concrete piece of public property. For Daley, it was a literal place where local taxpayers or residents could enjoy or express themselves if they followed the rules. Liberals saw public space as a symbolic place where individual rights took precedence. To them this meant that the demonstrators could do as they wished, with or without official approval. At the Democratic Convention, these visions collided.

The final element was how, through their dress and behavior, the demonstrators challenged middle-class social norms and moral traditions. Often the police vented anger (and possibly repressed envy) at the sexual ambiguity male hippies seemed to represent. "How would you like to fuck a man?" a group of officers yelled. The actions of the youthful demonstrators also seemed, to older policemen, like a rebellion against the authority of both the state and the family. Now they would receive a reminder of who was in charge both in the streets and at home. "If they'd gotten beaten like this when they were kids," said one officer, "they wouldn't be out here starting riots."

Two events highlighted the clash of generations and cultures. In June 1969, gays at the Stonewall Inn in Greenwich Village protested against police harassment and ignited five days of public demonstrations, which many have marked as the start of the gay rights movement. Liberals in general were tolerant and even supportive, seeing homosexuality as a private matter for consenting individuals. But conservatives were critical. In their view homosexuality was aberrant and abnormal. It violated the divine order of creation as established in the Bible. And it challenged the social order by weakening the nuclear family, which traditionalists saw as the cornerstone of civilization.

In August 1969, more than four hundred thousand young people gathered at a farm in upstate New York for a three-day music festival known as Woodstock. Although the rain fell periodically, it failed to dampen spirits as the concert-goers cavorted in the mud, smoked marijuana, and listened to the music of Janis Joplin, Jimi Hendrix, and many others. Some fans were nude. Some had sex in public. Virtually all were peaceful and relaxed.

Liberals saw Woodstock as a hopeful sign of better times. The noted anthropologist Margaret Mead, representing an older generation, praised the "spontaneous gentleness" of the participants. "This was the true happening at Woodstock," she wrote, "the realization by these 'Aquarians,' who think of themselves as the first generation in a new age of peace, that they have a voice, a viable style, a community of trust."[80] Perhaps it was possible to transcend violence and despair. And perhaps the counterculture could show the way.

Traditionalist conservatives were dismayed. Woodstock was possible only because of the affluence of American society and the leisure of American youth, who were unencumbered by jobs or responsibilities. Those in attendance had left massive waste and property damage so that, as a columnist in *National Review* put it, they could "indulge themselves in one vast paroxysm of mass infantilism—leaving it to the squares, of course, to feed them when they hunger, and doctor them when they bleed, and nurse them back from 'bad trips,' and clean up after them when they're gone."[81] If Woodstock was a sign of the future, asserted traditionalists, the United States was in trouble and the counterculture was responsible.

In the wake of Woodstock, an open debate on the decriminalization of marijuana emerged. Here liberals and libertarian conservatives found common ground. Both argued that marijuana was no more harmful than alcohol and that individuals deserved the freedom to choose. Both also asserted that the war on drugs was a failure, encouraged disrespect for the law, and weakened the credibility of government. And it needlessly ruined lives and led to a massive bureaucracy, a "prison-industrial" complex. The latter, of course, bothered libertarians more than liberals.

Traditionalist conservatives naturally disagreed with decriminalization. They believed that marijuana was addictive and dangerous, especially as a "gateway" drug to LSD and cocaine. They also contended that marijuana was a symbol of the counterculture and that legalization would constitute a stamp of legitimacy for a movement that traditionalists saw as eroding the moral fabric of American society. In their eyes, liberals had predictably placed personal freedom ahead of community values. More troubling to traditionalists was how the libertarians had become libertines, with no regard for the cost to civilization.

Even more troubling to traditionalists were changes in the family and the role of women. In the early 1960s, the modern feminist movement emerged, in part because more women than ever were in college and more than one in three married women worked outside the home, where they often faced discrimination and harassment. Yet the social model and domestic ideal for most remained marriage and motherhood. In 1963, Betty Friedan, a journalist, mother, and graduate of Smith College, challenged the model and ideal directly in *The Feminine Mystique*, which portrayed the suburbs as "comfortable concentration camps" where women were imprisoned and denied the opportunity to use their education and talents. The following year, the Civil Rights Act included an amendment—Title VII—which barred discrimination on the basis of sex as well as race. In 1966, Friedan and others formed the National Association for Women (NOW), which would become the main organization of liberal feminists.

The NOW Statement of Purpose declared that "the time has come for a new movement toward true equality for all women in America, and toward a fully equal partnership of the sexes." It also stated that "the time has come to confront, with concrete action, the conditions that now prevent women from enjoying the equality of opportunity and freedom of choice which is their right as individual Americans, and as human beings."[82] The basic premise of liberal feminism was that men and women shared a common humanity, that the similarities of men and women outweighed their differences. Accordingly, outside the home women should enjoy equal opportunity and receive equal pay for equal work, while inside the home men should treat their wives as equal partners and assume equal responsibility for cooking, cleaning, and childcare.

Conservatives—especially traditionalists—objected to both the premise and the conclusion. The biological differences between men and women outweighed the similarities. Their abilities and interests also differed. Therefore men should assume the role of primary breadwinner and women should embrace the role of primary caregiver, especially to children who were the future and most needed the nurturing that only mothers could provide. Few conservatives were completely opposed to women working for wages outside the home, especially as stagnant wages for male breadwinners made two incomes an economic necessity for most middle-class families. But inside the home the stability and success of the family, which was the bedrock of society, depended on women fulfilling their domestic duties as wives and mothers, while respecting their husbands as the ultimate authority in all matters, as the Bible and Christianity taught.

In the 1968 presidential election, law and order was the most important issue to the greatest number of white voters. The candidate who took the most extreme position was, not surprisingly, George Wallace, whose core followers consisted of Protestant Goldwater voters in the South and Catholic union members in the North, most of whom were on the lower margins of the middle class. The main cause of urban violence, he argued, was international communism, organized in the Soviet Union, aided by the Supreme Court, and abetted by "bearded beatnik bureaucrats" in Washington. The recommended response was the deliberate use of massive retaliation against rioters and protesters. "We don't have riots in Alabama," Wallace said at one rally. "[The] first one of 'em to pick up a brick gets a bullet in the brain, that's all. And then you walk over to the next one and say, 'All right, pick up a brick. We just want to see you pick up one of them bricks, now!'" If a riot began, he vowed to halt it by shooting arsonists and looters first, then asking questions later. One of his most popular lines was his promise that a demonstrator who laid down in front of his car once would never do it again.

The liberal candidate was Democratic nominee Hubert Humphrey, who promised to provide Americans with "order and justice" by attacking the root causes of crime. "There are two kinds of politics," the vice president said. "There is the politics of fear and despair, which I do not indulge in, and then there is the politics of hope and inspiration. That is more my kind." Unfortunately for him, his kind of politics had little appeal amid the chaos and confusion of 1968. Voters wanted firmness and reassurance, and although Humphrey repeatedly tried to show voters that he understood their fears, he rarely could find the right words or tone.

The conservative candidate was Republican nominee Richard Nixon, who pledged to restore order without violence by providing moral leadership and trimming social programs. He also promised to nominate conservative justices to the Supreme Court. Nixon stated that the "wave of crime is not going to be the wave of the future" and added that "the first civil right of every American is to be free from domestic violence." (See document 7.) The terms of debate had changed little since 1964. But the loss of social order had transformed the political climate. Despite a late surge by Humphrey, Nixon won by a narrow margin, comparable to what he had lost by in 1960.

Nevertheless, the victory for conservatism was significant. In 1964, Johnson had received more than 60 percent of the popular vote. In 1968, Nixon and Wallace had received almost 57 percent of the popular vote (the latter received more than 13 percent, the best showing by a third-party candidate since 1924, and carried the Deep South as well as Arkansas). More than twelve million voters, overwhelmingly white, had either abstained or defected from the Democrats to the Republicans. Nixon had reversed the results of 1964 in large part because a "silent majority" of white Americans believed that, unlike the liberals, conservatives could and would restore a society of authority, stability, and security. At last the social disorder of the past four years would come to an end.

Nixon would soon disappoint them. In July 1972, burglars with links to his reelection campaign were arrested in Democratic National Committee headquarters in the Watergate building. While there is no firm evidence that Nixon was aware of the break-in before it happened, there is clear proof—on the notorious tapes made in the Oval Office—that he immediately orchestrated a cover up of involvement by White House aides. For the next two years, the president used the powers of his office to obstruct investigations by the Senate Watergate Committee and Special Prosecutor Archibald Cox, whom the president fired during an infamous "Saturday Night Massacre" in October 1973. When the Supreme Court denied Nixon's claim of executive privilege and demanded that he produce the tapes, he had little choice. In August 1974, facing almost certain impeachment in the House followed by likely conviction in the Senate and removal from office, Nixon became the first president in history to resign.

Liberals saw Watergate as a constitutional crisis. Nixon had defied the legislative and judicial branches of the federal government in violation of the balance of powers. He had ordered the CIA to impede an FBI investigation and the IRS to harass his critics. He had violated his oath and obstructed justice. Liberals believed that Nixon's personality was partly to blame—he saw politics as a form of warfare and his opponents as enemies. He always sought to divide and conquer—his instinct was never to compromise—and ultimately his demons destroyed him. But liberals also saw Watergate as a logical outgrowth of the Cold War, which for three decades had placed a premium on executive power and secrecy. In a sense, then, Watergate was the inevitable outcome of the "imperial presidency."

Conservatives saw Watergate as a constitutional coup. Liberals had used the media to remove from office a leader who had carried forty-nine of fifty states in the election two years earlier and reflected what the people wanted. "The media storm over Watergate," declared *National Review*, "is not so much a natural reaction to the facts on view, but rather resembles the artificial storm flicked on by throwing a switch in a wind-tunnel. The point, of course, is to try to undo the results of the 1968 and 1972 elections . . . "[83] According to most conservatives, what Nixon had done was typical in electoral politics, where everyone was guilty of dirty tricks. At worst he had shown excessive loyalty to aides, who had failed to serve him well. Moreover, any steps Nixon had taken were justified. Domestic turmoil—protests and demonstrations—threatened the social order. In response to a real and serious threat, Nixon had reacted with excessive but understandable measures, perhaps because he saw the social crisis in the United States as beyond the reach of normal politics.

The impact of Watergate was mixed. In the short term, it stigmatized conservatives and revitalized liberals, who captured a slew of seats in Congress in 1974. Then in 1976 the Democrats reclaimed the White House when former Georgia Governor Jimmy Carter narrowly defeated Gerald Ford, who had signed his political death warrant when he pardoned Nixon, the man who had appointed him vice president. In the long term, Watergate contributed significantly to the continuing erosion of public faith in government and politicians, whether measured by polling data or voter turnout. In that respect, it may have strengthened the conservative cause and given the liberal camp false hope. Watergate also contributed to three decades of increasingly bitter partisan strife and a cycle of crisis in which many conservatives viewed the Clinton impeachment in 1998 as political payback. Finally, some felt that Watergate led to unfair and unconstitutional restrictions on the executive branch. In the George W. Bush administration, one such conservative was Vice President Dick Cheney, who had served briefly in the Nixon administration and strongly objected to the idea of restrictions on the power of the president in wartime.

Ironically, Nixon had risen to the White House on the appeal of law and order. But his fall should not disguise the important and lasting consequences of the issue. Law and order enhanced the popular appeal of conservatism and eroded the political viability of liberalism. It also enabled many Americans to make sense of a chaotic world filled with street crime, civil unrest, cultural change, and campus demonstrations. Above all, the issue demonstrated how widespread the anxiety over the loss of social order was. The legacy of law and order was a political arena in which grim expectations displaced grand ambitions.

CONCLUSION

The debates of the 1960s remain a defining feature in American politics. How one views the decade often reveals or determines how one views contemporary issues. Liberals believe that the 1960s was a decade of dreams, some realized and some not, which nonetheless brought badly needed and long-overdue change, especially for minorities and women. America is now a better place as a result. By contrast, conservatives believe that the 1960s was a nightmare decade, when the country took a wrong turn and abandoned traditional values. America is now a worse place as a result. As Bill Clinton, whom conservatives often depicted as the pot-smoking, draft-dodging embodiment of counterculture values, noted after his presidency, "If you look back on the 1960s and think there was more good than harm, you're probably a Democrat. If you think there was more harm than good, you're probably a Republican."[84]

In the 1960s, individuals frequently felt they were remaking society—and making history in the process. In his memoir, the radical activist turned liberal politician Tom Hayden wrote that "Times filled with tragedy are also time of greatness and wonder, times that really matter, and times truly worth living through." For him the decade was a transformative era, comparable only to the American Revolution and the Civil War.[85] He was not the only person to see similarities between the 1960s and the 1860s. As the conservative commentator George Will observed, "So powerful were—are—the energies let loose in the sixties there cannot be now, and may never be, anything like a final summing-up. After all, what is the final result of the Civil War? It is too soon to say."[86] Will is right. The "final result" of the 1960s remains ambiguous at best.

In electoral terms, the conservatives seemed victorious as of 2004. The emergence of the Christian Right in the 1970s and the popularity of Ronald Reagan in the 1980s enabled the New Right to take control of Congress by the middle of the 1990s. The conservative agenda was, in effect, to remove as many traces of the 1960s as possible. As the new Speaker of the House, Georgia Congressman Newt Gingrich, declared in 1994, "There are profound things that went wrong starting with the Great Society and the counterculture. . . . We simply need to erase the slate and start over."[87] Since 1968 only two Democrats, neither of them staunch liberals, have occupied the White House—Jimmy Carter, who in 1976 had the benefit of public outrage over Watergate, and Bill Clinton, who in 1992 had the benefit of independent candidate Ross Perot on the ballot. Conservatives have also dominated the political discourse by denouncing high taxes and big government while extolling the free market and traditional morality.

Meanwhile, aside from the Internet the radical voice has virtually disappeared from American politics and the liberal voice has become fainter. Even the word liberal has become toxic, so much so that most candidates shun it and instead favor the term progressive. Liberal programs like Medicare and Social Security remain popular, but the Democratic coalition of southern whites, northern workers, farmers, intellectuals, and minorities that the New Deal forged in the 1930s has not recovered from the chaos of the 1960s, when it splintered and shattered, perhaps permanently. Even the emergence of new groups and causes, like gay rights, did not revive liberal prospects, which seemed dim until 2006, when the Democrats narrowly regained control of Congress.

Yet in social and cultural terms the outcome is less clear. The civil rights movement has stalled, but the black middle class has expanded and race relations have improved, albeit unevenly and unsteadily. At the very least, it is no longer publicly acceptable to express racist ideas, and opposition to interracial marriage has largely disappeared. Few women may choose to identify themselves as feminists, but feminist concerns like equal opportunity and equal pay are now widely accepted. Title VII of the 1964 Civil Rights Act has also contributed to a considerable improvement in the economic and legal status of women. And personal tolerance of alternative lifestyles, a core value of the counterculture, has grown. Millions of gay and lesbian Americans now openly express their sexual orientation, and although gay marriage has generated a political backlash, polls indicate that a majority of those under thirty have no objections, which suggests that even this bitter flashpoint in the "culture wars" may eventually fade.

In a sense, the principal values of the counterculture—tolerance, freedom, individuality—have become mainstream. In personal and sexual matters, self-expression has increasingly trumped self-denial. Liberals tend to celebrate this trend. "Only a few periods in American history have seen such a rich fulfillment of the informing ideals of personal freedom and creativity that lie at the heart of the American intellectual tradition," asserted *The New York Times* in 1994. The counterculture, it concluded, was "part of us, a legacy around which Americans can now unite, rather than allow themselves to be divided."[88]

This verdict was premature. Most conservatives today vehemently reject any accommodation to the changes the counterculture of the 1960s has wrought. They equate social tolerance with cultural permissiveness and decry the harm it has supposedly wreaked on the family and society. Robert Bork, a law professor and failed nominee to the Supreme Court, spoke for many conservatives when in 1996 he declared, "There is no possibility that Americans will unite around that legacy. Those of us who regard the Sixties as a disaster are not 'allowing' ourselves to be divided; we insist upon it." According to Bork, the 1960s led to "an explosion of drug use and sexual promiscuity; it was a decade of hedonism and narcissism; it was a decade in which popular culture reached new lows of vulgarity."[89] It also contributed to a significant increase in abortion, which many conservatives saw and see as the most critical moral issue facing the nation. At bottom Bork and others maintain that American society is more violent, coarse, and explicit as a consequence of the 1960s.

Of course, many liberals, especially parents, hold a similarly negative view of contemporary culture as displayed on television, radio, or the Internet. But they tend to see the changes as due mostly to economic forces. In their view the counterculture deserves neither the primary credit nor the blame for the degradation of popular culture. Instead, the main fault rests with the free market, which promotes whatever sells, namely sex and violence. Therefore liberals often emphasize the social responsibility of corporate executives, although they concede that the rampant materialism of American consumers is also at fault. By contrast, conservatives stress personal responsibility, although they have also organized boycotts of networks that produce objectionable programs and companies that provide advertising sponsorship.

The debates of the 1960s remain as contested and controversial as the legacies. For instance, the War on Poverty is still a matter of some dispute, in large part because the outcome bears directly on policy issues like welfare reform. Liberals contend that the war was not won because it was never fought. Programs like Head Start made a difference for many—and could have served many more if the government had committed the resources required. By contrast, conservatives assert that the War on Poverty was fought and lost. Billions were spent and, in the end, the social problems were worse—more welfare dependency, more family disintegration, more teen pregnancy, more street crime.

In 2003, the invasion of Iraq refocused attention on Vietnam and led to frequent comparisons of the two wars, especially by liberals. Both began after murky allegations by the White House, whether it was the Gulf of Tonkin incident or the weapons of mass destruction Iraqi dictator Saddam Hussein was alleged to have. Both conflicts also began with great ambitions and unrealistic expectations—to stop the spread of communism or terrorism and bring democracy to oppressed peoples who would welcome U.S. intervention. And both began with no real understanding of the costs or consequences involved in fighting a civil and guerrilla war in a part of the world where the United States had little historical or cultural experience. Finally, both wars began with no exit strategy—no objective way to declare victory and depart until the governments of South Vietnam or Iraq were able, if ever, to handle matters on their own.

Conservatives since 2003 have usually rejected the analogy as outlined above. In their view Vietnam was a "noble cause," as President Reagan put it, and the proper lesson to draw was that the United States must avoid a premature retreat in Iraq. National security demanded that the United States "stay the course" and not "cut and run" in the face of international threats, whether in the form of communism or terrorism. Vietnam was also an unhealthy cancer in the sense that it had weakened national pride and power. In particular, it had weakened the power of the presidency, which conservatives like Vice President Dick Cheney were determined to restore. What was critical was that the United States display unity, not weakness, which might encourage the nation's enemies and discourage the nation's allies. In that context, patriotism was paramount—the country could not afford the divisive domestic debates that Vietnam had engendered.

Liberals typically embraced the analogy. In their view Vietnam was a tragic mistake, and it was imperative that the United States avoid a similar quagmire in Iraq. They had hoped that Vietnam would act as a healthy corrective to American arrogance and hubris, to the belief the United States could arrange the affairs of other nations, but it appeared that the antidote was temporary. Liberals also feared that another lengthy and costly foreign war would deflect attention and resources from domestic needs, such as health care. And it would renew the bitter controversy over civil liberties versus national security, while harming America's reputation in the international community. Finally, liberals raised alarms about the dramatic expansion of executive power and the possible return of the "imperial presidency," which Vietnam and Watergate had seemingly discredited.

The debates of the 1960s thus continue to cast a large shadow over American politics and society today. Perhaps no other decade in the twentieth century has had such a decisive and divisive impact. Novelist William Faulkner once wrote, "The past is not dead. It's not even past."[90] That is certainly the case with the 1960s. And it is probably the only point of agreement between liberals and conservatives, who still dispute the legacies of the era. In the twenty-first century, the debates of the 1960s will undoubtedly rage for the foreseeable future. When they will end only time will tell.

NOTES

I wish to thank Vincent Cannato, Donald Critchlow, Michael Kazin, James Patterson, Jonathan Schoenwald, David Stebenne, and Tim Thurber for their constructive comments and criticisms. Paul Burnam offered invaluable research assistance. I also wish to thank Columbia University Press for permission to use excerpts from *Law and Order: Street Crime, Civil Unrest, and the Crisis of Liberalism in the 1960s*, by Michael W. Flamm, copyright © 2005 Columbia University Press. Unless otherwise noted, the sources for all quotations can be found in that book or in the *Public Papers of the Presidents of the United States*.

1. Frank S. Meyer, "Hope for the '60s," *National Review*, 14 January 1961, 19.

2. Quoted in John A. Andrew III, *The Other Side of the Sixties: Young Americans for Freedom and the Rise of Conservative Politics* (New Brunswick: Rutgers University Press, 1997), 76.

3. Lionel Trilling, *The Liberal Imagination: Essays on Literature and Society* (New York: Viking Press, 1950), ix.

4. Russell Kirk, *The Conservative Mind: From Burke to Santayana* (Chicago: Regnery, 1953), 7–8.

5. William F. Buckley, Jr., "The Magazine's Credenda," *National Review*, 19 November 1955, 6.

6. Quoted in Andrew, *The Other Side of the Sixties*, 127.

7. Buckley, "The Young Americans for Freedom," *National Review*, 24 September 1960, 172.

8. Quoted in Mary C. Brennan, *Turning Right in the Sixties: The Conservative Capture of the GOP* (Chapel Hill: University of North Carolina Press, 1995), 63.

9. "National Review and the 1960 Elections," *National Review*, 22 October 1960, 233.

10. Quoted in Andrew, *The Other Side of the Sixties*, 7.

11. James T. Patterson, *Grand Expectations: The United States, 1945–1974* (New York: Oxford University Press, 1996), 558–60.

12. Ronald Reagan, *National Review*, 1 December 1964, 1055.

13. For the continuity interpretation, see among others Donald T. Critchlow, *Phyllis Schlafly and Grassroots Conservatism: A Woman's Crusade* (Princeton: Princeton University Press, 2005). For the change interpretation, see among others Brennan, *Turning Right in the Sixties*; Jonathan M. Schoenwald, *A Time for Choosing: The Rise of Modern American Conservatism* (New York: Oxford University Press, 2001); and Lisa McGirr, *Suburban Warriors: The Origins of the New American Right* (Princeton: Princeton University Press, 2001).

14. Quoted in Andrew, *The Other Side of the Sixties*, 5.

15. Quoted in Patterson, *Grand Expectations*, 531.

16. Quoted in McGirr, *Suburban Warriors*, 106.

17. Patterson, *Grand Expectations*, 538.

18. Buckley, "Mr. Goodwin's Great Society," *National Review*, 6 June 1964, 760.

19. Bulletin, *National Review*, 27 April 1965, 1.

20. James T. Patterson, *America's Struggle Against Poverty, 1900–1980* (Cambridge: Harvard University Press, 1981), 145.

21. Bulletin, *National Review*, 2 August 1966, 1.

22. Kurt Schuparra, "'A Great White Light': The Political Emergence of Ronald Reagan," in *The Conservative Sixties*, ed. David Farber and Jeff Roche (New York: Peter Lang, 2003), 104.

23. Quoted in Critchlow, *Phyllis Schlafly and Grassroots Conservatism*, 93.

24. Bulletin, *National Review*, 15 October 1968, B161.

25. http://www.cnn.com/SPECIALS/cold.war/episodes/10/interviews/sorensen/

26. "Cuba, RIP," *National Review*, 6 May 1961, 269.

27. Barry M. Goldwater, *With No Apologies: The Personal and Political Memoirs of United States Senator Barry M. Goldwater* (New York: William Morrow Company, 1979), 138–41.

28. Quoted in Andrew, *The Other Side of the Sixties*, 144.

29. "Has Cuba Defeated Us?" *National Review*, 25 September 1962, 217.

30. Quoted in Gregory L. Schneider, *Cadres for Conservatism: Young Americans for Freedom and the Rise of the Contemporary Right* (New York: New York University Press, 1999), 67–68.

31. James Burnham, "Is Disarmament Possible?" *National Review*, 30 January 1960, 67.

32. Quoted in Goldwater, *With No Apologies*, 133.

33. "At Home," *National Review*, 25 March 1969, B182.

34. Quoted in Rebecca E. Klatch, *A Generation Divided: The New Left, the New Right, and the 1960s* (Berkeley: University of California Press, 1999), 103.

35. Burnham, "What Chance in Vietnam?" *National Review*, 8 October 1963, 304.

36. "The American Way of Death," *National Review*, 19 November 1963, 424.

37. Burnham, "Laos and Containment," *National Review*, 8 April 1961, 213.

38. Quoted in Kenneth J. Heineman, *Campus Wars* (New York: New York University Press, 1993), 146.

39. Bulletin, *National Review*, 16 March 1965, 1.

40. J. William Fulbright, "The Great Society Is a Sick Society," *New York Times Magazine*, 20 August 1967, in *The 1960s: Opposing Viewpoints*, ed. William Dudley (San Diego: Greenhaven Press, 1997), 98–106.

41. Bulletin, *National Review*, 26 April 1966, 1.

42. Quoted in Christian G. Appy, *Working-Class War: American Combat Soldiers & Vietnam* (Chapel Hill: University of North Carolina Press, 1993), 42.

43. James W. Graham, "The Score for the Tet Match," *National Review*, 12 March 1968, 226.

44. Jeff Roche, "Cowboy Conservatism," in *The Conservative Sixties*, ed. Farber and Roche, 89.

45. "Notes and Comment," *New Yorker*, 20 December 1969, cited in James S. Olson and Randy Roberts, *My Lai: A Brief History with Documents* (New York: Bedford Books, 1998), 174.

46. "The Great Atrocity Hunt," *National Review*, 16 December 1969, 1253.

47. "Now Is the Time for All Good Men To Come to the Aid of Their President," *National Review*, 19 May 1970, 501.

48. M. Stanton Evans, "At Home," *National Review Bulletin*, 17 November 1972, B182.

49. Klatch, *A Generation Divided*, 226–28.

50. Meyer, "Libertarianism or Libertinism?" *National Review,* 9 September 1969, 910.

51. Patrick J. Buchanan, *Right from the Beginning* (Boston: Little, Brown & Co., 1988), 316.

52. Todd Gitlin, Afterword, in *Reassessing the Sixties: Debating the Political and Cultural Legacy,* ed. Stephen Macedo (New York: W.W. Norton & Company, 1997), 296.

53. Buchanan, *Right from the Beginning,* 305–06.

54. Allan Bloom, *The Closing of the American Mind* (New York: Simon & Schuster, 1987), 333–34.

55. Quoted in Klatch, *A Generation Divided,* 78.

56. Quoted in Patterson, *Grand Expectations,* 389.

57. Bulletin, *National Review,* 19 March 1960, 1.

58. Buckley, "Why the South Must Prevail," *National Review,* 24 August 1957, 148–49.

59. Bulletin, *National Review,* 16 October 1962, 1.

60. Buckley, "Birmingham and After," National Review, 21 May 1963, 397.

61. Quoted in Patrick Allitt, *Catholic Intellectuals and Conservative Politics in America, 1950–1985* (Ithaca: Cornell University Press, 1993), 116.

62. http://www.stanford.edu/group/King/publications/speeches/address_at_march_on_washington.pdf

63. "When the Plaints Go Marching In," *National Review,* 27 August 1963, 140.

64. Jerry Falwell, *Strength for the Journey: An Autobiography* (New York: Simon & Schuster, 1987), 290.

65. Quoted in Sara Diamond, *Roads to Dominion: Right-Wing Movements and Political Power in the United States* (New York: Guilford Press, 1995), 89.

66. Quoted in David Farber, "Democratic Subjects in the American Sixties: National Politics, Cultural Authenticity, and Community Interest," in *The Conservative Sixties,* ed. Farber and Roche, 10.

67. Meyer, "The Violence of Nonviolence," *National Review,* 20 April 1965, 327.

68. Buckley, "The Issue at Selma, *National Review,* 9 March 1965, 183.

69. Buckley, "Time for a Hiatus?" *National Review,* 18 October 1966, 1035; Frank S. Meyer, "The Negro Revolution—A New Phase," *National Review,* 4 October 1966, 998.

70. Quoted in Richard Kluger, *Simple Justice: The History of Brown v. Board of Education and Black America's Struggle for Equality* (New York: Alfred A. Knopf, 1976), 773.

71. Buchanan, *Right from the Beginning,* 284–85.

72. "The Thin Blue Line," *National Review,* 11 August 1964, 879.

73. Will Herberg, "Who Are the Guilty Ones?" *National Review,* 7 September 1965, 769–70.

74. Buckley, "Remarks to the NYPD Holy Name Society," *National Review* 20 April 1965, 326; Buckley, "Statement by Wm. F. Buckley Jr. Announcing His Candidacy for Mayor of New York, June 24, 1965," *National Review* 13 August 1965, 587.

75. Meyer, "Liberalism Run Riot," *National Review,* 26 March 1968, 283.

76. Russell Kirk, *The Sword of Imagination* (Grand Rapids, MI: William B. Eerdmans Publishing, 1995), 411.

77. "Anything Goes," *National Review,* 18 June 1968, 593.

78. Meyer, "The Right and Duty of Self-Defense," *National Review*, 17 May 1966, 471; "The Right of the People to Bear Arms," *National Review*, 2 July 1968, 657.

79. Burnham, "The Right to Riot," *National Review*, 8 October 1968, 1000; Meyer, "Richard Daley and the Will to Govern," *National Review*, 8 October 1968, 1015.

80. Margaret Mead, *Some Personal Views* (New York: Walker Press, 1979), in *The 1960s: Opposing Viewpoints*, ed. William Dudley (San Diego: Greenhaven Press, 1997), 152–57.

81. William A. Rusher, "Mass Infantilism, Anyone?" *National Review*, 7 October 1969, 1012.

82. National Organization of Women, http://www.now.org/history/purpos66.html

83. "Watergate as Power Struggle," *National Review*, 6 July 1973, 721.

84. Stephen Kinzer, "Clinton, On the Road Again, Stumps for a Book, Not a Seat," *The New York Times*, 4 June 2004, A16.

85. Tom Hayden, *Reunion: A Memoir* (New York: Random House, 1988), 507.

86. George Will, Foreword, in *Reassessing the Sixties: Debating the Political and Cultural Legacy*, ed. Stephen Macedo (New York: W.W. Norton & Company, 1997), 8.

87. Quoted in Sheldon Wolin, "The Destructive Sixties and Postmodern Conservatism," in *Reassessing the Sixties*, ed. Macedo, 129.

88. "In Praise of the Counterculture," *New York Times*, 11 December 1994, Sec. 4, 14.

89. Robert H. Bork, *Slouching Towards Gomorrah: Modern Liberalism and American Decline* (New York: HarperCollins, 1996), 35, 51.

90. William Faulkner, *Requiem for a Nun* (New York: Vintage Books, 1951), quoted in Maurice Isserman and Michael Kazin, *America Divided: The Civil War of the 1960s* (New York: Oxford University Press, 2000), 293.

Documents

1

THE SHARON STATEMENT
(SEPTEMBER 11, 1960)

In this time of moral and political crises, it is the responsibility of the youth of America to affirm certain eternal truths.

We, as young conservatives, believe:

That foremost among the transcendent values is the individual's use of his God-given free will, whence derives his right to be free from the restrictions of arbitrary force;

That liberty is indivisible, and that political freedom cannot long exist without economic freedom;

That the purpose of government is to protect those freedoms through the preservation of internal order, the provision of national defense, and the administration of justice;

That when government ventures beyond these rightful functions, it accumulates power, which tends to diminish order and liberty;

That the Constitution of the United States is the best arrangement yet devised for empowering government to fulfill its proper role, while restraining it from the concentration and abuse of power;

That the genius of the Constitution—the division of powers—is summed up in the clause that reserves primacy to the several states, or to the people, in those spheres not specifically delegated to the Federal government;

That the market economy, allocating resources by the free play of supply and demand, is the single economic system compatible with the requirements of personal freedom and constitutional government, and that it is at the same time the most productive supplier of human needs;

That when government interferes with the work of the market economy, it tends to reduce the moral and physical strength of the nation; that when it takes from one man to bestow on another, it diminishes the incentive of the first, the integrity of the second, and the moral autonomy of both;

That we will be free only so long as the national sovereignty of the United States is secure; that history shows periods of freedom are rare, and can exist only when free citizens concertedly defend their rights against all enemies;

That the forces of international Communism are, at present, the greatest single threat to these liberties;

That the United States should stress victory over, rather than coexistence with, this menace; and

That American foreign policy must be judged by this criterion: does it serve the just interests of the United States?

Source: Young Americans for Freedom (www.yaf.com/sharon.shtml)

2

PRINCIPLES OF THE JOHN BIRCH
SOCIETY (1962)

I

With very few exceptions the members of the John Birch Society are deeply religious people. A member's particular faith is entirely his own affair. Our hope is to make better Catholics, better Protestants, better Jews—or better Moslems—out of those who belong to the society. Our never-ending concern is with morality, integrity, and purpose. Regardless of the differences between us in creed and dogma, we all believe that man is endowed by a Divine Creator with an innate desire and conscious purpose to improve both his world and himself. We believe that the direction which constitutes improvement is clearly visible and identifiable throughout man's known history, and that this God-given upward reach in the heart of man is a composite conscience to which we all must listen.

II

We believe that the Communists seek to drive their slaves and themselves along exactly the opposite and downward direction, to the Satanic debasement of both man and his universe. We believe that communism is as utterly incompatible with all religion as it is contemptuous of all morality and destructive of all freedom. It is intrinsically evil. It must be opposed, therefore, with equal firmness, on religious grounds, moral grounds, and political grounds. We believe that the continued coexistence of communism and a Christian-style civilization on one planet is impossible. The struggle between them must end with one completely triumphant and the other completely destroyed. We intend to do our part, therefore, to halt, weaken, rout, and eventually to bury, the whole international Communist conspiracy.

III

We believe that means are as important as ends in any civilized society. Of all the falsehoods that have been so widely and deliberately circulated about us, none is so viciously untrue as the charge that we are willing to condone foul means for the sake of achieving praiseworthy ends. We think that communism as a way of life, for instance, is completely wrong; but our ultimate quarrel with the Communists is that they insist on imposing that way of life on the rest of us by murder, treason, and cruelty rather than by persuasion. Even if our own use of force ever becomes necessary and morally acceptable because it is in self-defense, we must never lose sight of the legal, traditional, and humanitarian considerations of a compassionate civilization. The Communists recognize no such compulsions, but this very ingredient of amoral brutishness will help to destroy them in the end.

IV

We believe in patriotism. Most of us will gladly concede that a parliament of nations, designed for the purpose of increasing the freedom and ease with which individuals, ideals, and goods might cross national boundaries, would be desirable. And we hope that in some future decade we may help to bring about such a step of progress in man's pursuit of peace, prosperity, and happiness. But we feel that the present United Nations was designed by its founders for the exactly opposite purpose of increasing the rigidity of government controls over the lives and affairs of individual men. We believe it has become, as it was intended to become, a major instrumentality for the establishment of a one-world Communist tyranny over the population of the whole earth. One of our most immediate objectives, therefore, is to get the United States out of the United Nations, and the United Nations out of the United States. We seek thus to save our own country from the gradual and piecemeal surrender of its sovereignty to this Communist-controlled supergovernment, and to stop giving our support to the steady enslavement of other people through the machinations of this Communist agency.

V

We believe that a constitutional republic, such as our founding fathers gave us, is probably the best of all forms of government. We believe that a democracy, which they tried hard to obviate, and into which the liberals have been trying for fifty years to convert our republic, is one of the worst of all forms of government. We call attention to the fact that up to 1928 the U.S. Army Training Manual still gave our men in uniform the following quite accurate definition, which would have been thoroughly approved by the Constitutional Convention that established our republic. "Democracy: A government of the masses. Authority derived through mass meeting or any form of direct expression results in mobocracy. Attitude toward property is communistic—negating property rights. Attitude toward law is that the will of the majority shall regulate, whether it be based upon deliberation or governed by passion, prejudice, and impulse, without restraint or regard to consequences. Results in demagogism, license, agitation, discontent, anarchy." It is because all history proves this to be true that we repeat so emphatically: "This is a republic, not a democracy; let's keep it that way."

VI

We are opposed to collectivism as a political and economic system, even when it does not have the police-state features of communism. We are opposed to it no matter whether the collectivism be called socialism or the welfare state or the New Deal or the Fair Deal or the New Frontier, or advanced under some other semantic disguise. And we are opposed to it no matter what may be the framework or form of government under which collectivism is imposed. We believe that increasing the size of government, increasing the centralization of government, and increasing the functions of government all act as brakes on material progress and as destroyers of personal freedom.

VII

We believe that even where the size and functions of government are properly limited, as much of the power and duties of government as possible should be retained in the hands of as small governmental units as possible, as close to the people served by such units as possible. For the tendencies of any governing body to waste, expansion, and despotism all increase with the distance of that body from the people governed; the more closely any governing body can be kept under observation by those who pay its bills and provide its delegated authority, the more honestly responsible it will be. And the diffusion of governmental power and functions is one of the greatest safeguards against tyranny man has yet devised. For this reason it is extremely important in our case to keep our township, city, county and state governments from being bribed and coerced into coming under one direct chain of control from Washington.

VIII

We believe that for any people eternal vigilance is the price of liberty far more as against the insidious encroachment of internal tyranny than against the danger of subjugation from the outside or from the prospect of any sharp and decisive revolution. In a republic we must constantly seek to elect and to keep in power a government we can trust, manned by people we can trust, maintaining a currency we can trust, and working for purposes we can trust (none of which we have today). We think it is even more important for the government to obey the laws than for the people to do so. But for thirty years we have had a steady stream of governments which increasingly have regarded our laws and even our Constitution as mere pieces of paper, which should not be allowed to stand in the way of what they, in their omniscient benevolence, considered to be "for the greatest good of the greatest number." (Or in their power-seeking plans pretended so to believe.) We want a restoration of a "government of laws, and not of men" in this country; and if a few impeachments are necessary to bring that about, then we are all for the impeachments.

IX

We believe that in a general way history repeats itself. For any combination of causes, similar to an earlier combination of causes, will lead as a rule to a combination of results somewhat similar to the one produced before. And history is simply a series of causes which produced results, and so on around cycles as clearly discernible as any of the dozens that take place elsewhere in the physical and biological sciences. But we believe that the most important history consists not of the repetitions but of the changes in these recurring links in the series. For the changes mark the extent to which man has either been able to improve himself and his environment, or has allowed both to deteriorate, since the last time around. We think that this true history is largely determined by ambitious individuals (both good and evil) and by small minorities who really know what they want. And in the John Birch Society our sense of gratitude and responsibility (to God and to the noble men of the past), for what we have inherited makes us determined to exert our influence, labor, and sacrifice for changes which we think will constitute improvement.

X

In summary, we are striving, by all honorable means at our disposal and to the limits of our energies and abilities, to bring about less government, more responsibility, and a better world. Because the Communists seek, always and everywhere, to bring about more government, less individual responsibility, and a completely amoral world, we would have to oppose them at every turn, even on the philosophical level. Because they are seeking through a gigantically organized conspiracy to destroy all opposition, we must fight them even more aggressively on the plane of action. But our struggle with the Communists, while the most urgent and important task before us today, is basically only incidental to our more important long-range and constructive purposes. For that very reason we are likely to be more effective against the Communists than if we were merely an ad hoc group seeking to expose and destroy so huge and powerful a gang of criminals. In organization, dedication, and purpose we offer a new form of opposition to the Communists which they have not faced in any other country. We have tried to raise a standard to which the wise and the honest can repair. We welcome all honorable allies in this present unceasing war. And we hope that once they and we and millions like us have won a decisive victory at last, many of these same allies will join us in our long look toward the future.

Source: *Congressional Record, App.*, 87 Cong., 2 Sess., pp. A4292–A4293

3

EXCERPTS FROM JOHN F. KENNEDY'S COMMENCEMENT ADDRESS, AMERICAN UNIVERSITY (JUNE 10, 1963)

I have . . . chosen this time and place to discuss a topic on which ignorance too often abounds and the truth too rarely perceived. And that is the most important topic on earth: peace. What kind of peace do I mean and what kind of a peace do we seek? Not a Pax Americana enforced on the world by American weapons of war. Not the peace of the grave or the security of the slave. I am talking about genuine peace, the kind of peace that makes life on earth worth living, and the kind that enables men and nations to grow, and to hope, and build a better life for their children—not merely peace for Americans but peace for all men and women, not merely peace in our time but peace in all time.

I speak of peace because of the new face of war. Total war makes no sense in an age where great powers can maintain large and relatively invulnerable nuclear forces and refuse to surrender without resort to those forces. It makes no sense in an age where a single nuclear weapon contains almost ten times the explosive force delivered by all the allied air forces in the Second World War. It makes no sense in an age when the deadly poisons produced by a nuclear exchange would be carried by wind and water and soil and seed to the far corners of the globe and to generations yet unborn.

Today the expenditure of billions of dollars every year on weapons acquired for the purpose of making sure we never need them is essential to the keeping of peace. But surely the acquisition of such idle stockpiles—which can only destroy and never create—is not the only, much less the most efficient, means of assuring peace. I speak of peace, therefore, as the necessary, rational end of rational men. I realize the pursuit of peace is not as dramatic as the pursuit of war, and frequently the words of the pursuers fall on deaf ears. But we have no more urgent task.

Some say that it is useless to speak of peace or world law or world disarmament, and that it will be useless until the leaders of the Soviet Union adopt a more enlightened attitude. I hope they do. I believe we can help them do it. But I also believe that we must reexamine our own attitudes, as individuals and as a Nation, for our attitude is as essential as theirs. And every graduate of this school, every thoughtful citizen who despairs of war and wishes to bring peace, should begin by looking inward, by examining his own attitude towards the possibilities of peace, towards the Soviet Union, towards the course of the cold war and towards freedom and peace here at home.

First examine our attitude towards peace itself. Too many of us think it is impossible. Too many think it is unreal. But that is a dangerous, defeatist belief. It leads to the conclusion that war is inevitable, that mankind is doomed, that we are gripped by forces we cannot control. We need not accept that view. Our problems are manmade; therefore, they can be solved by man. And man can be as big as he wants. No problem of human destiny is beyond human beings. Man's reason and spirit have often solved the seemingly unsolvable, and we believe they can do it again. I am not referring to the absolute, infinite concept of universal peace and good will of which some fantasies and fanatics dream. I do not deny the value of hopes and dreams but we merely invite discouragement and incredulity by making that our only and immediate goal.

Let us focus instead on a more practical, more attainable peace, based not on a sudden revolution in human nature but on a gradual evolution in human institutions—on a series of concrete actions and effective agreements which are in the interest of all concerned. There is no single, simple key to this peace; no grand or magic formula to be adopted by one or two powers. Genuine peace must be the product of many nations, the sum of many acts. It must be dynamic, not static, changing to meet the challenge of each new generation. For peace is a process—a way of solving problems.

With such a peace, there will still be quarrels and conflicting interests, as there are within families and nations. World peace, like community peace, does not require that each man love his neighbor, it requires only that they live together in mutual tolerance, submitting their disputes to a just and peaceful settlement. And history teaches us that enmities between nations, as between individuals, do not last forever. However fixed our likes and dislikes may seem, the tide of time and events will often bring surprising changes in the relations between nations and neighbors. So let us persevere. Peace need not be impracticable, and war need not be inevitable. By defining our goal more clearly, by making it seem more manageable and less remote, we can help all people to see it, to draw hope from it, and to move irresistibly towards it.

And second, let us reexamine our attitude towards the Soviet Union. It is discouraging to think that their leaders may actually believe what their propagandists write. It is discouraging to read a recent, authoritative Soviet text on military strategy and find, on page after page, wholly baseless and incredible claims, such as the allegation that American imperialist circles are preparing to unleash different types of war, that there is a very real threat of a preventive war being unleashed by American imperialists against the Soviet Union . . .

Yet it is sad to read these Soviet statements, to realize the extent of the gulf between us. But it is also a warning, a warning to the American people not to fall into the same trap as the Soviets, not to see only a distorted and desperate view of the other side, not to see conflict as inevitable, accommodation as impossible, and communication as nothing more than an exchange of threats.

No government or social system is so evil that its people must be considered as lacking in virtue. As Americans, we find communism profoundly repugnant as a negation of personal freedom and dignity. But we can still hail the Russian people for their many achievements in science and space, in economic and industrial growth, in culture, in acts of courage.

Among the many traits the peoples of our two countries have in common, none is stronger than our mutual abhorrence of war. Almost unique among the major world powers, we have never been at war with each other. And no nation in the history of battle ever suffered more than the Soviet Union in the Second World War. At least 20 million lost their lives. Countless millions of homes and families were burned or sacked. A third of the nation's territory, including two-thirds of its industrial base, was turned into a wasteland—a loss equivalent to the destruction of this country east of Chicago.

Today, should total war ever break out again—no matter how—our two countries will be the primary target. It is an ironic but accurate fact that the two strongest powers are the two in the most danger of devastation. All we have built, all we have worked for, would be destroyed in the first 24 hours. And even in the cold war, which brings burdens and dangers to so many countries, including this Nation's closest allies, our two countries bear the heaviest burdens. For we are both devoting massive sums of money to weapons that could be better devoted to combat ignorance, poverty, and disease. We are both caught up in a vicious and dangerous cycle, with suspicion on one side breeding suspicion on the other, and new weapons begetting counter-weapons. In short, both the United States and its allies, and the Soviet Union and its allies, have a mutually deep interest in a just and genuine peace and in halting the arms race. Agreements to this end are in the interests of the Soviet Union as well as ours. And even the most hostile nations can be relied upon to accept and keep those treaty obligations, and only those treaty obligations, which are in their own interest.

So let us not be blind to our differences, but let us also direct attention to our common interests and the means by which those differences can be resolved. And if we cannot end now our differences, at least we can help make the world safe for diversity. For in the final analysis, our most basic common link is that we all inhabit this small planet. We all breathe the same air. We all cherish our children's futures. And we are all mortal.

Third, let us reexamine our attitude towards the cold war, remembering we're not engaged in a debate, seeking to pile up debating points. We are not here distributing blame or pointing the finger of judgment. We must deal with the world as it is, and not as it might have been had the history of the last 18 years been different. We must, therefore, persevere in the search for peace in the hope that constructive changes within the Communist bloc might bring within reach solutions which now seem beyond us. We must conduct our affairs in such a way that it becomes in the Communists' interest to agree on a genuine peace. And above all, while defending our own vital interests, nuclear powers must avert those confrontations which bring an adversary to a choice of either a humiliating retreat or a nuclear war. To adopt that kind of course in the nuclear age would be evidence only of the bankruptcy of our policy—or of a collective death-wish for the world.

To secure these ends, America's weapons are nonprovocative, carefully controlled, designed to deter, and capable of selective use. Our military forces are committed to peace and disciplined in self-restraint. Our diplomats are instructed to avoid unnecessary irritants and purely rhetorical hostility. For we can seek a relaxation of tensions without relaxing our guard. And, for our part, we do not need to use threats to prove we are resolute. We do not need to jam foreign broadcasts out of fear our faith will be eroded. We are unwilling to impose our system on any unwilling people, but we are willing and able to engage in peaceful competition with any people on earth.

Meanwhile, we seek to strengthen the United Nations, to help solve its financial problems, to make it a more effective instrument for peace, to develop it into a genuine world security system—a system capable of resolving disputes on the basis of law, of insuring the security of the large and the small, and of creating conditions under which arms can finally be abolished. At the same time we seek to keep peace inside the non-Communist world, where many nations, all of them our friends, are divided over issues which weaken Western unity, which invite Communist intervention, or which threaten to erupt into war. . . .

Speaking of other nations, I wish to make one point clear. We are bound to many nations by alliances. Those alliances exist because our concern and theirs substantially overlap. Our commitment to defend Western Europe and West Berlin, for example, stands undiminished because of the identity of our vital interests. The United States will make no deal with the Soviet Union at the expense of other nations and other peoples, not merely because they are our partners, but also because their interests and ours converge. Our interests converge, however, not only in defending the frontiers of freedom, but in pursuing the paths of peace. It is our hope, and the purpose of allied policy, to convince the Soviet Union that she, too, should let each nation choose its own future, so long as that choice does not interfere with the choices of others. The Communist drive to impose their political and economic system on others is the primary cause of world tension today. For there can be no doubt that if all nations could refrain from interfering in the self-determination of others, the peace would be much more assured.

This will require a new effort to achieve world law, a new context for world discussions. It will require increased understanding between the Soviets and ourselves. And increased understanding will require increased contact and communication. One step in this direction is the proposed arrangement for a direct line between Moscow and Washington, to avoid on each side the dangerous delays, misunderstandings, and misreadings of others' actions which might occur at a time of crisis.

We have also been talking in Geneva about our first-step measures of arm[s] controls designed to limit the intensity of the arms race and reduce the risk of accidental war. Our primary long range interest in Geneva, however, is general and complete disarmament, designed to take place by stages, permitting parallel political developments to build the new institutions of peace which would take the place of arms. The pursuit of disarmament has been an effort of this Government since the 1920's. It has been urgently sought by the past three administrations. And however dim the prospects are today, we intend to continue this effort—to continue it in order that all countries, including our own, can better grasp what the problems and possibilities of disarmament are.

The only major area of these negotiations where the end is in sight, yet where a fresh start is badly needed, is in a treaty to outlaw nuclear tests. The conclusion of such a treaty, so near and yet so far, would check the spiraling arms race in one of its most dangerous areas. It would place the nuclear powers in a position to deal more effectively with one of the greatest hazards which man faces in 1963, the further spread of nuclear arms. It would increase our security; it would decrease the prospects of war. Surely this goal is sufficiently important to require our steady pursuit, yielding neither to the temptation to give up the whole effort nor the temptation to give up our insistence on vital and responsible safeguards.

. . . [T]o make clear our good faith and solemn convictions on this matter, I now declare that the United States does not propose to conduct nuclear tests in the atmosphere so long as other states do not do so. We will not—We will not be the first to resume. Such a declaration is no substitute for a formal binding treaty, but I hope it will help us achieve one. Nor would such a treaty be a substitute for disarmament, but I hope it will help us achieve it.

Finally, my fellow Americans, let us examine our attitude towards peace and freedom here at home. The quality and spirit of our own society must justify and support our efforts abroad. We must show it in the dedication of our own lives—as many of you who are graduating today will have an opportunity to do, by serving without pay in the Peace Corps abroad or in the proposed National Service Corps here at home. But wherever we are, we must all, in our daily lives, live up to the age-old faith that peace and freedom walk together. In too many of our cities today, the peace is not secure because freedom is incomplete. It is the responsibility of the executive branch at all levels of government—local, State, and National—to provide and protect that freedom for all of our citizens by all means within our authority. It is the responsibility of the legislative branch at all levels, wherever the authority is not now adequate, to make it adequate. And it is the responsibility of all citizens in all sections of this country to respect the rights of others and respect the law of the land.

. . . All this is not unrelated to world peace. "When a man's way[s] please the Lord," the Scriptures tell us, "he maketh even his enemies to be at peace with him." And is not peace, in the last analysis, basically a matter of human rights: the right to live out our lives without fear of devastation; the right to breathe air as nature provided it; the right of future generations to a healthy existence?

While we proceed to safeguard our national interests, let us also safeguard human interests. And the elimination of war and arms is clearly in the interest of both. No treaty, however much it may be to the advantage of all, however tightly it may be worded, can provide absolute security against the risks of deception and evasion. But it can, if it is sufficiently effective in its enforcement, and it is sufficiently in the interests of its signers, offer far more security and far fewer risks than an unabated, uncontrolled, unpredictable arms race.

The United States, as the world knows, will never start a war. We do not want a war. We do not now expect a war. This generation of Americans has already had enough—more than enough—of war and hate and oppression.

We shall be prepared if others wish it. We shall be alert to try to stop it. But we shall also do our part to build a world of peace where the weak are safe and the strong are just. We are not helpless before that task or hopeless of its success. Confident and unafraid, we must labor on—not towards a strategy of annihilation but towards a strategy of peace.

Source: Public Papers of the Presidents of the United States: John F. Kennedy, 1963 (Washington, D.C.: Government Printing Office, 1964), pp. 459–64.

4

EXCERPTS FROM LYNDON B. JOHNSON'S COMMENCEMENT ADDRESS, UNIVERSITY OF MICHIGAN (MAY 22, 1964)

I have come today from the turmoil of your Capital to the tranquility of your campus to speak about the future of your country.

For a century we labored to settle and to subdue a continent. For half a century we called upon unbounded invention and untiring industry to create an order of plenty for all of our people.

The challenge of the next half century is whether we have the wisdom to use that wealth to enrich and elevate our national life, and to advance the quality of our American civilization.

Your imagination, your initiative, and your indignation will determine whether we build a society where progress is the servant of our needs, or a society where old values and new visions are buried under unbridled growth. For in your time we have the opportunity to move not only toward the rich society and the powerful society, but upward to the Great Society.

The Great Society rests on abundance and liberty for all. It demands an end to poverty and racial injustice, to which we are totally committed in our time. But that is just the beginning.

The Great Society is a place where every child can find knowledge to enrich his mind and to enlarge his talents. It is a place where leisure is a welcome chance to build and reflect, not a feared cause of boredom and restlessness.

It is a place where the city of man serves not only the needs of the body and the demands of commerce but the desire for beauty and the hunger for community.

It is a place where man can renew contact with nature. It is a place which honors creation for its own sake and for what it adds to the understanding of the race. It is a place where men are more concerned with the quality of their goals than the quantity of their goods.

But most of all, the Great Society is not a safe harbor, a resting place, a final objective, a finished work. It is a challenge constantly renewed, beckoning us toward a destiny where the meaning of our lives matches the marvelous products of our labor.

So I want to talk to you today about three places where we begin to build the Great Society—in our cities, in our countryside, and in our classrooms.

Many of you will live to see the day, perhaps 50 years from now, when there will be 400 million Americans—four-fifths of them in urban areas. In the remainder of this century urban population will double, city land will double, and we will have to build homes, highways, and facilities equal to all those built since this country was first settled. So in the next 40 years we must rebuild the entire urban United States.

The catalog of ills is long: there is the decay of the centers and the despoiling of the suburbs. There is not enough housing for our people or transportation for our traffic. Open land is vanishing and old landmarks are violated.

Our society will never be great until our cities are great. Today the frontier of imagination and innovation is inside those cities and not beyond their borders.

A second place where we begin to build the Great Society is in our countryside. We have always prided ourselves on being not only America the strong and America the free, but America the beautiful. Today that beauty is in danger. The water we drink, the food we eat, the very air that we breathe, are threatened with pollution. Our parks are overcrowded, our seashores overburdened. Green fields and dense forests are disappearing.

A few years ago we were greatly concerned about the "Ugly American." Today we must act to prevent an ugly America.

For once the battle is lost, once our natural splendor is destroyed, it can never be recaptured. And once man can no longer walk with beauty or wonder at nature his spirit will wither and his sustenance be wasted.

A third place to build the Great Society is in the classrooms of America. There your children's lives will be shaped. Our society will not be great until every young mind is set free to scan the farthest reaches of thought and imagination. We are still far from that goal.

Each year more than 100,000 high school graduates, with proved ability, do not enter college because they cannot afford it. And if we cannot educate today's youth, what will we do in 1970 when elementary school enrollment will be 5 million greater than 1960? And high school enrollment will rise by 5 million. College enrollment will increase by more than 3 million.

In many places, classrooms are overcrowded and curricula are outdated. Most of our qualified teachers are underpaid, and many of our paid teachers are unqualified. So we must give every child a place to sit and a teacher to learn from. Poverty must not be a bar to learning, and learning must offer an escape from poverty.

These are three of the central issues of the Great Society. While our Government has many programs directed at those issues, I do not pretend that we have the full answer to those problems.

The solution to these problems does not rest on a massive program in Washington, nor can it rely solely on the strained resources of local authority. They require us to create new concepts of cooperation, a creative federalism, between the National Capital and the leaders of local communities.

For better or for worse, your generation has been appointed by history to deal with those problems and to lead America toward a new age. You have the chance never before afforded to any people in any age. You can help build a society where the demands of morality, and the needs of the spirit, can be realized in the life of the Nation.

So, will you join in the battle to give every citizen the full equality which God enjoins and the law requires, whatever his belief, or race, or the color of his skin?

Will you join in the battle to give every citizen an escape from the crushing weight of poverty?

Will you join in the battle to build the Great Society, to prove that our material progress is only the foundation on which we will build a richer life of mind and spirit?

There are those timid souls who say this battle cannot be won; that we are condemned to a soulless wealth. I do not agree. We have the power to shape the civilization that we want. But we need your will, your labor, your hearts, if we are to build that kind of society.

Source: Public Papers of the Presidents of the United States: Lyndon B. Johnson, 1964 (Washington, D.C.: Government Printing Office, 1965), pp. 704–7.

5

EXCERPTS FROM BARRY GOLDWATER'S ACCEPTANCE SPEECH, REPUBLICAN NATIONAL CONVENTION (JULY 16, 1964)

. . . In this world no person, no party can guarantee anything, but what we can do and what we shall do is to deserve victory, and victory will be ours. The good Lord raised this mighty Republic to be a home for the brave and to flourish as the land of the free—not to stagnate in the swampland of collectivism, not to cringe before the bully of communism.

Now, my fellow Americans, the tide has been running against freedom. Our people have followed false prophets. We must, and we shall, return to proven ways—not because they are old, but because they are true.

We must, and we shall, set the tide running again in the cause of freedom. And this party, with its every action, every word, every breath, and every heartbeat, has but a single resolve, and that is freedom.

Freedom made orderly for this nation by our constitutional government. Freedom under a government limited by laws of nature and of nature's God. Freedom balanced so that liberty lacking order will not become the slavery of the prison cell; balanced so that liberty lacking order will not become the license of the mob and of the jungle.

Now, we Americans understand freedom; we have earned it, we have lived for it, and we have died for it. This nation and its people are freedom's models in a searching world. We can be freedom's missionaries in a doubting world.

But, ladies and gentlemen, first we must renew freedom's mission in our own hearts and in our own homes.

During four, futile years the administration which we shall replace has distorted and lost that faith. It has talked and talked and talked and talked the words of freedom, but it has failed and failed and failed in the works of freedom.

Now failure cements the wall of shame in Berlin; failures blot the sands of shame at the Bay of Pigs; failures marked the slow death of freedom in Laos; failures infest the jungles of Vietnam; and failures haunt the houses of our once great alliances and undermine the greatest bulwark ever erected by free nations, the NATO community.

Failures proclaim lost leadership, obscure purpose, weakening wills, and the risk of inciting our sworn enemies to new aggressions and to new excesses.

And because of this administration we are tonight a world divided. We are a nation becalmed. We have lost the brisk pace of diversity and the genius of individual creativity. We are plodding at a pace set by centralized planning, red tape, rules without responsibility, and regimentation without recourse.

Rather than useful jobs in our country, people have been offered bureaucratic make-work; rather than moral leadership, they have been given bread and circuses; they have been given spectacles, and, yes, they've even been given scandals.

Tonight there is violence in our streets, corruption in our highest offices, aimlessness among our youth, anxiety among our elderly; and there's a virtual despair among the many who look beyond material success toward the inner meaning of their lives. And where examples of morality, should be set, the opposite is seen. Small men seeking great wealth or power have too often and too long turned even the highest levels of public service into mere personal opportunity.

Now, certainly simple honesty is not too much to demand of men in government. We find it in most. Republicans demand it from everyone . . . no matter how exalted or protected his position might be.

The growing menace in our country tonight, to personal safety, to life, to limb and property, in homes, in churches, on the playgrounds and places of business, particularly in our great cities, is the mounting concern—or should be—of every thoughtful citizen in the United States. Security from domestic violence, no less than from foreign aggression, is the most elementary and fundamental purpose of any government, and a government that cannot fulfill this purpose is one that cannot long command the loyalty of its citizens.

History shows us, demonstrates that nothing, nothing prepares the way for tyranny more than the failure of public officials to keep the streets from bullies and marauders.

Now, we Republicans see all this as more—much more—than the rest: of mere political differences or mere political mistakes. We see this as the result of a fundamentally and absolutely wrong view of man, his nature and his destiny.

Those who seek to live your lives for you, to take your liberty in return for relieving you of yours, those who elevate the state and downgrade the citizen, must see ultimately a world in which earthly power can be substituted for divine will. And this nation was founded upon the rejection of that notion and upon the acceptance of God as the author of freedom.

Now, those who seek absolute power, even though they seek it to do what they regard as good, are simply demanding the right to enforce their own version of heaven on earth, and let me remind you they are the very ones who always create the most hellish tyranny.

Absolute power does corrupt, and those who seek it must be suspect and must be opposed. Their mistaken course stems from false notions, ladies and gentlemen, of equality. Equality, rightly understood as our founding fathers understood it, leads to liberty and to the emancipation of creative differences; wrongly understood, as it has been so tragically in our time, it leads first to conformity and then to despotism.

Fellow Republicans, it is the cause of Republicanism to resist concentrations of power, private or public, which enforce such conformity and inflict such despotism.

It is the cause of Republicanism to ensure that power remains in the hands of the people—and, so help us God, that is exactly what a Republican president will do with the help of a Republican Congress.

It is further the cause of Republicanism to restore a clear understanding of the tyranny of man over man in the world at large. It is our cause to dispel the foggy thinking which avoids hard decisions in the delusion that a world of conflict will somehow resolve itself into a world of harmony, if we just don't rock the boat or irritate the forces of aggression—and this is hogwash.

It is further the cause of Republicanism to remind ourselves, and the world, that only the strong can remain free: that only the strong can keep the peace. . . .

It was during those Republican years [under former President Dwight Eisenhower] that the thrust of Communist imperialism was blunted. It was during those years of Republican leadership that this world moved closer not to war but closer to peace than at any other time in the last three decades.

And I needn't remind you—but I will—that it's been during Democratic years that our strength to deter war has been stilled and even gone into a planned decline. It has been during Democratic years that we have weakly stumbled into conflicts, timidly refusing to draw our own lines against aggression, deceitfully refusing to tell even our people of our full participation and tragically letting our finest men die on battlefields unmarked by purpose, unmarked by pride or the prospect of victory.

Yesterday it was Korea; tonight it is Vietnam. Make no bones of this. Don't try to sweep this under the rug. We are at war in Vietnam. And yet the president, who is the commander in chief of our forces, refuses to say . . . whether or not the objective over there is victory, and his secretary of defense continues to mislead and misinform the American people, and enough of it has gone by.

And I needn't remind you—but I will—it has been during Democratic years that a billion persons were cast into Communist captivity and their fate cynically sealed.

Today, today in our beloved country, we have an administration which seems eager to deal with communism in every coin known—from gold to wheat, from consulates to confidence, and even human freedom itself. . . .

Now, we here in America can keep the peace only if we remain strong. Only if we keep our eyes open and keep our guard up can we prevent war. And I want to make this abundantly clear—I don't intend to let peace or freedom be torn from our grasp because of lack of strength, or lack of will—and that I promise you Americans.

I believe that we must look beyond the defense of freedom today to its extension tomorrow. I believe that the communism which boasts it will bury us will instead give way to the forces of freedom. And I can see in the distant and yet recognizable future the outlines of a world worthy of our dedication, our every risk, our every effort, our every sacrifice along the way. Yes, a world that will redeem the suffering of those will be liberated from tyranny. . . .

It is a goal far, far more meaningful than a moon shot. It's a truly inspiring goal for all free men to set for themselves during the latter half of the twentieth century. I can also see, and all free men must thrill to, the events of this

Atlantic civilization joined by a straight ocean highway to the United States. What a destiny! What a destiny can be ours to stand as a great central pillar linking Europe, the Americas, and the venerable and vital peoples and cultures of the Pacific!

. . . Now, I know this freedom is not the fruit of every soil. I know that our own freedom was achieved through centuries by unremitting efforts by brave and wise men. And I know that the road to freedom is a long and a challenging road, and I know also that some men may walk away from it, that some men resist challenge, accepting the false security of governmental paternalism. . . .

My fellow Republicans, we do no man a service by hiding freedom's light under a bushel of mistaken humility. I seek an America proud of its past, proud of its ways, proud of its dreams, and determined actively to proclaim them. But our examples to the world must, like charity, begin at home.

In our vision of a good and decent future, free and peaceful, there must be room, room for the liberation of the energy and the talent of the individual, otherwise our vision is blind at the outset.

We must assure a society here which while never abandoning the needy, or forsaking the helpless, nurtures incentives and opportunity for the creative and the productive. . . .

This nation, whose creative people have enhanced this entire span of history, should again thrive upon the greatness of all those things which we—we as individual citizens—can and should do. . . .

We Republicans see in our constitutional form of government the great framework which assures the orderly but dynamic fulfillment of the whole man as the great reason for instituting orderly government in the first place.

We see in private property and in economy based upon and fostering private property the one way to make government a durable ally of the whole man rather than his determined enemy. We see in the sanctity of private property the only durable foundation for constitutional government in a free society.

And beyond all that we see and cherish diversity of ways, diversity of thoughts, of motives, and accomplishments. We don't seek to live anyone's life for him. We only seek to secure his rights, guarantee him opportunity, guarantee him opportunity to strive, with government performing only those needed and constitutionally sanctioned tasks which cannot otherwise be performed.

We Republicans seek a government that attends to its inherent responsibilities of maintaining a stable monetary and fiscal climate, encouraging a free and a competitive economy, and enforcing law and order.

Thus do we seek inventiveness, diversity, and creative difference within a stable order, for we Republicans define government's role where needed at many, many levels—preferably, though, the one closest to the people involved: our towns and our cities, then our counties, then our states, then our regional contacts, and only then the national government.

That, let me remind you, is the land of liberty built by decentralized power. On it also we must have balance between the branches of government at every level. . . .

This is a party—this Republican Party is a party for free men. Not for blind followers and not for conformists. . . .

Anyone who joins us in all sincerity, we welcome. Those, those who do not care for our cause, we don't expect to enter our ranks, in any case. And let our Republicanism so focused and so dedicated not be made fuzzy and futile by unthinking and stupid labels.

I would remind you that extremism in the defense of liberty is no vice! And let me remind you also that moderation in the pursuit of justice is no virtue!

The beauty of the very system we Republicans are pledged to restore and revitalize, the beauty of this federal system of ours, is in its reconciliation of diversity with unity. We must not see malice in honest differences of opinion, and no matter how great, so long as they are not inconsistent with the pledges we have given to each other in and through our Constitution.

. . . Our Republican cause is to free our people and light the way for liberty throughout the world. Ours is a very human cause for very humane goals. This party, its good people, and its unquestionable devotion to freedom will not fulfill the purposes of this campaign which we launch here now until our cause has won the day, inspired the world, and shown the way to a tomorrow worthy of all our yesteryears.

I repeat, I accept your nomination with humbleness, with pride, and you and I are going to fight for the goodness of our land. Thank you.

Source: The Personal and Political Papers of Senator Barry M. Goldwater, Arizona Historical Foundation

6

EXCERPTS FROM RONALD REAGAN, "A TIME FOR CHOOSING" (OCTOBER 27, 1964)

I have spent most of my life as a Democrat. I recently have seen fit to follow another course. I believe that the issues confronting us cross party lines. Now, one side in this campaign has been telling us that the issues of this election are the maintenance of peace and prosperity. The line has been used "We've never had it so good."

But I have an uncomfortable feeling that this prosperity isn't something on which we can base our hopes for the future. No nation in history has ever survived a tax burden that reached a third of its national income. . . . We have raised our debt limit three times in the last twelve months, and now our national debt is one and a half times bigger than all the combined debts of all the nations in the world. . . .

As for the peace that we would preserve, I wonder who among us would like to approach the wife or mother whose husband or son has died in South Vietnam and ask them if they think this is a peace that should be maintained indefinitely. Do they mean peace, or do they mean we just want to be left in peace? There can be no real peace while one American is dying some place in the world for the rest of us. We are at war with the most dangerous enemy that has ever faced mankind in his long climb from the swamp to the stars, and it has been said if we lose that war, and in doing so lose this way of freedom of ours, history will record with the greatest astonishment that those who had the most to lose did the least to prevent its happening. . . .

This is the last stand on Earth. And this idea that government is beholden to the people, that it has no other source of power except to sovereign people, is still the newest and most unique idea in all the long history of man's relation to man. This is the issue of this election. Whether we believe in our capacity for self-government or whether we abandon the American revolution and confess that a little intellectual elite in a far-distant capital can plan our lives for us better than we can plan them ourselves.

You and I are told increasingly that we have to choose between a left or right, but I would like to suggest that there is no such thing as a left or right. There is only an up or down—up to a man's age-old dream, the ultimate in individual freedom consistent with law and order—or down to the ant heap of totalitarianism, and regardless of their sincerity, their humanitarian motives, those who would trade our freedom for security have embarked on this downward course.

In this vote-harvesting time, they use terms like the "Great Society," or as we were told a few days ago by the President, we must accept a "greater government activity in the affairs of the people." . . . And Senator Clark of Pennsylvania, another articulate spokesman, defines liberalism as "meeting the material needs of the masses through the full power of centralized government." Well, I for one resent it when a representative of the people refers to you and me—the free man and woman of this country—as "the masses." This is a term we haven't applied to ourselves in America. But beyond that, "the full power of centralized government"—this was the very thing the Founding Fathers sought to minimize. They knew that governments don't control things. A government can't control the economy without controlling people. And they knew when a government sets out to do that, it must use force and coercion to achieve its purpose. They also knew, those Founding Fathers, that outside of its legitimate functions, government does nothing as well or as economically as the private sector of the economy. . . .

We have so many people who can't see a fat man standing beside a thin one without coming to the conclusion that the fat man got that way by taking advantage of the thin one. So they are going to solve all the problems of human misery through government and government planning. Well, now, if government planning and welfare had the answer and they've had almost 30 years of it, shouldn't we expect government to almost read the score to us once in a while? Shouldn't they be telling us about the decline each year in the number of people needing help?

But the reverse is true. Each year the need grows greater, the program grows greater. We were told four years ago that 17 million people went to bed hungry each night. Well, that was probably true. They were all on a diet. But now we are told that 9.3 million families in this country are poverty-stricken on the basis of earning less than $3,000 a year. Welfare spending is 10 times greater than in the dark depths of the Depression. We are spending $45 billion on welfare. Now do a little arithmetic, and you will find that if we divided the $45 billion up equally among those 9 million poor families, we would be able to give each family $4,600 a year, and this added to their present income should eliminate poverty! Direct aid to the poor, however, is running only about $600 per family. It would seem that someplace there must be some overhead.

So now we declare "war on poverty". . . Now, do they honestly expect us to believe that if we add $1 billion to the $45 billion we are spending . . . that poverty is suddenly going to disappear by magic?

. . . Yet anytime you and I question the schemes of the do-gooders, we are denounced as being against their humanitarian goals. They say we are always "against" things, never "for" anything. Well, the trouble with our liberal friends is not that they are ignorant, but that they know so much that isn't so. We are for a provision that destitution should not follow unemployment by reason of old age, and to that end we have accepted Social Security as a step toward meeting the problem.

But we are against those entrusted with this program when they practice deception regarding its fiscal shortcomings, when they charge that any criticism of the program means that we want to end payments to those who depend on them for livelihood. They have called it insurance to us in a hundred million pieces of literature. But then they appeared before the Supreme Court and they testified that it was a welfare program. They only use the term "insurance" to sell it to the people. And they said Social Security dues are a tax for the general use of the government, and the government has used that tax. . . .

At the same time, can't we introduce voluntary features that would permit a citizen who can do better on his own to be excused upon presentation of evidence that he had made provisions for the non-earning years? Should we allow a widow with children to work, and not lose the benefits supposedly paid for by her deceased husband? Shouldn't you and I be allowed to declare who our beneficiaries will be under these programs, which we cannot do? I think we are for telling our senior citizens that no one in this country should be denied medical care because of a lack of funds. But I think we are against forcing all citizens, regardless of need, into a compulsory government program, especially when we have such examples, as announced last week, when France admitted that their Medicare program was now bankrupt. They've come to the end of the road. . . .

I think we are for an international organization, where the nations of the world can seek peace. But I think we are against subordinating American interests to an organization that has become so structurally unsound that today you can muster a two-thirds vote on the floor of the General Assembly among the nations that represent less than 10 percent of the world's population. I think we are against the hypocrisy of assailing our allies because here and there they cling to a colony, while we engage in a conspiracy of silence and never open our mouths about the millions of people enslaved in Soviet colonies in the satellite nation.

I think we are for aiding our allies by sharing our material blessings with those nations which share in our fundamental beliefs, but we are against doling out money government to government, creating bureaucracy, if not socialism, all over the world. We set out to help 19 countries. We are helping 107. We spent $146 billion. With that money, we bought a $2 million yacht for Haile Selassie. We bought dress suits for Greek undertakers, extra wives for Kenyan government officials. We bought a thousand TV sets for a place where they have no electricity. In the last six years, 52 nations have bought $7 billion worth of our gold, and all 52 are receiving foreign aid from this country.

No government ever voluntarily reduces itself in size. Government programs, once launched, never disappear. Actually, a government bureau is the nearest thing to eternal life we'll ever see on this Earth. Federal employees number 2.5 million, and federal, state, and local, one out of six of the nation's work force is employed by the government. These proliferating bureaus with their thousands of regulations have cost us many of our constitutional safeguards. How many of us realize that today federal agents can invade a man's property without a warrant? They can impose a fine without a formal hearing, let alone a trial by jury, and they can seize and sell his property in auction to enforce the payment of that fine. . . .

Well, what of this man [Goldwater] that they would destroy? And in destroying, they would destroy that which he represents, the ideas that you and I hold dear. Is he the brash and shallow and trigger-happy man they say he is? Well, I have been privileged to know him "when." I knew him long before he ever dreamed of trying for high office, and I can tell you personally I have never known a man in my life I believe so incapable of doing a dishonest or dishonorable thing.

This is a man who in his own business, before he entered politics, instituted a profit-sharing plan, before unions had ever thought of it. He put in health and medical insurance for all his employees. He took 50 percent of the profits before taxes and set up a retirement program, a pension plan for all his employees. He sent checks for life to an employee who was ill and couldn't work. He provided nursing care for the children of mothers who work in the stores. When Mexico was ravaged by floods from the Rio Grande, he climbed in his airplane and flew medicine and supplies down there.

. . . This is not a man who could carelessly send other people's sons to war. And that is the issue of this campaign that makes all of the other problems I have discussed academic, unless we realize that we are in a war that must be won.

Those who would trade our freedom for the soup kitchen of the welfare state have told us that they have a utopian solution of peace without victory. They call their policy "accommodation." And they say if we only avoid any direct confrontation with the enemy, he will forget his evil ways and learn to love us. All who oppose them are indicted as warmongers. They say we offer simple answers to complex problems. Well, perhaps there is a simple answer— not an easy answer—but simple.

If you and I have the courage to tell our elected officials that we want our national policy based upon what we know in our hearts is morally right. . . . Let's set the record straight. There is no argument over the choice between peace and war, but there is only one guaranteed way you can have peace— and you can have it in the next second—surrender.

Admittedly there is a risk in any course we follow other than this, but every lesson in history tells us that the greater risk lies in appeasement, and this is the specter our well-meaning liberal friends refuse to face—that their policy of accommodation is appeasement, and it gives no choice between peace and war, only between fight and surrender. If we continue to accommodate, continue to back and retreat, eventually we have to face the final demand— the ultimatum. And what then? . . . You and I know and do not believe that life is so dear and peace so sweet as to be purchased at the price of chains and slavery. . . . The martyrs of history were not fools, and our honored dead who gave their lives to stop the advance of the Nazis didn't die in vain. Where, then, is the road to peace? Well, it's a simple answer after all.

You and I have the courage to say to our enemies, "There is a price we will not pay." There is a point beyond which they must not advance. This is the meaning in the phrase of Barry Goldwater's "peace through strength."

. . . You and I have a rendezvous with destiny. We will preserve for our children this, the last best hope of man on Earth, or we will sentence them to take the last step into a thousand years of darkness.

We will keep in mind and remember that Barry Goldwater has faith in us. He has faith that you and I have the ability and the dignity and the right to make our own decisions and determine our own destiny.

Source: Courtesy of the Ronald Reagan Presidential Foundation

7

EXCERPTS FROM RICHARD NIXON'S ACCEPTANCE SPEECH, REPUBLICAN NATIONAL CONVENTION (AUGUST 8, 1968)

The choice we make in 1968 will determine not only the future of America but the future of peace and freedom in the world for the last third of the Twentieth Century.

And the question that we answer tonight: can America meet this great challenge?

For a few moments, let us look at America, let us listen to America to find the answer to that question.

As we look at America, we see cities enveloped in smoke and flame.

We hear sirens in the night.

We see Americans dying on distant battlefields abroad.

We see Americans hating each other; fighting each other; killing each other at home. . . .

Listen to the answer. . . . It is another voice. It is the quiet voice in the tumult and the shouting.

It is the voice of the great majority of Americans, the forgotten Americans—the non-shouters; the non-demonstrators.

They are not racists or sick; they are not guilty of the crime that plagues the land.

They are black and they are white—they're native born and foreign born— they're young and they're old. . . . They give drive to the spirit of America. They give lift to the American Dream. They give steel to the backbone of America. They are good people, they are decent people; they work, and they save, and they pay their taxes, and they care. . . .

Let's never forget that despite her faults, America is a great nation. And America is great because her people are great.

America is in trouble today not because her people have failed but because her leaders have failed. And what America needs are leaders to match the greatness of her people.

When the strongest nation in the world can be tied down for four years in a war in Vietnam with no end in sight;

When the richest nation in the world can't manage its own economy;

When the nation with the greatest tradition of the rule of law is plagued by unprecedented lawlessness;

When a nation that has been known for a century for equality of opportunity is torn by unprecedented racial violence;

And when the President of the United States cannot travel abroad or to any major city at home without fear of a hostile demonstration—then it's time for new leadership for the United States of America. . . .

We shall begin with Vietnam. . . .

For four years this Administration has had at its disposal the greatest military and economic advantage that one nation has ever had over another in any war in history.

For four years, America's fighting men have set a record for courage and sacrifice unsurpassed in our history.

For four years, this Administration has had the support of the Loyal Opposition for the objective of seeking an honorable end to the struggle.

Never has so much military and economic and diplomatic power been used so ineffectively.

And I pledge to you tonight that the first priority foreign policy objective of our next Administration will be to bring an honorable end to the war in Vietnam. We shall not stop there—we need a policy to prevent more Vietnams.
. . .

The American Revolution was a shining example of freedom in action which caught the imagination of the world.

Today, too often, America is an example to be avoided and not followed.

A nation that can't keep the peace at home won't be trusted to keep the peace abroad.

A President who isn't treated with respect at home will not be treated with respect abroad.

A nation which can't manage its own economy can't tell others how to manage theirs.

If we are to restore prestige and respect for America abroad, the place to begin is at home in the United States of America. . . .

So let us have order in America—not the order that suppresses dissent and discourages change but the order which guarantees the right to dissent and provides the basis for peaceful change.

Let us always respect, as I do, our courts and those who serve on them. But let us also recognize that some of our courts in their decisions have gone too far in weakening the peace forces as against the criminal forces in this country and we must act to restore that balance.

Let those who have the responsibility to enforce our laws and our judges who have the responsibility to interpret them be dedicated to the great principles of civil rights.

But let them also recognize that the first civil right of every American is to be free from domestic violence, and that right must be guaranteed in this country.

The wave of crime is not going to be the wave of the future in the United States of America.

We shall re-establish freedom from fear in America so that America can take the lead in re-establishing freedom from fear in the world.

And to those who say that law and order is the code word for racism, there and here is a reply:

Our goal is justice for every American. If we are to have respect for law in America, we must have laws that deserve respect.

Just as we cannot have progress without order, we cannot have order without progress, and so, as we commit to order tonight, let us commit to progress.

And this brings me to the clearest choice among the great issues of this campaign.

For the past five years we have been deluged by government programs for the unemployed; programs for the cities; programs for the poor. And we have reaped from these programs an ugly harvest of frustration, violence and failure across the land.

And now our opponents will be offering more of the same—more billions for government jobs, government housing, government welfare.

I say it is time to quit pouring billions of dollars into programs that have failed in the United States of America.

We are a great nation. And we must never forget how we became great. America is a great nation today not because of what government did for people— but because of what people did for themselves over a hundred-ninety years in this country. . . .

Government can pass laws. But respect for law can come only from people who take the law into their hearts and their minds—and not into their hands.

Government can provide opportunity. But opportunity means nothing unless people are prepared to seize it . . . .

My fellow Americans, the long dark night for America is about to end.

The time has come for us to leave the valley of despair and climb the mountain so that we may see the glory of the dawn—a new day for America, and a new dawn for peace and freedom in the world.

Source: Courtesy of the Richard M. Nixon Library and Birthplace

SELECTED READINGS

Allitt, Patrick. *Catholic Intellectuals and Conservative Politics in America, 1950–1985*. Ithaca: Cornell University Press, 1993.

Anderson, Terry H. *The Movement and the Sixties*. New York: Oxford University Press, 1996.

Andrew, John A. III. *The Other Side of the Sixties: Young Americans for Freedom and the Rise of Conservative Politics*. New Brunswick: Rutgers University Press, 1997.

Bailey, Beth. *Sex in the Heartland*. Cambridge: Harvard University Press, 1999.

Bloom, Alexander. *Long Time Gone: Sixties America Then and Now*. New York: Oxford University Press, 2001.

Bloom, Alexander, and Wini Breines, eds. *"Takin' It to the Streets: A Sixties Reader*. New York: Oxford University Press, 2003.

Bloom, Allan. *The Closing of the American Mind*. New York: Simon & Schuster, 1988.

Bork, Robert H. *Slouching towards Gomorrah: Modern Liberalism and American Decline*. New York: Regan Books, 1996.

Branch, Taylor. *At Canaan's Edge: America in the King Years, 1965–68*. New York: Simon & Schuster, 2005.

———. *Parting the Waters: America in the King Years, 1954–63*. New York: Simon & Schuster, 1988.

———. *Pillar of Fire: America in the King Years, 1963–65*. New York: Simon & Schuster, 1998.

Breines, Wini. *The Great Refusal: Community Organization in the New Left: 1962–1968*. New York: Praeger, 1982.

Brennan, Mary C. *Turning Right in the Sixties: The Conservative Capture of the GOP*. Chapel Hill: University of North Carolina Press, 1995.

Buchanan, Patrick J. *Right from the Beginning*. Boston: Little, Brown & Co., 1988.

Buckley, William F. *Happy Days Were Here Again: Reflections of a Libertarian Journalist*. New York: Random House, 1993.

————. *The Jeweler's Eye*. New York: Putnam, 1968.

Burner, David. *Making Peace with the 60s*. Princeton: Princeton University Press, 1998.

Cannato, Vincent J. *The Ungovernable City: John Lindsay and His Struggle to Save New York*. New York: Basic Books, 2001.

Cannon, Lou. *President Reagan: The Role of a Lifetime*. New York: Simon & Schuster, 1991.

Chalmers, David. *And the Crooked Places Made Straight: The Struggle for Social Change in the 1960s*. Baltimore: Johns Hopkins University Press, 1996.

Dallek, Matthew. *The Right Moment: Ronald Reagan's First Victory and the Decisive Turning Point in American Politics*. New York: Free Press, 2000.

Dallek, Robert. *Flawed Giant: Lyndon Johnson and His Times, 1961–73*. New York: Oxford University Press, 1998.

————. *An Unfinished Life: John F. Kennedy, 1917–1963*. Boston: Little, Brown & Co., 2003.

Diamond, Sara. *Roads to Dominion: Right-Wing Movements and Political Power in the United States*. New York: Guilford Press, 1995.

Edsall, Thomas Byrne, and Mary D. *Chain Reaction: The Impact of Race, Rights, and Taxes on American Politics*. New York: Norton, 1991.

Falwell, Jerry. *Strength for the Journey*. New York: Simon & Schuster, 1987.

Farber, David. *The Age of Great Dreams: America in the 1960s*. New York: Hill & Wang, 1994.

————. ed. *The Sixties: From Memory to History*. Chapel Hill: University of North Carolina Press, 1994.

Farber, David, and Beth Bailey. *The Columbia Guide to America in the 1960s*. New York: Columbia University Press, 2001.

Farber, David, and Jeff Roche. *The Conservative Sixties*. New York: Peter Lang, 2003.

Fischer, Klaus. *America in White, Black and Gray: The Stormy Sixties*. New York: Continuum Press, 2006.

Flamm, Michael W. *Law and Order: Street Crime, Civil Unrest, and the Crisis of Liberalism in the 1960s*. New York: Columbia University Press, 2005.

Foley, Michael S. *Confronting the War Machine: Draft Resistance During the Vietnam War*. Chapel Hill: University of North Carolina Press, 2003.

Formisano, Ronald P. *Boston Against Busing: Race, Class, and Ethnicity in the 1960s and 1970s*. Chapel Hill: University of North Carolina Press, 1991.

Freedman, Lawrence. *Kennedy's Wars: Berlin, Cuba, Laos, and Vietnam*. New York: Oxford University Press, 2000.

Freedman, Samuel G. *The Inheritance: How Three Families and the American Political Majority Moved from Left to Right*. New York: Simon and Schuster, 1996.

Frost, Jennifer. *An Interracial Movement of the Poor: Community Organizing and the New Left in the 1960s*. New York: New York University Press, 2001.

Gitlin, Todd. *The Sixties: Years of Hope, Days of Rage.* New York: Bantam Books, 1987.

Goldwater, Barry. *With No Apologies.* New York: Morrow, 1979.

Gosse, Van. *Where the Boys Are: Cuba, Cold War America, and the Making of the New Left.* New York: Verso, 1993.

Greenberg, David. *Nixon's Shadow: The History of an Image.* New York: W. W. Norton & Company, 2003.

Heineman, Kenneth J. *Campus Wars: The Peace Movement at American State Universities in the Vietnam Era.* New York: New York University Press, 1992.

Howard, Gerald, ed. *The Sixties: Art, Politics and Media of Our Most Explosive Decade.* New York: Paragon House, 1982, 1991.

Isserman, Maurice, and Michael Kazin. *America Divided: The Civil War of the 1960s.* New York: Oxford University Press, 2000.

Jackson, Rebecca. *The 1960s: An Annotated Bibliography of Social and Political Movements in the United States.* Westport, CT: Greenwood Press, 1992.

Klatch, Rebecca E. *A Generation Divided: The New Left, The New Right, and the 1960s.* Berkeley: University of California Press, 1999.

———. *Women of the New Right.* Philadelphia: Temple University Press, 1987.

Lytle, Mark Hamilton. *America's Uncivil Wars: The Sixties Era from Elvis to the Fall of Richard Nixon.* New York: Oxford University Press, 2006.

Macedo, Stephen, ed. *Reassessing the Sixties: Debating the Political and Cultural Legacy.* New York: W. W. Norton & Company, 1997.

Marwick, Arthur. *The Sixties.* New York: Oxford University Press, 1998.

Matusow, Allen J. *The Unraveling of America: A History of Liberalism in the 1960s.* New York: Harper, 1984.

McGirr, Lisa. *Suburban Warriors: The Origins of the New American Right.* Princeton: Princeton University Press, 2000.

Morrison, Joan and Robert K. *From Camelot to Kent State: The Sixties Experience in the Words of Those Who Lived It.* New York: Oxford University Press, 1987.

Murray, Charles. *Losing Ground.* New York: Basic Books, 1984.

Nash, George. *The Conservative Intellectual Movement in America.* New York: Basic Books, 1976.

O'Neill, William L. *Coming Apart: An Informal History of America in the 1960s.* New York: Random House, 1971.

Patterson, James T. *America's Struggle Against Poverty.* Cambridge: Harvard University Press, 1981.

———. *Grand Expectations: The United States, 1945–1974.* New York: Oxford University Press, 1996.

Perlstein, Rick. *Before the Storm: Barry Goldwater and the Unmaking of the American Consensus.* New York: Hill & Wang, 2001.

Rossinow, Doug. *The Politics of Authenticity: Liberalism, Christianity, and the New Left in America.* New York: Columbia University Press, 1998.

Rusher, William A. *The Making of a New Majority Party.* New York: Sheed and Ward, 1975.

Schneider, Gregory L. *Cadres for Conservatism: Young Americans for Freedom and the Rise of the Contemporary Right.* New York: New York University Press, 1999.

———. *Conservatism in America Since 1930.* New York: New York University Press, 1993.

Schoenwald, Jonathan M. *A Time for Choosing: The Rise of Modern American Conservatism.* New York: Oxford University Press, 2001.

Steigerwald, David. *The Sixties and the End of Modern America.* New York: St. Martin's Press, 1995.

Sugrue, Thomas. *The Origins of the Urban Crisis: Race and Inequality in Postwar Detroit.* Princeton: Princeton University Press, 1996.

Suri, Jeremi. *Power and Protest: Global Revolution and the Rise of Détente.* Cambridge: Harvard University Press, 2003.

Tischler, Barbara L., ed. *Sights on the Sixties.* New Brunswick: Rutgers University Press, 1992.

Tyson, Timothy. *Radio Free Dixie: Robert F. Williams and the Roots of Black Power.* Chapel Hill: University of North Carolina Press, 1999.

INDEX

ABOUT THE AUTHORS

Michael W. Flamm is associate professor of history at Ohio Wesleyan University. He is a scholar of modern U.S. political history with a research focus on the 1960s. He is the author of *Law and Order: Street Crime, Civil Unrest, and the Crisis of Liberalism in the 1960s* (2005) and coauthor of *The Chicago Handbook for Teachers* (1999). He is currently writing a book on the Harlem Riot of 1964 titled *In the Heat of the Summer*.

David Steigerwald is associate professor of history at Ohio State University and teaches at the university's Marion Campus. Among his books is *The Sixties and the End of Modern America*. He is finishing a book on American intellectuals and the affluent society.